Stuart Coupe is an author, music commentator, independent artist publicist and radio broadcaster who has been involved with music all his life. Among the books he has written, edited or collaborated on are *The New Music* (1980), *The New Rock 'n' Roll* (1983), *The Promoters* (2003), *Gudinski* (2015) and *Tex* (2017).

ROADIES

– THE SECRET HISTORY OF –
AUSTRALIAN ROCK'N'ROLL

STUART COUPE

hachette
AUSTRALIA

hachette
AUSTRALIA

Published in Australia and New Zealand in 2018
by Hachette Australia
(an imprint of Hachette Australia Pty Limited)
Level 17, 207 Kent Street, Sydney NSW 2000
www.hachette.com.au

10 9 8 7 6 5 4 3 2 1

A catalogue record for this
book is available from the
National Library of Australia

ISBN 978 0 7336 3874 9 (paperback)

Cover design by Luke Causby, Blue Cork Designs
Cover photograph courtesy of Stewart Riddick
Author photograph courtesy of Susan Lynch
Internal photographs courtesy author's collection
Text design by Bookhouse, Sydney
Typeset in 11.5/15.7 pt Sabon LT Pro by Bookhouse, Sydney
Printed and bound in Australia by McPherson's Printing Group

MIX
Paper | Supporting
responsible forestry
FSC
www.fsc.org   FSC® C001695

The paper this book is printed on is certified against the
Forest Stewardship Council® Standards. McPherson's Printing
Group holds FSC® chain of custody certification SA-COC-005379.
FSC® promotes environmentally responsible, socially beneficial
and economically viable management of the world's forests.

For Susan Lynch – just kids . . . forever.
And in memory of Iain Shedden –
friend, writer, music lover.

Contents

Prologue

Cold Chisel are exhausted. After close to two hours they stagger off the stage at Brisbane's Entertainment Centre. It's 13 December 2011. The final night of the Light the Nitro national tour which had started in Newcastle exactly two months earlier.

It's the band's first tour without drummer Steve Prestwich who passed away in January. Charlie Drayton is sitting in the drummer's seat.

'Flame Trees' rolls into 'Khe Sanh' and on to 'Bow River'. The capacity crowd is in a sweaty frenzy as the band wave and walk offstage. Of course it's not the end. It's been a good gig and everyone – audience and band – know that there'll be more.

While the band wander around backstage, having a quick drink and gathering their breath, there is activity on the stage. The lights are down. The crowd is chanting. 'Chisel! Chisel! Chisel!'

Onstage the road crew are busy. Very busy. Mischievously busy. They have a plan in motion. A big plan. They are preparing a thank you to the five musicians who they've toured with for the past two months – the band they've set up gear for night after night, stage after stage, then loaded off from the stage and into trucks and semitrailers and on to the next city and the next gig.

Chisel have a reputation for respecting their road crew. And a road crew that's treated well is a very, very loyal bunch of people.

There is a long history of crews giving a little gift to the bands they work with on the last night of a tour – if they've been treated well. And Chisel have treated these guys well. It's thank you time.

Earlier in the day while setting up the equipment and stage for the show the crew had removed two six-foot-by-four-foot sections of the stage, and replaced them with Perspex flooring so that everything below these sections of the stage was visible. They'd also gone under the stage and set up some lights.

They knew they had to be careful with end-of-tour hijinks. On a previous tour strippers had appeared onstage at the Sydney Entertainment Centre. These beautifully dressed and adorned creatures had preened and pranced around the stage during Chisel's encore, at one point turning to the band and bending over provocatively for those in the front rows.

As the strippers disrobed further it became obvious that two of the trio were male, causing some of the audience members to confront their notions of beauty and sexuality.

Not all of Cold Chisel had been happy about this caper. At least one member thought that it was undermining their image as a credible rock'n'roll band.

The Light the Nitro tour crew knew this and didn't want to open any old wounds so their 'gift' was to take place below stage level, visible only to the band members onstage. It had to be funny, and in the great tradition of road crew end-of-tour gifts to a band it had to totally fuck with their heads without completely detracting from the performance.

Cold Chisel have walked offstage. The audience are screaming. With all bar a few lights down, the crew remove the carpet that had covered the Perspex staging. At the same time some figures emerge from a room backstage, and when it is clear that none of the Cold Chisel members are within eyesight, these figures are shown to the area created below the stage. Everything is in place.

The stage lights go up. Cold Chisel walk onstage, waving to the audience and preparing to launch into 'Saturday Night', the first song of the encore.

Jimmy Barnes walks to his microphone stand and looks down. He does a double take, blinks in the glare of the stage lighting. He looks down again. Did someone spike his drink during the break? He looks again. And then a massive grin spreads across his face. He's thinking that this is just what he doesn't need right at the start of an encore – but that it's extremely funny. He motions to Ian Moss to wander over. Moss looks down, shakes his head, and they hit the opening chords of the song.

From 'Saturday Night' the band move in to 'Letter To Alan', their ode to two of their long-serving crew members who had died in a motor vehicle accident. Then it's 'Four Walls', and 'Goodbye (Astrid Goodbye)'. The band are trying to concentrate on the show at hand, the road crew are in hysterics, all the musicians gravitate to the area around Barnes's microphone stand, Don Walker peers over his keyboard to check out the action below the stage. The normally unfazable keyboard player is completely distracted.

What the members of Cold Chisel can clearly see are a number of very, very scantily clad women cavorting with each other. Such was the blur of flesh that no one is sure how many women were involved. And this being roadie and musician world, everything is embellished with the telling and retelling. Some say four women. Others say eight. Jimmy Barnes recalls that 'there was a lot going on'. Ian Moss thinks they were on a bed. There was oil. There was no oil. They were completely naked. They were wearing G-strings. They were having sex. They were embracing suggestively. There were sex toys. There were no sex toys.

The show finishes, the band and their road crew quickly enjoy some backstage laughter and back slapping.

Then the band disappear into the night. The crew start doing what they do every night after a show. Dismantling all the sound equipment and lights and loading it all into trucks. It'll be a good four hours before their workday is over.

Welcome to the world of the road crew.

Introduction

The famous rock'n'roll performer Tom Petty, who knew a thing or two about the trials, tribulations and rigours of the live music world, once observed: 'I think the general public has no idea what roadies do. Bless 'em all. I just play the songs. They make the show happen.'

There are thousands of roadies scattered around the globe. You may even know one or two. Even then you probably have only the vaguest idea of what they do. You probably think they set up equipment for musicians and cart it to and from concerts and pubs. And you'd be right – partially.

There's a little more to it than that. In fact, there's a *lot* more.

Yes, roadies generally need to be strong enough to move, position, reposition, pack and unpack usually heavy equipment. But pretty much anyone with biceps and a strong back can do that. What defines the roadie is really the highly skilled, meticulously detailed work that goes with moving and setting up that equipment – and the unpredictable beasts (aka musicians) who accompany it pretty much everywhere. Spot an amplifier, drum kit or guitar case and chances are a musician will turn up sooner or later.

The circumstances of a gig are unpredictable. You have to consider the musicians themselves, the audience, the location, the climate, the power supply – and these are all things that arise at every concert or event.

Roadies know how equipment works. They can plug it in, set it up, and get it working again when it breaks down mid-show. They are an ingenious bunch of people. They are problem solvers. Lateral-thinking wizards who don't understand the concept of something *not* being possible. Their minds are simply focused on what it will take to *make* it happen. They have no comprehension that you can't hang this there, that something doesn't fit or that it won't work in this situation. They find a way to get it done.

It doesn't matter what your musical preferences or your favourite performers are. Going to concerts, gigs, shows and events is usually thrilling. That's what it's all about. It's *meant* to be life-changing. And often it is.

Imagine walking into a big outdoor concert with 50,000 other people. You walk through the entrance and head towards your seat or ideal standing position with hopes of being transported out of your everyday life to somewhere truly special.

There's a magnificent stage setting. There are video screens so you can see whatever's happening onstage even if you're in the cheap seats. There are huge stacks of sound equipment. There are thousands of lights around the stage, and people perched a hundred feet in the air in little cockpits to operate them. There is a wall of equipment, all finely tuned and ready for show time.

The construction before you is a glittering, sparkling marvel. And – in most cases, anyway – none of it was there a few days before. Over a hundred people will have spent a week building the huge stage, and those same arms and legs will be starting to dismantle it half an hour after the last song is played, while you, exhausted, shuffle out through the venue gates and make your way home. Those roadies and crew people will be working feverishly for hours after you've gone to bed, loading trucks and then driving them towards the next concert event.

Every aspect of staging a concert performance is intricate, demanding, highly skilled work. And at any stage of the process there are so many things that can go wrong. The wiring for a big concert looks like an explosion at a spaghetti factory. But backstage there are roadies who know every bit of that tangle of wires and cables. Every metre of it has a function in the overall structure of the two-hour show. And at any point any of it might decide to malfunction. Someone needs to know what to do – and then act quickly – when that happens. That person is a roadie.

When an amplifier splutters and stops – or when smoke starts billowing from the back of it – someone must resuscitate or replace it, fast. That person is a roadie.

When the over-enthusiastic fan next to you drinks his eight-eenth beer and decides it's a really good idea to climb onto the stage and race towards the singer, tripping over cords as he staggers forward, someone has to grab him, get him safely off the stage, and then sort out whatever complications have arisen from the thirty-second rampage. That person is a roadie.

Or when the lead singer decides to throw herself from the stage for an unscheduled crowd surf, still clutching a micro-phone, someone has to deal with the problems caused by this foray into thousands of fans, all of whom seem intent on grab-bing the singer and the microphone. That person is a roadie.

Positioned at various spots around the stage and venue are a variety of highly skilled technicians. One is controlling the sound you hear, another oversees the lighting, others are responsible for each of the musicians onstage, their instruments and amplifiers. If a guitarist needs to change their guitar every second song, there needs to be someone at the side of the stage keeping all the instruments in tune, and knowing exactly when each one is required. That person is a roadie.

And when the performance is over, someone has to dismantle and organise all the bits and pieces that made the magnificent show you've just experienced, tightly packing cords and leads into boxes and removing everything from the stage, and loading that equipment into trucks and vans in ways that resemble the intricacies of the logic of a Rubik's cube. Everything has to go in *exactly* the right spot – as that's the way it will be unloaded for the next show. One box at a time. One truck at a time. All happening at once. Then the truck doors are shut tight and those trucks pull out of the backstage area and are dispatched onto highways and freeways, moving on to another town or venue, followed by all those exhausted human beings. Those people are roadies.

The bones of the concert bird will be deposited in the next backstage area in another city or town where the same crew will arrange for the skeleton to be unloaded, unpacked and rebuilt. It could be hours away, or days – or weeks. But the phoenix will rise again. The roadies give it wings. Sometimes people climb mountains just because they are there.

In carnival conditions, it's hyped-up adrenalin surging bursts of activity. Extreme highs and hard comedowns. It's addictive. And like any addiction, once you get on, it's hard to stop. The personal costs – of putting the band, the set-up, the show, above everything else – can be great. Roadies do what they do so that *you*, the audience, have the best possible experience at a live music event – be that a good old-fashioned beer barn pub or a massive outdoor love festival or concert. If the artist sounds too soft, too loud or too distorted, you're not going to have a great time. If the sounds and lights aren't operating properly, you'll notice. You'll be disappointed. You'll feel like you've wasted your money.

Good roadies are invisible. The better they do their job at a show, the less you see of them. If you catch sight of a roadie scrabbling across the stage and fiddling with a piece of equipment, that usually means something has gone wrong.

Roadies are a unique breed. They are fiercely individual and non-conformist, but also collegiate and accommodating. They are, and have to be, real team players. Like the pieces they assemble, they rely on each other to create the whole. It's not going to work unless they all work together.

Roadies are literally always on the road, constantly on the move. They've run away to join the circus that is the world of rock'n'roll. They immerse themselves in it. And they are, for the most part, protected by it. They are in turn protective of the artists they work with. Some are fugitives on the run from their own emotions, from themselves. Others, quite literally, are on the run. Despite the day-to-day hammering their bodies take, and the emotional disruption they may experience, they keep doing it.

The classic roadie image is a stereotype. He has long, straggly hair, wears singlets and tattered jeans, has a ring of keys on his back pocket, bears a few tattoos, and has the pallor of someone who takes far too many drugs, drinks too much and has a girl in every town. That's right – roadie culture is predominantly male. It's never been exclusively that, and it's slowly changing, but it's still a testosterone-fuelled world, even if many roadies have a gentleness – almost an old-world chivalry – that's not immediately apparent.

And there's one thing every musician will tell you that goes a long way to explaining why musicians – at least the smart ones – are always very, very nice to their roadies. Cross a roadie and anything can happen, because roadies know everything. Absolutely *everything*.

Misbehaved on the road? The roadies know about it. And they know who with. And they probably have their number and beat you to it anyway. Overdoing it with the pharmaceuticals? The road crew have almost certainly been there, done that and are better at it than you. Do you have a fetish for albino sheepdogs bred in remote European villages? The road crew will know how to source one – and will shut up about your little secret. They may piss themselves with laughter when you're not around, but when you are, it's: 'Mate, the babe is waiting. No, you don't owe me anything.'

•

As Jimmy Barnes knows only too well, a good road crew is one of the essentials of the rock'n'roll world. You need songs, a singer, a band, an audience – and a first-rate road crew.

'Most of the guys who do this job are very clever,' he says, 'and very resourceful. Necessity makes it happen. The show *has* to happen and they'll do absolutely whatever it takes for that to happen. Our key roadies – like Gerry Georgettis, Nicky Campbell and Harry Parsons – not only introduced us to lots of music, but they were as instrumental in making Chisel the band we were as the actual band members were. They deserve an equal share. We couldn't do it without them. They work harder than anyone I've met in my life.

'Everyone in the business knows how integral they are to a show. They make it seamless. Cold Chisel would drive for three hours and there it would all be, set up and ready to go. Then we get all the glory and they tear it down, pack it up, transport it and set it up again before we get to the next town. That's pretty amazing in itself.'

And as Barnes knows better than most, you don't mess with your road crew. Ever. And if you do it's at your own peril.

'They know your darkest secrets. They know your weakest points. They know your strong points. They know more about you than any of the audience. And they know how they've had to prop you up and make you seem good so many times.

'For years I'd be a mess and the crew would slap me around and get me onstage. Give me just enough to drink or a line to get me going and then push me out onto the stage.

'When we were doing seven or eight shows a week – sometimes three on a Saturday night – we were fucked. It was just so much work. We were seeing stars, and to think they set up and took down the gear from morning till night, sometimes three times a day. And they had the same level of enthusiasm. If they didn't have their shit together we didn't come across onstage.

'The crew were like the contact point for us with the audience. Crews plug everyone in the band into the audience.'

•

I've been around roadies for decades. During my years managing bands such as the Hoodoo Gurus and Paul Kelly and The Messengers/Coloured Girls, I hired a lot of them. I shared hotel rooms and vans with them. I've been yelled at by them, been looked after by them, and sadly had to fire or not rehire some of them.

Like every artist and manager, I've been guilty of taking them for granted. I've assumed they were bulletproof and capable of doing things that were clearly impossible. Even if the truck loaded with the crew and equipment drove at 300 kilometres an hour, they were not going to get from Gig A to Gig B in ten hours.

Over the years I've drunk far too much beer with roadies and bought far too many drugs from them. A good roadie always knows how and where to score. And they score good. Some of the crew from those days are still my friends.

I've only lost one friend to the rigours of the roadie world – and that was a woman trying her hand in the very blokey world of the mid-1980s Australian road crew. Genevieve Farmer was killed in a car accident near Coffs Harbour while working for The Johnnys. My obituary for her and a rumination on roadies was published in the *Sun-Herald*.

Really, I'm lucky to have known just one roadie who's lost their life. Given the hundreds of thousands of kilometres driven by roadies over the decades, often on less-than-ideal roads and frequently with a bloodstream fuelled by alcohol and ampheta-mines – and just one or two (or three) joints – it's astonishing that the road toll has been so low. The real carnage has been in the area of mental health. And it's frightening. Very frightening.

When I was researching my biography of Michael Gudinski, I received invaluable assistance about the Melbourne music scene in the late 1960s and early 1970s from Adrian Anderson, who had worked extensively as a roadie. During one conversation he told me about the Australian Road Crew Association (ARCA), which was launched in 2013 by working and retired roadies to try to stall the staggering rate of suicide among former roadies. In basic terms, Australian road crew members suicide at four to five times the national rate. Internationally the rate is nowhere near as high.

Why have legions of Australian roadies been ending their own lives? There are some basic reasons. Physical incapacity. Poverty. Mental illness. Decreased demand. A changing work-place. A lot of the older generation began working in the business in their late teens. There was no occupational health and safety, and no training. They spent ten or twenty years pushing their bodies to breaking point.

And their bodies did break. Many former roadies suffer signif-icant back and muscular-skeletal problems. They've had multiple surgeries, and body parts replaced. That's if they can afford it. Others live with chronic pain. Too many roadies have passed away simply neglecting their own physical and mental health, or because they lack the means to get proper medical attention.

Sometimes the work just dries up. The artist a roadie has been committed to moves on, or a band breaks up. The Australian live scene is not what it was in the 1960s, '70s, '80s and even into the '90s. There is less work, and more competition for it.

Until recent times there was no superannuation for roadies. Some roadies were paid comparatively well for the work they did, others not so well. There is still no holiday pay. Beyond watching great rock'n'roll, and a lifestyle that many enjoyed, there were no other benefits. Except maybe a sense of purpose, and of family and belonging. But when it's all over, that can be lost too. For some, there is no one waiting at home, or no home at all.

Like the musicians they work for, roadies have a tendency to overuse alcohol, stimulants and other drugs. Often whatever they can get their hands on. Ultimately, though, using stimulants for short-term escapes or as pick-me-ups often masks deep-seated issues, which some roadies put off dealing with for years and years.

It's an understatement but years on the road makes it hard to maintain long-term relationships. Find a former roadie who has a stable, longstanding relationship and you've found a roadie who is probably not in danger of self-harm. Sadly, there are many who don't have stable relationships and family support.

Then there's the issue of gaining other employment. Sure, there's security work or corporate events for some, but for others many doors are closed because they have no recognised qualifications.

'Mate, I can get Guns N' Roses around the country, onstage and not missing a gig – but apparently I'm not qualified to do anything,' said one former roadie.

The tragic suicide of Gerry Georgettis ten years ago galvanised the roadie community, and led to the formation of ARCA. The mantra of the organisation is that a roadie should call another roadie each week and check in on them, and this – along with financial assistance, in conjunction with the Support Act organisation – has dramatically reduced the suicide rate. Former roadies are learning that they're not alone.

●

Why did I decide to write the stories of Australian roadies? Partly because I know and love the world they inhabit. I was stunned by the suicides, and acutely aware that with each passing we lost not only a great individual but a key part of Australian music and popular-culture history.

No one was recording oral histories with these roadies. No one was preserving their memories and stories, some of them hysterically funny, others beyond poignant.

Roadies know Australian music history in ways that no one else does. Not even the artists who make the music. Roadies know the real road stories, the successes, the disasters, the fuck-ups and the triumphs. They speak a language that is distinctly Australian. It's direct, and often laden with expletives. And they tell a secret history of music in this country – from small pub bands to the mainstream success stories and the international tourists. Artists are only at their own gigs; roadies are at everybody's gigs. That makes them custodians of a unique history of Australian and international rock'n'roll.

The roadies featured in this book have worked with dozens, often hundreds, of artists, across all musical styles. There is nothing they haven't seen, fixed, set up or packed up. The world of the roadie is about providing a special service: it's about making musicians look and sound as good as they possibly can, night after night after night.

Roadies are great storytellers. They have hundreds and hundreds (make that thousands) of yarns – almost all of them embellished to some degree by years of retelling. Theirs is in the classic oral-history tradition, apocryphal yarns passed along in seedy bars, backstage, in hotel rooms and cramped trucks. Many of those stories and shared reminiscences are in this book. Of course hundreds of them aren't.

This book can't hope to feature every Australian roadie, or tell all their stories. They could probably fill ten thick volumes and still only touch the surface. What I have attempted to do is bring you into the world of some amazing characters, and let them have a yarn about their journey on the road with Australian and international artists. It isn't definitive, but I have no doubt that it is representative.

By the end of this book, I hope you never view a rock'n'roll concert the same way again. You'll be looking around for the road crew. You'll realise just what has taken place behind the scenes so you could witness this musical event – and what will continue to take place long after you've gone home.

One roadie I spoke to for this book commented that everyone admires a Ferrari – it looks magnificent and runs like a dream. But the real essence of a Ferrari is the engine under the bonnet. Without that, it's just a good-looking piece of metal.

Road crew are the engine under the bonnet of every rock'n'roll performer.

1

In the Beginning

Unfortunately, and romantic though it may sound, on the seventh day God did not create roadies. Economics and the need for strong arms and increased mobility between a myriad of gigs created roadies.

Life before roadies? Yes, of course there was such a thing. That was a world where musicians carried their own gear and set it up themselves.

But in the rock'n'roll era the amount of equipment increased and musicians found themselves having to carry sound equipment, mixing desks, amps and occasionally even lights.

This all needed to be loaded in and out of vehicles, carted in and out of venues, and set up and operated. Enter the need for a roadie.

Who was the very first roadie? No one can answer that with any degree of certainty, but one artist who's prepared to put their hand up and give a name to possibly the first Australian roadie is singer Col Joye. And he's *very* definitive about it, explaining that before he started in the entertainment business, travelling artists – mostly country performers, such as Buddy Williams, Tex Morton and Slim Dusty – all transported their own equipment from town to town, loaded it onstage and got it working.

The first Australian roadie, according to Col Joye, was James Robert Doyle – Jim Doyle – and he emanated from the Bronte Surf Club in Sydney where he began working with The Joy Boys and their singer.

'Jim Doyle was the first roadie in Australia and he moved equipment, set up equipment and worked the spotlight,' Joye says emphatically.

Joye is adamant that he had a roadie well before Johnny O'Keefe.

'We were among the first rock'n'roll bands to tour Australia. O'Keefe had only been out once or twice and they played rooms with an existing sound set-up. But we took all our own sound and lights. We had a six-by-four box trailer and a ute and another vehicle and we carried everything.'

What Joye is uncertain about is whether the roadie who became better known as 'Spider' Doyle started working with him in the very late 1950s or early '60s. That specific detail is buried in the mists of time.

But what he does recall is that he and the Joy Boys used to play a dance on Sunday nights at the Bronte Surf Club.

'One night a copper came up to me and said, "We've got this young bloke here and he's going to get himself into trouble so see if you can find something for him to do because he's on a downhill slide."'

This potentially wayward youth, as Joye recalls, was both young and headstrong. Joye went up to Doyle and told him he was on the payroll and to pick up all the guitars and amplifiers and stick them in the back of the band's utility. He said that the next night they had a dance at Lakemba and that Doyle needed to be there when the musicians arrived and unload the gear.

'Spider' Doyle, who was a teenager at the time he started, worked with Joye for the next decade and a half before eventually moving on to work at Telecom.

Even though he started roadying some years after 'Spider' Doyle, another pioneering Australian figure in this world was John Highlands, who began working with Max Merritt and the Meteors, soon after the band members left hospital and recuperated following a horrible car accident in June 1967.

A head-on collision on the way to a gig in Morwell in Victoria resulted in singer Merritt losing his right eye; saxophonist Bob Bertles was left with a permanent limp; and drummer Stewart Speer never regained full mobility after his legs were crushed.

Highlands and his mate Lee Dillow had come to know Bertles and Speer at the Spanish Club in the Latin Quarter in Sydney. Dillow had relocated to Melbourne and kept up contact with the musicians in their new band with Merritt.

Following the accident Dillow called Highlands, who was working in a cocktail bar in Sydney, and said there was work going in Melbourne with this band if he wanted it.

Prior to the accident Merritt and the Meteors did what most bands did – set up all their own gear and equipment – but now that was more complicated because of their injuries.

Highlands started carrying their gear in and out of gigs. Speer taught him how to set up the drum kit. It was basic stuff and Highlands didn't even refer to himself as a 'roadie'.

'I just took care of them,' he says. 'They treated me as a part of the band. As it went on I was introduced to people as both their roadie and their mate.

'I'm not sure about other states but I'm pretty sure I was the first full-time roadie in Melbourne. I 24/7 lived and breathed Max Merritt and the Meteors. I was constantly busy with up to twenty gigs a week.

'In those days it was just so primitive. Little valve amps which were pretty easy to move in and out of gigs. You had to learn very quickly how to solve problems and have a back-up plan if the first one failed. You learnt from day one and there was hardly anyone to show you what to do. I'd set everything up – they just walked onstage and off.'

In 1968, when Max Merritt was taking a break from live work, Highlands also worked with Billy Thorpe.

'I enjoyed Thorpie but I really loved Max,' is how Highlands views it.

Highlands isn't particularly fazed by claims of who came first in the roadie scene. He recalls Mick Cox, Wayne 'Swampy' Jarvis, Norm Swiney, Nick Campbell, John D'Arcy and others being around at a similar time, along with Daryl Kavanagh, another member of the first wave of serious, full-time roadies and the man who took over as Billy Thorpe's main roadie.

Kavanagh – who was best man at Thorpe's wedding – came out of the world of boxing, particularly on TV.

'I used to fight on *TV Ringside* when Ron Casey started the TV show,' Kavanagh says. 'I was on the very first night, the same night Lionel Rose and Johnny Famechon boxed an exhibition bout of three rounds, the only time they were ever in a ring together.'

Next Kavanagh came into the orbit of Billy Thorpe. Apparently Thorpe had watched Kavanagh fight on TV and when the two met at the Thumpin' Tum disco, the singer asked Kavanagh if he was interested in some work.

'I started driving for him. None of them could drive after a gig because they were usually pretty full. I don't drink or smoke, so I used to pick them up and drive them around. The band worked for wages, so I'd collect all the money from gigs and pay them whatever was agreed. I guess I was sort of like their manager.

'I thought of myself more as a caretaker. And I got up during the day. No one else got up in daylight. I'd go and set up all the gear in the places we were playing and organise things.

'And I drove everywhere – usually with Lobby Loyde, who would never fly. He was frightened, so he used to come in the van with me. I used to drive a dual-wheel transit van with the speaker boxes in the back.

'After I'd set up the gear I'd go and wake them up and get them food or whatever was needed. I was like a caretaker, a bit of a gopher. I was the one everyone spoke to because I collected the money, set up the gear and did the lighting. I organised the food for the band and Billy's dry-cleaning. That was my job.

'I can remember at times having $20,000 or $30,000 in cash in a bag under the front seat of the car.'

Kavanagh drove Thorpe and the band everywhere – Sydney, Melbourne, Canberra, Brisbane and a lot of trips to Adelaide, because that was the closest major city to their home base.

When it came time for Thorpe to venture overseas he offered Kavanagh the opportunity to come to America with him, but the roadie decided to stay and did a stint with the New Zealand band Compulsion before moving out of the music industry caper.

'I finished up when my wife told me that I could either stay working with bands or go with her – and she looked a lot better than they did, so my decision was made.'

Kavanagh was certainly not the last roadie to have to make that decision.

2

The First Woman

Howard Freeman remembers being at a Sunbury Music Festival with Tana Douglas. The memory still makes him smile – and bristle.

'Someone didn't want her backstage in the security area and I told them to get fucked,' he says. 'That was the first time I got to say the words: "Fuck off – *she* is a roadie." For Douglas to get through all that was pretty amazing. She did it by the size of her balls. And she was *very* good at her gig.'

Tana Douglas can lay a strong claim to being the world's first female roadie. And not only was she a roadie, she also spent an extended period doing sound for AC/DC. Yes, that's right. Sound. For. AC/DC. But doing things that hadn't been done before was what Tana Douglas did best.

From the age of nine or ten, Douglas began running away from home and school. Eventually she was put in boarding school, which was harder to run away from. At boarding school in 1969 Douglas heard about the upcoming Woodstock festival and wanted to go. She called her dad and told him she wasn't coming home for the holidays – she wanted to go and see Janis

Joplin sing. She was about eleven at the time. This wasn't going to happen.

Of course, Douglas's father hopped in his car and drove to the school immediately, thinking his daughter had gone mad. She was too young even to know where Woodstock was. So Douglas and her father had a serious sit-down. She told him that if she could go to Woodstock, she would study hard and get A grades in everything, and she'd never ask for anything ever again. She figured she had to go because it'd be the only chance she'd ever have of seeing Janis. Sadly, she was right about that: Joplin died just a few months after the festival.

Eventually, Douglas did a runner and made her way to Nimbin, in northern New South Wales – 'Australia's answer to Woodstock', as she calls it, 'for everyone else who felt ripped off by not being able to go'.

Soon Douglas was doing the whole hippie thing. In 1973 in Nimbin she met a French guy called Philippe Petit, who a year later would walk across a tightrope between the two World Trade Center buildings in New York City. In Nimbin he and a coterie of friends were planning a less ambitious but still audacious venture. Petit was intending to do a tightrope walk between the northern pylons of the Sydney Harbour Bridge – just for practice, to get into the swing of things before tackling the World Trade Center.

To Douglas, this seemed beyond exciting, so instead of staying in the rainforests and growing pot she joined Petit's gang and headed to Sydney, where she had a small but important role in the walk.

'I didn't do any of the rigging because obviously that's really technical and they had their own crew for that,' she recalls. 'I was part of the ground crew – one of the people who caught the cans of film as they dropped them down off the edge and then took off like I was in *The Great Escape* so they didn't get confiscated.'

After the thrill of the bridge walk, Douglas left Sydney and headed to Kuranda, growing pot and settling into the hippie lifestyle once again, but the lure of Sydney was strong and she soon returned.

'I'd been running around naked pretty much, in the forest. It was the whole "Kumbaya" thing up there, playing guitar by the fire every night looking at the stars thing up there,' she says. 'Everyone was telling me not to go back to Sydney, and certainly not to Kings Cross, but by now I was curious and my response was: "Why not?" So, off I went.'

By chance, Douglas ended up sharing an apartment with two other young women who were into the Sydney nightlife. They started club-hopping together, and it was at the Whiskey A Go Go in William Street, just down from the main drag of Kings Cross, that Douglas met a man who would play a major role in her life: the already legendary Wayne 'Swampy' Jarvis.

'He was working with some R&B band from the States playing for all the American soldiers. It was really the dregs of that scene, with lots of servicemen coming through. But I was pretty interested as the music was completely electric, whereas in the forest where I came from it was all acoustic. I was asking Swampy questions and he was telling me things, and then he asked if I wanted to come back the next night, which I did.'

Douglas rocked up late. Everyone involved with the band and the show had gone out and got trashed the night before. The gear was staying at the club for the next night's show, so there was no packing up and loading out to do. Party time.

That was why the sound guy figured he could arrive at the very last minute, along with the band – but the cleaning ladies at the venue had thought they'd do the right thing and clean his desk for him, so all the settings had been changed from the way he left it. When Douglas arrived the guy was freaking out, running backwards and forwards between his desk and the band and trying to get everything back the way it was.

'Swampy's running around too,' Douglas remembers. 'I asked what happened and he said, "The fucking sound guy isn't happening – that's what happened!" The show that night was terrible, and I only stayed to see if he could get it together in time.'

The next day Swampy and the band were heading to Melbourne. Douglas was amazed that people actually got paid to travel with bands.

Not long afterwards, one of the women Douglas was sharing her flat with said that some friends of hers from a Melbourne band, Fox, were coming to Sydney for some gigs. This flatmate was driving Douglas crazy, forever carrying on about how great Melbourne was, and how her parents would take care of her if she moved back. Douglas started praying that Fox would give her flatmate a lift back down south.

At their last Sydney gig of that run she introduced the idea to the band's guitarist, Peter Laffey, who said that if all the band's gear was packed and they got on the road that night, the flatmate could come with them. Now Douglas was on a mission.

'I looked at the stage and all the gear, and everyone was wandering around in circles and doing nothing, so I offered to help. Everyone in the band laughed, knowing the reaction I'd get from their crew guys, so I wandered over to the stage and told them I'd give them a hand and asked what I could do. They showed me how to coil cables. There is a definite way to do it correctly and I learnt how.'

As Douglas worked, the other roadies started picking up their game: they didn't want to be shown up by some girl. In no time they had everything loaded into the truck. Douglas threw her flatmate into the front seat, and off she went.

The next time Fox returned to Sydney for more gigs, they called Douglas and said they were a guy short: did she want to come and do the gig? It was that casual. She thought it was hilarious that they asked, and figured they just wanted to see if she could do it again.

During Fox's run of Sydney shows, Douglas met a roadie who would mentor her: the already established, already bordering on legendary, and certainly infamous $crooge Madigan. He was the roadie for Daddy Cool, with whom Fox was doing a show. Swampy Jarvis was also at the gig as he was working for the promoter. These guys took Douglas seriously.

'No one acted like, "What the fuck is going on?" – they just told me what went where, and I just went and did it. I was just sponging everything up, and I didn't want to make a fool of myself. Then Fox said they were going back to Melbourne and asked if I wanted to go back with them.'

Fox's booking agent worked in what was known at the time as Mushroom House, and that was where Douglas met a young Michael Gudinski. She went to the office every week to collect Fox's worksheets, which explained the details of the gigs they had coming up. Fox was doing okay for a band of their level, with three or four shows a week in and around Melbourne. Douglas thought that was a lot – until she saw the work schedule of the next band she would get involved with.

The roadie world at this time was still comparatively small. There was $crooge, Swampy, John D'Arcy and a handful of others. They all knew each other and knew the lifestyle. They were all blokes until Douglas came along. And because she was accepted by the 'cool guys', other roadies accepted her as well.

Fox began to run out of steam, so booking agent Bill Joseph started to look around for other work for Douglas. Joseph became a father figure to her. 'He was kind, always letting me into his office and telling me things and teaching me stuff,' she says. 'Gudinski would fly in and out of rooms and I'd listen to what I could from him, too. I think everyone got used to me just being around. It's like a stray kitten that wanders in and someone feeds it, and before you know it everyone's feeding it. Then it's, "Oh yeah, that's our cat."'

One day Joseph mentioned to Douglas that there was a band coming to town and they'd be looking for a full crew, and he thought it'd be an interesting job. Douglas felt loyal to the Fox guys but still she didn't really hesitate.

It was definitely interesting – and more. The band was called AC/DC.

Joseph hooked Douglas up with their manager, Michael Browning, and she went round to the band's house in Lansdowne Road, East St Kilda. It was late 1974. There she met Bon Scott, and Angus and Malcolm Young. Also there were Harry Vanda and George Young. After the introductions were made, they told Douglas the band needed someone to be their stage roadie, and asked if she wanted to do it. 'I can do that,' she replied.

They also needed a PA, so Douglas went and picked it up. She was thereafter in charge of looking after it.

Initially, Douglas was AC/DC's roadie. There was a lot of equipment that needed moving around. The only person who had more equipment was Billy Thorpe.

'In the beginning we had an amazing couple of months just hanging around the house, auditioning people,' Douglas says. 'They were writing songs and also recording. They'd take off for a couple of days and go to Sydney to record some things, and then they'd come back down to Melbourne. George and Harry would trade bass or drum parts. And that's how it was. It wasn't really a band then.'

In Douglas's opinion, the AC/DC the world knows started at that time in the house in St Kilda. The glam rock period – when they dressed in pink satin and Dave Evans fronted the band – was over. Bon Scott was singing, and the dress – with the exception of Angus's perennial schoolboy outfit – was working-class and 'rock'.

'They'd been in Sydney, and George and Harry had had the "You know what, this isn't going to work" chat. That's when they decided on the change of direction. The big vision started at Lansdowne Road.'

Douglas was AC/DC's roadie for their first shows with Bon Scott fronting the band. 'Bon was still friends with his wife, even though they'd just separated. After the gig we went to her house and had a barbecue. That's where Bon announced that he'd joined the band!'

According to Douglas, the passing of time has distorted some versions of this period of AC/DC. Even those very close to the band don't have totally accurate recollections of the time. She laughs as she recalls a Sunbury Music Festival that AC/DC *didn't* play at.

'We didn't have a proper bass player then,' she says. 'George was going to play bass but we ended up having a fight with Deep Purple backstage, and we just went, "Fuck it, we're not playing."'

Douglas was with AC/DC for about 18 months, and as well as being their roadie she did the front-of-house sound. In those days, the roadies did everything that the band didn't do.

'I was with them for the first three albums,' she says. 'We went back to Sydney as returning heroes. They invited me to stay with their families for a night before we started a run of Bondi Lifesaver shows. I think we did four or five nights there and 12 shows in total. Then we came back to Melbourne and did the Myer Music Bowl, and we started doing Festival Halls and the like.'

But things were changing rapidly in AC/DC's world. Their audiences were growing, and the sound requirements at the larger gigs meant that the band's old PA system just wasn't cutting it anymore. 'It got to the point where they needed a lighting rig and a bigger PA, because the one we had just couldn't handle Bon's voice. He just couldn't cut through it.' The band decided they needed a production company.

With the exception of Bon Scott, AC/DC was a very young rock'n'roll band. The police would often turn up at pubs to arrest Angus because they assumed he was underage with his schoolboy uniform, even though he was 19 at the time and allowed into pubs, and Douglas – who at 16 *was* underage – would run interference so he could avoid the cops.

Douglas was a fine sound person, particularly as – like all road crew from that era – she'd learnt on the job, with no formal training.

'I was out of my depth with sound at this stage and there was no one to show me,' she reflects. 'There was no time to refine things. There was a minimum of ten shows a week. I sabotaged the tops on Angus's amp because it was the only way I could get Bon's voice above it. I had to do it. That's how desperate it was.'

Things were escalating rapidly. The band was living at the Freeway Gardens Motel in Melbourne, and according to Douglas it was a free-for-all. Girls broke in through the windows hoping they'd be in the room of one of the band members. People wanted to fight her at gigs, particularly female fans jealous of her closeness to the band.

'They'd go, "Who the fuck are you?" so it got a little hairy there for a while and I had to rethink things. Then we got this horrible bus thing. That was also pretty much the beginning of the end for me, because it was just horrible. The travel thing that I'd signed on for wasn't this. The bus kept breaking down all the time, and it was freezing and horrible. You'd have to actually cuddle someone to avoid freezing to death on the road. I went to myself, "You know what, this isn't happening."'

At the end of 1975 Douglas was also starting to get a bit disillusioned with AC/DC and what was happening. It was all moving too fast, and she felt she couldn't see clearly where she was going. She needed to stop and think, but that meant stepping away from the band because they weren't stopping for anyone.

Douglas was closest to Malcolm Young, although she had a strong bond with Angus as well, and with their families. On reflection, she thinks that family was – and is – so important to the Youngs that it might have been a factor in why they enjoyed having her on the road. 'With a girl on their crew, it gave them a little semblance of home,' she says, 'because with me around it didn't just seem like a bunch of guys on the road going for it.'

Eventually, Malcolm took Douglas aside and told her that they felt they needed someone more experienced to do their sound. He asked her if she wanted to take over doing lights, but she decided instead to leave and find a place where she could learn more.

Still not even 18 years of age, Douglas said farewell to AC/DC – but they parted on good terms. Now she had to sort out what she was going to do – and find somewhere to live, as during her AC/DC time all that had been taken care of.

In the end she had virtually no time off. The promoter and tour manager Ron Blackmore had taken over a PA system that the American band Blood, Sweat & Tears had left in Australia in 1973. Instead of shipping it back to America it was decided to leave it in Australia with Bruce Jackson, the sound engineer who had formed Jands, and then use it for an upcoming Johnny Cash tour. It was pretty much the best PA system in the world at the time, a mythical beast known as a Clair Brothers System. That became Ron Blackmore's calling card. With it, he and promoter Paul Dainty secured 90 per cent of the international tours coming to Australia in the era. Everyone wanted to use a Clair Brothers PA.

And Blackmore picked a superlatively talented array of young Australian road crew to work with it: Wyn Milsom, Peter Wilson, Howard Page, Peter Rooney, Nicky Campbell, Michael Oberg and others. They needed a lighting person, and Douglas got the gig.

'That was amazing,' she recalls. 'Out of all the people in Australia who could have got that job, I did. And I've got Peter Wilson teaching me electricity, and I've got Swampy and all these other guys – I've got the cream to learn from.

'There were no rules, and people were making shit up as they went along. And that attitude stays with you – that's why so many Australians got snapped up by international bands. It was because they couldn't believe the ingenuity. It's the stuff people joke about now. "Just drive a six-inch nail in there so the fuse won't blow? Okay, let's try it. It has a wooden handle, doesn't it? Step back – it might make a noise."

'That's what kept me going in those early years. It was simply that I didn't know any better.'

Eventually, Douglas moved to England. She wanted to go to America but circumstances dictated that the UK was her next stop. There she shared a flat with Swampy Jarvis, who was working with Status Quo, and also making a name for himself for other reasons.

'He was quite the lad with the girls,' Douglas laughs.

That reputation landed Jarvis in all sorts of trouble, including being shot at by an American singer/songwriter after he suspected the Australian tour manager was having an affair with his recently ex-wife.

Not long after, Jarvis suffered a massive heart attack in the UK and returned to Australia, but Douglas stayed on, working as a lighting person with Status Quo. Through this she ended up working for TASCO, one of the world's biggest sound production companies, which ended up buying the Quo's lighting system so that when the band wasn't working they could offer both sound and lighting equipment and crews.

While running the lighting, Douglas worked with an astonishing array of artists, and on events such as Prince Andrew's 21st birthday party at Windsor Castle, where Elton John was the entertainment.

'Everyone's off their head, Elton wouldn't get off the stage, it was a nightmare,' she laughs now.

Douglas still harboured an ambition to get to the States, but she kept working with Status Quo and a myriad of other acts. She even returned to Australia a few times with the Quo.

'You came back a conquering hero,' she says. 'And it made the local crew people feel really good to see us doing it, because Australia was so isolated back then. It was such a small industry, and a hard industry in Australia. People drove everywhere – there was no flying. They didn't get enough sleep, and cars and trucks were running off the road. It was tough touring in Australia.'

After years working in the UK, Douglas decided that England's weather was miserable and cold: she needed to get out. There'd also been an enjoyable nine-month stint in Paris, working with French superstar Johnny Hallyday. Setting up and running his lighting system was a challenge Douglas enjoyed.

'We were working with this massive lighting system, and there was a discussion about whether or not something could be done. Everyone looked at me and I said, "If you can think it, then it can be done."

'Paris was nice but you're not seeing a lot of it. You get up at 5 pm, go and do the show and get to bed at 6 am. You don't really see daylight for months, and that's not healthy.'

Hallyday wanted Douglas to be his mistress. She replied by saying that as soon as she permanently relocated to Paris, she was sure he'd dump her. His reply was priceless: 'Tana, we leave our wives, but not our mistresses.'

Douglas had by this stage moved to America. TASCO had a sound equipment office in New York, but when they opened a lighting division on the west coast in the 1980s, Douglas moved to LA. There she ended up working with lots of heavy rock and metal bands.

'I hated a lot of it,' she recalls. 'I got stuck with one US performer's first solo tour, with him and his partner crawling on the floor and puking everywhere and vowing their undying love. It was ugly. Very ugly. But they had a great road crew and that's probably why everyone stayed.'

With the exception of a brief sojourn back in Australia, Douglas has been based in Los Angeles ever since, running her own tour logistics business. If you have a lot of concert equipment that needs to be freighted anywhere in the world, Douglas is your go-to woman.

Today Douglas is semi-retired, but something keeps dragging her back – and it's not always the money. She still loves music, concerts, production, lighting – the excitement and the challenge of it all. And it all started with AC/DC.

'I've never really felt normal anywhere else,' she laughs, although perhaps with a hint of poignancy. 'People would see me working and say, "What are you doing, bitch?" And I'd look at them and say, "Well, I'm loading a truck – would you like to give me a hand?"'

3

$crooge

'$crooge' Madigan has a real first name – it's Graham – but no one uses it. In fact, very few people use his surname either. He's just $crooge. He writes it that way. Yes, with the dollar sign at the front. He's one of the most legendary roadies ever to load a van and set up a stage in this country. And he's still working.

Ask him where the nickname came from and he quickly becomes circumspect. He mutters about being brought up in a tough environment, and being associated with people 'who later became TV shows'. But clearly there was a time when it wasn't such a good idea for him to use his real name.

$crooge may be a little guy but, make no mistake, he's tough. Very tough. He can look after himself in any situation, and anyone who mistakes him for a pint-sized pushover does so at their peril.

He was one of the pioneers of the 'one man, one van, one band' era. $crooge's band was Daddy Cool. He lived for them, had their back, did their business. Of course, Daddy Cool became one of the most famous rock'n'roll bands Australia has ever produced, but when $crooge became their roadie he was belittled for getting involved with them.

'When I started with Daddy Cool, you had Coxy and D'Arcy and Jiva – they were the fucking roadies, the kings of the road,' he says. 'They asked me who I was with, and when I said Daddy Cool they just looked at me and said, "Who are they?" But I just turned to them and said, "One of these days they'll be one of the biggest bands in Australia."'

And $crooge was right.

As Daddy Cool grew, so did he. $crooge walked the walk. In fact, he swaggered. And he talked a million miles an hour with a don't-fuck-with-me attitude. He talked like that even before he discovered amphetamines; combine the two and it was nonstop verbiage.

After leaving school, $crooge worked at a travel agency. The Valentines' truck would blow up on a regular basis, and when it did, who did their roadie, John D'Arcy, call? $crooge. The two were mates who went way back – $crooge grew up in Brunwsick in Melbourne, while D'Arcy was a Coburg boy. They hung around together during the sharpie era.

$crooge's company, Parlor Cars and Coaches, ran interstate buses to Adelaide, Sydney and Brisbane. When the Valentines' van exploded (it was a regular occurrence), $crooge would tell D'Arcy to bring the band's gear into the office. He'd stash it under a bus, and D'Arcy and the band would climb aboard, sitting up the back blowing joints, drinking and having a mighty fine time.

In 1970 $crooge started doing martial arts. He already knew how to handle himself; this was just a case of getting better at it. His instructor was Bob Jones, who used to be a bouncer at the Southern Cross Hotel and had a team of guys who looked after the security at the majority of clubs in the city. One night Jones asked $crooge if he'd work the door at the T. F. Much Ballroom. That was where he met Wayne Duncan, Ross Wilson and Gary Young. They were in a band with a guy called Ross Hannaford. They were called The Sons of the Vegetal Mother, a trippy outfit, but late in 1970, when an exploration of 1950s rock'n'roll started to feel pretty good, they became Daddy Cool.

One night the band were outside a venue with $crooge, and Wilson asked if the van was his. Affirmative from $crooge. Wilson asked if he'd like a gig with the band – not onstage, but they'd give him $10 to drive them and the gear to Adelaide – and they'd pay for petrol. $crooge had just become a roadie. But he still had to go through the motions to be a full-time roadie with Daddy Cool.

'With Wilson, even in those days you had to apply for the position,' he says. 'The drive to Adelaide wasn't considered enough of a commitment for me to become their roadie. I had to go for an interview with Ross. Ross the Boss – all business. They'd used someone before but that was with the earlier band.

'There were three guys going for the job. They all had a van. That was the thing. You *must* have a van. No van, no gig. What made you a roadie was that you had a van. Simple as that.'

Also essential was an ability to handle yourself. $crooge had the former and was getting even better at the latter.

'If you weren't able to take care of yourself you were in trouble, because you had to be able to take care of the band. The band was your income. So, if you weren't strong enough to guard your band, then you were going to have problems.

'It didn't happen all the time but you'd have to deal with idiots wanting to fight – and people trying to get onstage. Sherbet and Skyhooks would have been worse. We had a reputation as tough guys because that was our gig. And then the band felt okay because they knew we were there. They felt protected.'

And another requirement was to operate normally despite being in a state of altered consciousness.

'Daddy Cool were probably the most out of it band around,' $crooge says. 'They weren't drunks. Wilson not so much, but as for the others . . . we were well known for our ability to consume pretty much anything. In the early days our drugs were pot and acid.'

But $crooge's true drug of choice was speed. He *loved* speed. Having first taken it at 14, he was already known as the Speed King.

'There's a famous colour,' he says. 'It's roadie grey. That was the colour of the roadies because many were speed freaks. It was the colour of our skin. You could pick us a mile away. Speed became a huge drug because of one thing – the amount of work we had to do.

'When "Eagle Rock" came out and became such a big hit, it meant only one thing to me: 14 gigs a week with one roadie, and that roadie was me. You'd do a lunchtime gig and then Bertie's or Sebastian's or the Tum on Friday, and on Saturday three gigs starting somewhere like Ringwood Town Hall. On Sunday there was usually only one gig – but then you'd drive to Adelaide that night to be set up by noon. Adelaide Uni was always your first gig, and at lunchtime. So, we drove from Melbourne and went straight to the gig. How the fuck do you think we were going to stay awake?

'Roadies were notorious in my day. We were the drug suppliers. Simple as that. Apart from being good roadies, we were good drug suppliers.'

Life on the road for Australian rock'n'roll bands and their crews was frequently violent, particularly in smaller towns. $crooge tells the story of one memorable night:

'I remember sitting in a dual transit van with the doors open after we'd done one of the most famous gigs in Australia. Every roadie knows about Shepparton. Our route out of that town was the one fucking road south, and the local fucking kids would wait until you'd finished work for the night and then try and bash the fuck out of you. You were usually by yourself, but this particular night I was lucky as I was with Mickey Christian, who had quite a reputation. He told me he'd do the gig with me. He knew what was going to happen.

'So Daddy Cool played and we're leaving town, driving down the only road, and then we'd look ahead and the only thing we could see was the lights from all the cars blocking the road. Why? Because they wanted to fight us. Why? Because we came to town and because we looked at their girlfriends the wrong way. From that moment on, we're fucked.

'They'd be as polite as they could be early in the day while you're setting up the gear. You'd go out the back for a cigarette and they'd be, "Matey, how you going? Everything good, matey?" They just waited for you to pack up and then it was on. They wanted to kill you.

'So I had Mickey Christian sitting in the back of the van with a sawn-off shotgun, and the two doors open. We drove at the road block and he went *kabang, kabang, kabang*! He was a bad man. But he liked Daddy Cool and he'd come along with me so he could fire his fucking shotgun as we tried to get out of town.'

Then there were the girls. In $crooge's opinion, other bands had more girls 'because Daddy Cool has as much sex appeal as Canned Heat'. But they did okay. $crooge himself and Gary Young did particularly well – at least the way $crooge recalls it. 'There were critical fucking gymnastic activities,' he says. 'Gary and I were known for that. Our presentations at the end of the night were always of a very high level.'

For $crooge, the hit record that was 'Eagle Rock' only meant more gigs – but for the band it meant enough cash to buy a bigger form of transport. They invested in a Chrysler six-cylinder heavy engine Dodge van. This gave them more room for their gear – and the band was starting to carry more by now out of necessity, given the bigger venues. The band members started to fly between cities, but Gary Young continued to accompany

$crooge on the drives with the equipment. They both liked it that way.

And they put in the miles – hundreds of thousands of miles. This was a different sort of touring for pop and rock'n'roll artists. One that doesn't exist anymore.

$crooge brings up a more contemporary example to illustrate his point. He gets annoyed that people bagged out John Farnham for an ultra extensive tour he billed as The Last Time tour.

'He wasn't saying this was his last tour – but it was the last time he was doing it like the old days. He did it, we *all* did it. Someone would start in Cairns and finish in Perth, others would start in Perth and finish in Cairns and you'd always be passing each other on the road. We did every fucking country town.

'Look at the Farnsey Last Time tour – what he did was what we all used to do. Kalgoorlie, Geraldton, Bunbury, Perth, Albany, Whyalla, Adelaide, Mildura, Broken Hill, Ballarat, Bendigo, Melbourne, Mt Gambier, Albury. That's what we ALL USED TO DO. No one does that now. In those days you worked from Rockhampton to Perth and you did every fucking town you could,' $crooge says.

When the tour arrived in a new town, $crooge did everything himself. 'I never had an extra roadie with Daddy Cool,' he explains. 'I couldn't tolerate it. I tried it once with Mighty Kong but the guy didn't work out. Fuck off, I don't need help. But still a lot of us would work with each other and help each other out for no money. If you have a Hammond B3 organ you can't carry that by yourself, so if I wasn't working for Daddy Cool I'd call a mate like Swampy and say I'd come and work with him for the night.

'But it all started to change. One guy became two guys. There was more gear. And then someone said, "Fuck, we'll get lights," and then the crew increased again . . .

'With lights it's still red, green, blue and yellow. There's still going to be those basic colours so it doesn't matter if you've got 20 semitrailers full of lights – there's still the same basic colours. And really, no one goes home humming lights. They go home humming songs. Things just got bigger and bigger.'

On the back of 'Eagle Rock', Daddy Cool became the biggest band in Australia. The money wasn't exactly rolling in but it was okay – an average of $100 a gig. As the unofficial fifth member of the band $crooge was doing just fine. 'I was the highest-paid roadie in the country at the time,' he says. 'Twenty dollars a gig – less tax. As I said, Ross was all business.'

Daddy Cool was also $crooge's ticket to America. Mind you, he didn't go on their first visit to the States when they made a brief visit to Los Angeles for some showcase gigs at the Whisky a Go Go. $crooge was almost 21 years old and his mother was extremely ill. He told the band he couldn't go with them for the week. A few days after they got back, his mother died, on his birthday.

Ross Wilson told him that Daddy Cool would never tour overseas without him again. This was a big deal, as very few Australian bands had performed overseas, especially in America – among the only ones were the Easybeats and the Bee Gees. Taking an Australian roadie overseas with you was a very new concept.

$crooge ended up doing a number of American tours with Daddy Cool, playing with the likes of Little Feat, Captain Beefheart, Harvey Mandel, Jo Jo Gunne, the Stone Poneys, Earth, Wind & Fire, Ten Years After and others. He learnt the hard way – and very quickly – that things worked very differently in America.

'We were playing at Madison Square Garden in New York with Deep Purple and Fleetwood Mac,' he recalls. 'I carried a speaker box through the little backstage area that we had there and plonked it on the stage. Then all hell broke loose.

'All the crews from the big bands came up to me demanding to know what I was doing. I told them that I was doing what it looked like I was doing – bringing our gear in. But they said I wasn't allowed to. It was all unionised.

'Two guys from Deep Purple's crew, who I subsequently became good friends with, said, "Listen, you're doing 15 fucking minutes – don't touch a fucking thing." They asked who I was and I told them I was the roadie. Then I asked them what they did. One said he was the production manager and the other said that he was the tour manager. That's when I discovered "Life After Roadie". Where I came from it was still one man, one van, one band. And if you were the roadie, when the band split up you either went with the brain surgeon from that band or you gave the game away.'

When Daddy Cool did split up in mid-1972, $crooge went with the brain surgeons from that band – Ross Wilson and Ross Hannaford – to Mighty Kong. Then when that band broke up, our intrepid and enterprising roadie reached for the phone and called Eric Robinson at Jands Production Services. This was the beginning of the era where large production houses – another was Ron Blackmore's Artist Concert Tours (ACT) – would offer a one-stop shop for concert promoters: an all-in-one price for sounds, lights, trucks and road crew.

Jands changed the world of concert production in Australia, and this changed the way road crews worked. 'In the old days, when international bands used to tour, Jands had a really, really good crew of people who had toured a lot with international acts, and word spread that we were good and could do the job.'

$crooge worked tirelessly both in Australia and overseas. There were big names and not so big names. Seemingly endless runs through Australia or America, and short international tours. His focus was always on looking after the artists – even though, like most other crew members, having to accommodate the stars' frequent and lavish indulgences was demanding.

'Barbra Streisand wanted the backstage area to be a recreation of her house, with a covered walkway to the stage,' he recalls.

'Everything there was meant to be exactly how it was at home – even the fucking air temperature had to be identical to wherever she came from. The flowers, the white couch – all just like home.'

One that sticks in $crooge's memory is when he worked on a Stevie Wonder tour being promoted by Paul Dainty. 'I have a look at the rider [the list of requirements for the artist] and then I go and tell Dainty that there's one thing missing with the rider for Stevie. In that posh English accent he has, Dainty asks me what it is. I go, "Paul, the cunt's fucking blind – is there an itinerary in Braille for him?" There wasn't, so I went down to the Institute for the Blind and got an itinerary done in Braille for him, didn't I.

'I took it to the first Australian gig, at the Hordern Pavilion. I find Stevie standing up against the wall in the dressing room. I asked him what he was doing, and he told me he had been told to stand there and not move. I gave him the Braille itinerary and there were some big changes after that. A lot of the indulgent and excessive stuff on the backstage rider disappeared. Until then, he had no idea what was going on.

'That's one of the reasons Jands got so much work. It was because they hired crew that could really talk to artists – be it getting them drugs or anything. They just made sure it was the right combination of people on the road. That's why those international acts kept coming back and asking for certain crew members.'

$crooge is a road crew lifer. That's what he knows, and what he does. He's had some tough times financially, and the years of amphetamine use and the rigours of the road have taken their toll. But he's still working. A gig here, a gig there.

He still works on the production of the entertainment for the AFL Grand Final, something he's done for many years. For the past 14 years he's also been a key figure in the production of the RMIT Graduation ceremony at Etihad Stadium. Yes, even graduation ceremonies need crew. And as he points out, there are 7000 students on the ground and 40,000 in the grandstands.

What could possibly go wrong? Lots of things, that's what.

'People ask what I do at events like that and the Grand Final. I say that if anything goes wrong I will fix it. That's what I do. I'm a roadie. We sort shit out.'

4

Enjoy Your Trip

Picture this. It's early one morning. Nick Campbell, roadie for Spectrum, is flying to Melbourne after the band appeared the day before at Myponga, an outdoor festival in Adelaide. They have no time to drive as they are due to appear at the Sunbury Music Festival later that day. Campbell looks across the terminal and sees his friend Mick Cox, a roadie for Doug Parkinson in Focus. They've already played Sunbury and are arriving in Adelaide for a gig.

'Curley, how are you?' says Cox.

Everyone calls Campbell by his nickname. They chat briefly, before it's time to go their separate ways.

'Stick your tongue out, Curley,' says Cox. Curley does what he's told, and Cox places a tab of LSD on his tongue and smiles. 'Enjoy your trip, Curley,' he says as he walks away to collect the band's gear.

Cox is one of *the* great characters of the Australian road crew scene of the 1960s and '70s. He travelled the highways, loaded and unloaded the gear, did the gigs, smoked the dope and took the acid. Just like you did in that era.

Cox comes from Newcastle, and first drifted into the world of entertainment in the mid-1960s. Trained as a carpenter, he built a stage for an English guy called Phil Clark who rented the premises above a local cafe and opened a disco called Shindig Village in 1964, a big deal for the time.

Clark used to bring a group called Steam Packet up from Sydney to play as his resident band, and on weekends he booked bigger names such as Max Merritt. Then he'd send Steam Packet on the road to do extra gigs in places like Armidale and Tamworth. Cox was the guy who drove them there and back.

'I didn't even know I was a roadie! I'm just driving people around and doing all this shit,' Cox laughs.

Cox's close mate was Wayne 'Swampy' Jarvis, who went on to become a revered roadie and tour manager. At the time Jarvis was working for a band called the Tellmen, the resident band at the Belmont Hotel.

With a few friends, Cox and Jarvis were living in a house near the yacht club at Lake Macquarie. Then they got busted. 'Drug ring smashed' screamed the headlines in the local newspaper after a major police raid.

'It had been Swampy's 21st birthday,' recalls Cox. 'His mum and dad lived in Ashfield, so we came down from Newcastle to Sydney and had this party. We were shitfaced but we got in the car and drove back to Newcastle. Everyone went to bed, and the next minute the door gets kicked in and it's the police. They found an ice cream container full of pot.'

They knew they were never going to be left alone now if they stayed in Newcastle. The two returned to Sydney, where they started working with bands like the La De Das.

The spectre of the drug bust haunted Cox for a long time. Many years later he would apply for a gun licence. He'd not been in any trouble since, but his application was refused.

After working in Sydney for a while, Cox and Jarvis, now the proud owners of a transit van, decided to go to Melbourne and advance their careers as roadies. As out-of-towners it wasn't easy at first, but then Wayne de Gruchy gave them a gig driving Zoot on a tour around Victoria. When they returned they were paid not with cash but with 50 tickets to Bertie's nightclub. This was not much use to Jarvis and Cox – until they put their heads together.

'We were desperate and broke so we head down to Bertie's and stood outside on Friday night and scalped these tickets to the joint. This is how we met Bob Jones and all his karate guys because they came outside and told us they were going to fucking kill us if we didn't stop selling tickets to the joint. But they didn't kill us and we became good mates with them.'

The two roadies started looking for bands to work with. Jarvis ended up continuing with Zoot, while Cox got the Avengers, a Brisbane band who had just won a Hoadley's Battle of the Sounds final.

The driving between cities and town was relentless, and Cox remains amazed that bands and roadies had so few road accidents.

'The thing is that we were always off our heads,' he says. 'Trips and smoking dope. If you could get some speed you were lucky, but one way or the other we were always off our tits.

'One night we left Sydney and it's about midnight. We're heading to Melbourne. It's pissing down the whole way. We get to Gundagai and we come swinging around the corner and the river has flooded and it's the middle of the night so we don't see it, and the next thing the van – with us inside – is submerged in water. It's *freezing* cold. We get out, get ashore, freezing our nuts off, and then a semi comes along, cutting through the water. We explain that we're a band and that we have gear in the van. The driver says that if I can go back into the water and put the chain around the axle he'll pull us out.

'Of course I will do this. I'm the roadie. It's pitch-black and in the middle of the night, but I manage to get the chain connected. The truck driver drags us out and pulls us to a servo in Gundagai, where we sit freezing until daybreak until the servo opens and the guy drains the motor.'

The gear in the van included some of the first transistorised amps, and they were soaked. The band headed back to Brisbane and spent a week drying the gear out in their flat.

Cox and his Avengers played around Melbourne and Sydney for a year before deciding to go into recess for six months. Stuck without a gig, Cox ran into a promoter who was running a tour through remote areas of Queensland, featuring a bunch of Brisbane pop stars of the day: Mike Furber, Tony Worsley, April Byron and others, along with a band called the Sect, which backed them all.

The tour crisscrossed Queensland and even went into the Northern Territory, playing shows in towns such as Longreach, Cloncurry, Mataranka, Darwin and Mount Isa.

'There were two guys as an advance party driving an Avis Rent-a-Car that was never meant to leave Brisbane,' Cox remembers. 'They're doing advance publicity, posters, radio interviews and things like that, and then the rest of us turn up.

'It was really basic. We were doing cattle stations and everything. We had a semitrailer that the band would set up on and you'd get all the people from the stations and the cowboys standing up the back. It was that whole trip.

'I remember as we started getting into the outback, someone said, "We should buy a gun," so we bought one gun and then everybody wanted a gun, so in every town we passed through or played in we'd put out the word that we were looking for guns. We ended up with all these .303s and .22s with bits welded on. We brought them all, and after a while it looked like we were travelling in an armoured vehicle with guns hanging out every window. And yes of course we're shooting at every fucking sign and thing that we could. Anything that moved – or didn't.'

Naturally, the travelling party of roadies and musicians got themselves into endless trouble.

'At one of the towns the singer from the Sect fucked this girl and that night her family attacked the hotel that we were staying in. They were trying to crawl up the banisters to get us. Then the publican has come out and gone BOOM BOOM BOOM, firing his double-barrelled shotgun and telling them to fuck off, so off they went.'

Then the Avengers came calling, and Cox needed to get back to Brisbane quickly or miss out on that gig.

'The guys doing the advance work had rolled the hire car,' he recalls. 'It's buckled and all the doors are squashed, the windows broken, the roof is crushed in and these cunts tell me they need me to drive it back to Brisbane and re-roll it on the outskirts of Brisbane, as it's never meant to have left the city.

'It took me four or five days, sleeping, driving, sleeping, driving. I got back, sorted the car and hooked back up with the Avengers, and soon after they pretty much dissolved. So I went on to a band called the Browns, who were shit-hot – they featured a few singers like Leo De Castro.'

After that, Cox joined Doug Parkinson in Focus in 1967, and worked with them until they went overseas to record.

Cox had some extreme experiences on the road with Parkinson, none more off-the-wall than a New Year's weekend in Queensland.

'Our first gig was at the Cabbage Patch Hotel in Coolangatta,' he remembers. 'The second was the Skyline, which was at the Chevron at Surfers Paradise, then one on the beach and then we had to drive to Brisbane to do this place called the Red Orb at 3 am. It was four gigs in a day but that's nothing unusual. We used to do three or four gigs every Saturday, and two or three on Fridays.

'Anyway, Doug had this old girlfriend at Surfers, and she invited us around for dinner before the first gig at the Cabbage

Patch. We were sitting around when this surfie mate of hers turns up with these magic mushrooms, a pile of them. Doug had magic mushrooms on toast and I had a bowl of mushroom soup. We all dig in and realise – to our surprise – they were very potent magic mushrooms.

'After we ate, we get in the car and start driving to the gig. We get to the Currumbin bird sanctuary and Doug says he's completely gone, so we get out of the car. This stuff is coming on and it's full-on, so we're trying to spew it all up.

'Eventually we get to the Cabbage Patch, and I get half the gear set up onstage but it's hopeless. I start foaming at the mouth, so the rest of the band take me out and put me in the car.

'The band set up the rest of the gear and they do half a set before Doug collapses. He's put in the car with me and it's over, so we lose three of the biggest jobs of the year. We had to give all the money back. It was *the* worst fuck-up ever. The headline in the paper the next day said "Band suffers food poisoning", which was sort of true. It took ages to live that one down.'

Part of a roadie's work in those days was to collect the money after a gig. That wasn't always straightforward. There were a lot of fly-by-night promoters, and some would try pretty much any ruse to avoid paying.

'We were up in Queensland again doing a week's work for a promoter,' Cox says. 'We finished on the Saturday night and the next day I go to get our money, as we're booked on the plane to go to Melbourne.

'I go to the promoter's office, and of course he's not there. The girl working on the desk says, "Oh, John got killed in a car accident coming back from the Gold Coast last night." I don't believe her, so I say, "So, the money died with him did it?" They just want us to get out of town, and I know if we leave we'll never see the money.

'So, Doug and everybody else flies to Melbourne, and I'm left to hang around Brisbane and try and track the promoter down to get the money. He hadn't died. It was just a scam. Just a typically scurrilous promoter. I'm up there for four days, and I ring Doug and tell him I can't find the guy.

'Eventually I go down to his office again. It's in Fortitude Valley above a shop. I was so angry I put his filing cabinet and chairs and table and everything else I could through the window or down the stairs into the courtyard below his office, and then went and got the plane and flew home. Bands were just easy meat in those days.'

Cox took a break from working with Parkinson when he and the band headed overseas. They weren't going to perform in the UK, so they didn't need their roadie. Cox soon found himself working with Billy Thorpe and his band the Aztecs after their roadie, the already legendary Norm Swiney, was involved in a car accident and was off the road. Cox worked with the Aztecs until Doug Parkinson returned from the UK and put together the band Fanny Adams.

Cox had been lucky on the road but he was involved in a nasty car accident in Sydney while driving the Aztecs around.

'We were in the van,' he says. 'We'd already done a show at Caesar's in the city, and we had to go to the Narrabeen Surf Club or somewhere like that on the Northern Beaches. The van has a single bench seat, and it's me driving, with Pig [Warren Morgan], Paul [Wheeler], Kevin Murphy – who was, like, seven foot tall and the biggest roadie you've ever seen – and Billy [Thorpe] and Lobby [Loyde]. We're all sitting over each other's knees and we're out around Mona Vale when we T-boned this other car. Pig nearly had his ear sliced off, but luckily he was the only one hurt.

'So, we're waiting for the coppers, and there's a milk bar on the corner. We all get a milkshake and then the coppers turn up. Suddenly someone says, "What about the dope?" So before the copper could see we're throwing all this dope – hash and all sorts of stuff – into Pig's milkshake.'

Caesar's Palace was the scene of a number of memorable gigs for Cox. In the 1960s and early 1970s there were two locations for the venue in Sydney. When Fanny Adams returned from England, the first job they did in Sydney was at Caesar's in the city.

Johnny Dick had come back from overseas with a massive bass drum. The day before the gig, Cox set it up in the club as the band were told they could rehearse there. Overnight, however, the place went up in flames, along with Dick's new drum and all the other gear the band had left there. Dick used to joke that Cox himself was behind the fire as he didn't want to keep setting up the bass drum.

Earlier, Cox had been at the other Caesar's, working with the Browns. 'It was a basement place,' he recalls. 'They had a bouncer up on street level and a ticket office down the stairs. I'm down there, and the next thing I see is the bouncer from up the top coming flying down the stairs backwards. He's been knocked out.

'It was Neddy Smith and his guys, who were running a protection racket on the clubs. They knocked the chick in the ticket booth out and then came into the club and started bashing patrons. They're throwing tables and chairs around and making a real mess. There's a full-on riot, so I tell the band to hide in the kitchen and that's what we do.

'Then I hear a yell that they're taking the band's gear, so I run out. I grab the first thing I see, which is one of those long steel things you sharpen knives on. What the fuck was I thinking? I've also managed to throw a bottle in their direction and yelled, "Leave that fucking guitar there!" And the next thing I hear are the words, "Shoot the cunt," and then I see the guns come out and I run back to the kitchen and hide in the coolroom till they've gone.

'We knew a couple of figures in the underworld ourselves in those days, so the guitars were returned a few days later by

Fast Eddy and the Argentinian Ant, but the amps and speaker boxes were ruined as they'd just thrown them into the crowd and smashed them up.'

It wasn't only organised crime gangs that roadies had to contend with. These were violent times at nightclubs and venues, with patrons getting out of control on a regular basis, or just doing really stupid things. A roadie had to be prepared to fight – and fight often. He was there to protect not only the band but himself. And usually the odds weren't stacked in his favour.

'There was a night at Ringwood Town Hall. I was working with Billy Thorpe and the Aztecs. Billy's onstage and there's these young punks down the front with matchboxes, and they're lighting matches and flicking them at Billy. He asks a couple of them to come towards the stage and then he smacks them in the head. I thought to myself, *This is not going to be good*.

'Because of the venue size that night, I'm working with some extra roadies. I have Frank Milan, who's one of Bob Jones's karate guys, and a guy called Bob Oakley. At the end of the night we're loading the gear out the back and I see about eight or ten of the punks coming towards us. Lobby saw them coming too, so he's jumped in the van and locked himself in, so it was just me, Frank and Bob.

'Frank took the biggest and ugliest one first with a mic stand and T-bones him straight in the face. He's out cold. I grab a hammer and we laid into them. Eventually we all get in the van and drive around the corner to get onto the main road, and as we come around the bend, once again there's all these guys waiting for us, so we jump out of the van and give this lot a go too.

'Another night at Bertie's there were all these sharpies. There were only two bouncers, then two at the Tum and two at the Catcher. And a hundred sharpies all waiting out the front. So a call has gone out to get all the guys from the other discos and clubs in the area – about eight of them – so when they've arrived we open the door to let them in. The first ones fall all over themselves and it was on. It was a fucking massacre. Nothing better than seeing them licking their wounds.'

While there were lots of fights, and the hours they worked were ridiculously long, there were plenty of other compensations for roadies at the time. There were drugs. Lots of drugs. And lots of girls, too.

'We had a flat in St Kilda and somehow they always seemed to know when we were coming back. We were on the second floor and there was an outside staircase. We'd pull up and I swear there were twenty chicks sitting on the steps waiting for the band to arrive back. It was full-on free love in those days. It couldn't have been a better time.

'There was a time I remember. We were doing a university ball with Billy Thorpe, and we came back to the hotel with all the chicks. And all the beds were in the one room. And Billy fancied this chick I'd pulled. We had a nice time together and then Billy thought he'd try too but she turned him down. That was great, as I loved to see Billy's ego slapped down as it was pretty large.'

In the early days when Cox was first on the road, there was lots of pot, LSD and speed – but the only amphetamines available were real pills from real chemists. There were no little bags of white powder. They came later.

'I remember Tony Worsley turned up one day with a brown medicine bottle full of little pills,' Cox says. 'They were so strong. I took some and it was a disaster. There were these go-go girls in Newcastle and I'd been trying to latch onto one of them for ages. As it happens, the night I took the amphetamine I get her, but I was so out of it I spent about eight hours trying to jab my soft cock into her but never did. I made up for it the following week, mind you.

'But there was lots of acid. One night I was working with Thorpie, and I called in on these guys I knew before I went to work. It was a busy night – I had Coburg, Frankston, Sebastian's and Catcher – school hall dances and then on to the discos. I had a cup of tea and a smoke, and then hopped in my car and then it hit me. They'd put a trip in my cuppa. I was so pissed off. I wanted to beat them up as it made working so hard.'

Good pot was pretty easy to find, according to Cox. He and John D'Arcy had a mate called Paddy Beach, the drummer from the Valentines, the band Bon Scott fronted at the time.

'After the Valentines broke up Paddy went to South Africa for a while, and decided he was going to import some Durban Poison. They were like corn cobs. He got on this cargo ship in South Africa to come back to Australia, and shared a cabin with four other guys with his long hair shoved under a wig so he didn't look like your typical dope-smuggling hippie. The boat docked in Fremantle, Adelaide, Melbourne and Sydney, and as he didn't have to go through customs until he finally disembarked, he'd just walk off the boat and go to the post office and mail four or five of these cobs to me and D'Arcy.

'Later he got busted – I think it was the second time he did it. A couple of roadies bailed him out, and then the three of them walked around Melbourne cemetery until they found the grave of a young guy who had just died. Then they got his details and went to Births, Deaths and Marriages and got Paddy a passport to get out of the country. Nothing was computerised in those days, so he went back to South Africa and lived out his days there.

Looking back on the gigs, the fights, the drugs and the precarious and hair-raising drives, Cox admits there were many times he and his fellow roadies and musicians could have lost their lives, but most of them got through it.

'It was hard yakka, but fun,' he says.

Cox got off the road in 1975. 'I was done and dusted with it. It had gone from one man, one van, one band and really changed. In those days we were like the fifth or sixth member of the band. When I started, we were treated the same. In some ways the roadies were probably more important than the band, because without us they were never going to get to the gigs because they were all so fucking hopeless – all of them. We never really questioned the work. We just did it.'

Cox had been in the roadie game for a decade by the time he quit. 'I got married and had kids and got the carpenter's tools back on. The crews were getting bigger by this stage. Skyhooks came along and had 15 to 20 crew guys. They started to produce decent PA systems so you needed more people to carry them around. It was different. In my era there were very few crew guys, so you looked after each other. The bigger crews meant that you were more remote from the band as well.

'I became I think the highest-paid roadie in Australia at that time. When I first started we were on $60 a week, and then it gradually went up to $100, which back then was a fucking lot of money. You could fill a Safeway trolley for $10; our rent in Melbourne was $17.

'I wouldn't have missed those times for the world. We were all mates. If my band was off the road I'd go out with Curley Campbell and help him with Spectrum. Same with the other guys. We didn't get paid, we just did it for fun, as the bands wouldn't pay for another crew guy. It was just good to have a mate out with you. I'm still like brothers with everyone I worked with – there's a really strong bond.'

When Cox quit the road he sold his van and bought his first house. He had a furniture manufacturing business and stayed in Melbourne till 1980, when he moved up to Coffs Harbour and bought 60 acres of rainforest. He built a house, then bought the 60 acres next to it as well.

For Cox it has been a comparatively good trip. He's now 70, in good health. 'I feel like I was lucky to get out when I did,' he says. 'I'd had enough. I'd had the best time on the road but it was time to move on.'

5

How Weird

If you tell anyone who's interested that you're writing a book about Australian roadies, you can pretty much guarantee the first six words that come out of their mouth: 'Have you talked to Howard Freeman?'

Howard Freeman is the king of the roadies. People say he's indestructible. His escapades over the course of six decades in Australian music are the stuff of legend. He's brash, tough, in your face, a ridiculously hard worker and a phenomenal motivator. He's very experienced with martial arts, approaching 70 years of age, and a formidable, tattooed physical presence. And he's just a little crazy.

'I remember my assistant Irene coming around for her first job interview,' recalls manager Roger Davies, who employed Freeman as his tour manager when he was looking after Sherbet. 'Howard was walking around the office in a tutu and not much else, doing the vacuuming. He opened the door and said to Irene, "Hi, I'm How Weird." That's Howard.'

When he's not on the road – which for most of his life has been the majority of the time – Freeman lives in the Dandenongs, outside of Melbourne, with Lil, his wife of 46 years. Part of him wants to retire but he can't. When I visit, he has just finished a stint with Green Day. Rather unconvincingly, he says that's his last tour.

He talks enthusiastically about the ongoing Freeman dynasty in show business. His eldest son, 42-year-old Paul, runs a staging company in Melbourne, and youngest son, 38-year-old Lee, works as a production manager and has just been employed to work worldwide with the Foo Fighters.

Freeman immediately launches into his philosophy of working on the road and managing tours. His articulation of his world is direct and loud.

'If you surround yourself with really smart people, you get away with it every day of your fucking life,' he says. 'That was the joy of what we had in the early days. None of us was particularly brilliant at everything. Some of us were pretty good at little things – but we all *got* what the other guy did. So if somebody fell over, the gig would still go on.'

Unlike most road crew of his era, Freeman came from an established business and one involving showbiz. His father and grandfather were both ballroom dance promoters. He has a photo from 1905 of Stan Freeman's third annual ball.

'My family has been in this business for 112 years, four generations in entertainment. It's been a gypsy lifestyle. There's been wealth, there's been poverty. It's been madness. I worked on the door for a dance my old man ran at the Masonic Ballroom in Collins Street when I was 14. I wanted a drum kit and that was how I was going to earn the money for it.'

Freeman's father ran dances not only at the Masonic Ballroom but also at the St Kilda Town Hall and Collingwood Town Hall. He had buses running between each venue when dances were on, which was every Thursday, Friday, Saturday and Sunday night. This was the era when the pubs closed at 6 pm, so for evening entertainment there were really only two options – you went to the movies or to a dance.

When Howard was ten, his father was offered the opportunity to run dances on Brampton Island, off the Queensland
coast. 'I still remember the conversation around the dinner
table, my mother saying that they couldn't drag us kids out of
school. I was expelled five years later – fuck that.'

Freeman flips backwards and forwards through his life as
he chats. The memory of wanting that drum kit at 14 somehow
connects with touring with The Rolling Stones, something he's
done a few times.

'The first time I toured with the Stones – I've done it four
times. It sounds big-headed but it's sort of like a mechanic
talking about cars. When I was 14 and 15 I wanted to be Charlie
Watts. I wanted to have facial surgery to look like fucking
Charlie Watts, because he was the guy who had the jazz chops
that played great rock. And then I met him and he's this tiny
little man who looked like he was made out of cigarette papers.
He looked like he could tear. And he was fucking grey. And
he was tiny. Just like Ronnie Wood – you could put him down
the front of your pants. All of them were so small.

'So many of the guys from that era are little motherfuckers,
and all relentlessly badarses because they've got this "fuck you"
small man's thing. It's like, "Fuck you – bring it on."'

Freeman's real introduction to the music and entertainment business was running a venue in suburban Melbourne,
which he'd inherited from his father. Q Club was the biggest
suburban dance in Melbourne. Held in the Kew Civic Centre,
it went through three or four incarnations and at various times
hosted jazz dances and late mod dances. Freeman's father and
his cousin Ron Cronin had opened it in 1961.

Q Club was typical of the venues of the time, a large circuit
of discotheques, dances and clubs. They were part of a contin-
uous tradition of local dances run by church and community
groups with a history that can be traced back to the 19th
century. The nature of these dances was dictated by where they

were held, which was usually in church, municipal and community halls, and sometimes police boys' clubs. None sold alcohol and all were supervised, so were open to all ages.

Freeman's father had died when Howard was 18, and he and his brother inherited the business. Did they ever think about not continuing in the family tradition? Not likely.

'We kept it going because we loved it – and what were we going to do? As Billy Thorpe sang: cigarettes, whiskey and wild, wild women. That was it.'

In a hint of what was to come, Freeman and his brother made some innovations. He suggests Q Club was probably the first venue in Melbourne where the PA came off the floor and went on scaffolding to give the sound more oomph. There were two stages – one at either end of the room – to remove any gaps in the night's entertainment. And they drew some big artists, such as English blues legend John Mayall, even if Freeman almost certainly paid too much to promoter Michael Gudinski for the show – 'because I was a kid'. Q Club ended up going broke, and Howard went bankrupt and lost everything.

'I was in partnership with my brother, and his penchant for the drug-fucked lifestyle with the opposite sex – and later dying from AIDS – put the mocker on our relationship. I was meant to be running the gig and he was meant to be doing the books, and I was doing quite well running the gig. He hated violence and I fucking *loved* it. I loved the sharpies coming to the gig.'

Even in those formative years, Freeman had a feeling for what should be done. The simple things, like looking after artists after they'd performed. Not a big deal maybe, but to Freeman it was an important aspect of doing business, and it became something that he'd carry with him in his days as a roadie and band manager.

'We started putting out pizza and beer for the bands,' he says. 'I used to go up to the pizza shop in the middle of the night and fight my way through the sharpies who wanted to fight me, and get half a dozen large pizzas and put them in the band room.'

During this time, Freeman was also branching out into quasi management roles and a security venture. 'I was looking after Buster Brown and Angry [Anderson]. He was in a band called Peace Power and Purity, that evolved into Buster Brown. Then I did the Sunbury festivals, where I had a security business with "Tony the Wog". Bob Jones Corporation did some of it and so did we. That went on for a couple of years.'

Enter Sherbet. Freeman was doing security at Dallas Brooks Hall, and one night when Sherbet was playing he was approached by the band's manager, Roger Davies, who asked if he wanted to be what Freeman refers to as 'sort of a tour manager'. He would be replacing Wayne 'Swampy' Jarvis, who had moved on to other ventures.

Freeman thought about it for maybe four seconds. 'Count the money and look after the band. Fucking easy. Really fucking easy. I made a great fist of it, didn't I. The first gig I did was on a national tour, and the band were in Cairns. I managed to get really, really fucked up at the gig. I had a white suit on, John Travolta style. I couldn't find my way back to the motel so I slept on the mud flats on the beach, and pulled a little boat over me to hide the light. The sea knocked me around as the fucking tide came in. So, I woke up the next morning, went back to the band bus and we were gone. Yeah, I'm your tour manager. What a hit that was. But in saying that, I've probably saved bands more money than I've lost.'

This was the early days for Australian roadies: Freeman estimates that there were maybe 20 in the country. In fact, everything about the Australian music industry was rudimentary – the equipment, the management, the booking agencies. Everyone was making it up as they went along. It was a world of attitude-strong cowboys blazing a trail.

And it was tough and violent, in the cities but especially in country towns. In those times bands played in every town that had a television set, because shows like *Countdown* were the main way that contemporary music reached regional audiences. Local country radio stations weren't exactly embracing new Australian music.

'You'd walk through town and the local guys just wanted to belt you, just because you looked different,' Freeman recalls. 'And you're treated like shit because you get no respect from anyone at hotels or venues or anywhere else for that matter. You're treated like second-class citizens, and all the guys are going, "You're just here to root my sister," and I'm going, "Abso-fucking-lutely." And then it's on.

'A guy looked at me once – I was five or six years older than him. He was maybe 16 or 17 years old, and we were in Deniliquin South near a saw-milling place, just having a beer. He said to me, "Do you want to know how to start a fight in a pub?" And I said, "Yeah, show me." And he walked into the men's shithouse and there were three guys having a piss – and he pissed on the back of their legs. That's how you start a fight in a pub. How do you stop a fight in a pub around there? With a chainsaw. It's a pretty simple apprenticeship, really.

'You'd check in to second-rate hotels in small towns in the middle of nowhere on these tours, and you'd have the local guys driving around the motel in their utes, yelling obscenities, so you'd be looking for something to break that cycle, if you know what I mean. You were bored and this was something to do, you know.

'It *was* violent. You were treated worse than bikers in these places. You also had your own code, your own look, and no one in these places understood anything about it. You were like the first pirates, the first gypsies. You had to be able to think pretty good, work pretty hard, fight pretty well. You seriously never thought you'd make next week, let alone further beyond that.

'I mean, there were people *dying* and there were some pretty bad accidents. People were going down all the time on the road. We were going to a gig at the Lifesaver in Sydney one night, and Billy Rowe and Alan Dallow died. The truck catches fire and they burnt to death.

'It was tough, fucking hard work. You would take some speed so you could get to the next gig so you could keep going and make your living. Brisbane to Sydney to Melbourne in three nights. You fucking try and do it and throw in a gig every one of those nights.'

Freeman felt a sense of brotherhood with both crew guys and musicians, simply because he'd grown up in band rooms. 'It's simple. If the crew are loading out, I'll load out with the crew. If you're managing the act, once you've got the money you give the crew a hand, because the quicker you can get the shit out, the quicker you can get to the next gig and make some more money. Or everyone can go and have some fun – the quicker you can get to the drugs and the chicks. "Quit fucking around here, you're eating into my drinking time!"'

Working for a band with a massive teen following, as Sherbet had, was a logistical nightmare. Simply keeping the band members safe was a full-time job.

'I was putting bands into armoured cars to get them out of gigs, because if you had three limos or hire cars the aeriels would be stolen, they'd be scratched or dented and it would cost more than the vehicle was worth, so you'd go to Armaguard and get a vehicle. Sherbet were the first band to have to do this, but later you'd do it for bands like the Bay City Rollers.

'That was the era. "I'm a 14-year-old chick and you're the star, and I want some of your fucking hair." So they have a pair of fucking scissors, they would pull your hair up and try to cut some off. One mistake, there goes your neck – just to cut off a lock of your hair and put it in their locket. Tell me that's not dangerous.'

Sherbet finished up in 1978, after which Freeman ran an agency with Harvey Lister, trying to get 'real' music into Brisbane. But this was the era of Joh Bjelke-Petersen, and after six months, despite the support of community radio station 4ZZZ, it was obvious that the venture wasn't going to work.

Freeman also did stints on the road with Ted Mulry. And with that came all the chaos and hijinks of the era.

'We did a regional show, and I'm sharing a room with Ted. I've got the bed near the toilet and Ted's got the one near the window. I go to sleep, fucking smashed, as Ted loved a bottle of Scotch – and his Tally Ho's.

'So it's 6.30 or 7 am and the door is being hammered on. OPEN THE FUCKING DOOR. It's the local sergeant of police looking for his daughter, isn't it. I opened the door and went YOU ARE FUCKING KIDDING and then I glance across and there's Ted with half an erection and a doona stuck between the window and the bed. It's sort of positioned weirdly.

'I've told the cop to have a look around, he glances in and then slams the door and storms off. As I hop back into bed the doona lifts up and a chick stands up and says, "I'd better go home." That's how you lived. A tram ticket away from being stabbed, run over or put in jail.'

Then Dragon's manager Sebastian Chase called up and asked if Freeman wanted to tour-manage a band that were considered close to unmanageable. This was the sort of challenge Freeman thrived on. He was in. Freeman managed to get Dragon – and himself – out of scrapes around the world. Who was there in Texas when, from the stage, the band's lead singer, Marc Hunter, decided to say, 'All Texans are faggots and John Wayne fucks his horse'? That would be Howard. As glasses began flying around, he got Hunter off the stage and into a car with the rest of the band. 'I think we hit four other cars getting out of there. I could hear the rifles cocking. And you thought it was hard getting out of Shepparton.'

By now Freeman had the reputation that continues to this day: he was the guy who looked after the wildcards, the seemingly untameable.

'If someone had a band they thought was unkempt, unreasonable or hard to control, I would get the call. And I'd continue getting those calls right through the era of the Big Day Out and onwards. "Here's fucking Courtney Love, here's some other fucking basketcase. Here's Ministry – better get Howard."

'Take Dragon – no one wanted to work with them. They and their fucking crew were smacked off their fucking tits. Robert Taylor on guitar and Todd Hunter were okay, but Marc and Paul Hewson – *phew!* Fucking monsters with smack.

'But on their night . . . Look, I never worked with anyone where I didn't like their music. If you're going to stand there and listen to it every night, you've got to be fucking into it. And when Dragon were really on, they were frighteningly good, world-class.

'But that was only part of it. I stopped the car so many times and brought Hewson back to life. We were always going to hospitals and clinics. We were regulars at St Vincent's Hospital in Sydney. Once they shot him full of Narcan and then I threw him in the car and we drove to a festival show. I used to clean the spew off him when they lived at the Squire Inn.'

Not only was Freeman trying to sort out the day-to-day screw-ups of the band members, but there was an equally out-of-it, drug-fuelled road crew to deal with.

'When I started working with Dragon, I had to go to the crew and say, "Look, I know you've been nicking shit – we're missing microphones and a lot of gear." I'm assuming they'd hocked it to buy smack. I knew the shit was missing because they owned their own PA in those days. They owned everything. I asked the crew to bring back what they'd fucking stolen.

'The next day a station wagon turned up with half a dozen microphones, stands, a couple of amps and other bits and pieces – maybe five or six grand's worth of shit. Then a transit van turned up with speakers from the PA. And you tell me it's a good drug.

'One of the crew robbed the Flying Pieman in Bondi one night when he was off his tits. He got locked up for five years. Thought he was a tough guy. Brandished a gun. And you know what he stole? The fucking calculator, because he was so off his tits he had no idea what he was doing.'

Dragon and their crew lived tough, wild and crazy life-styles. One famous story involves them all buying guns and other weapons while on tour in Queensland. That's true – but Dragon's gun escapades weren't exceptional. Most bands and their crew bought guns in Queensland. It was just what you did.

'Queensland had no guns laws in those days,' Freeman says, 'so when you went over the border you could buy a pump-action repeating thing that would blow your tits off, and shoot at everything you wanted to. But once you came back across the border you had to throw it in the bin. The same with every-thing else. You could also buy hunting bows and arrows. I once had a band member – lovely man – mandraxed off his head one night with a bow and arrow pointed at my head. I was thinking, "This is it."

'You'd do a lot of shit to amuse yourselves on the road, and not all of it was really safe or smart. You'd be powering down the highway and the games would include getting cracker guns with ball bearings in them and leaning out of the vehicle and firing at cars that had their high beams on. Or you'd swap vehi-cles while you were driving. You'd have two cars driving side by side with the windows down, and you'd climb out of your car and climb through the window of the other one – while the car was doing 80 k's. Possibly not the safest thing to be doing.'

Along the way, Freeman has worked with a cavalcade of major – and aspiring – Australian and international artists. To each he brings a take-no-prisoners attitude and a sense of humour. Everyone knows when Howard Freeman is working a tour. He represents old-school values on the road. Hard work – lots of it – and a sense of fun.

He's not a big fan of kids coming out of colleges and wanting to be 'event managers' just because they've done a few courses. 'Most of them couldn't run their dicks through custard,' he says dismissively of those who haven't done the hard yards.

'They get a certificate saying they're qualified in "Event Management" and all they end up doing is fucking Carols By Candlelight at a local football oval or some other event in the middle of nowhere.

'This job is *all* about dealing with people. That's it.

'The first major load-out I did at Etihad Stadium was when they had a football game scheduled there two days later. Someone from stadium management was there, and he was waving the flag for it by being out on the ground during the load-out. I was running the gig, and I came out wearing a German war helmet with fluoro paint on it and a woman's summer dress.

Freeman's mate $crooge recalls it being 'an off-the-shoulder number – with polka dots'.

As Freeman recalls: 'The guy said, "What the fuck do you think you're doing?" and I went, "Mate, I'm in charge, and everybody here knows who I am. No one has a fucking clue who you are."

'The backside of that is that at two o'clock in the morning, using a percentage of humour and a point of difference you engender your troops to strive a little bit harder, and that's what it's all about. Because at three o'clock in the morning if you go up to someone and yell at them and say, "Fucking pick that up," they go, "You're a fucking prick – I've had enough, see you later." And off they go and you're a human down. Then you're picking it up yourself.

'So, embrace and enthuse – that's the point. And contain people. It doesn't matter how many event courses you do and how many universities and colleges you go to, unless they teach you how to interact with humanity and how to treat people and what to watch for, and seeing who's whingeing and who's not whingeing and working out why, and getting that balance right, you'll never be able to do this. That's what you do. You use people and you get the best out of people.'

Freeman dismisses any suggestion that the road crew business is full of guys who – as the stereotype goes – are simply musclebound types with not a great deal of smarts, taking lots of drugs and carrying shit around. He knows from experience that there are phenomenally talented people within the ranks of road crews. They're just people who have chosen this lifestyle and career over other options.

'There are guys in this industry who have been attracted to it and who could build cities. There's guys who can build houses. There's boat builders, carpenters, engineers. They have skills you wouldn't believe. They're great artisans. They're *really* good at what they do. And they're people that, given a choice, would ride a high-powered motorbike before a motorcycle. It's a world that attracts people of independence, of independent spirit. And independent minds that then embrace other people of a similar ilk.'

Freeman knows what makes the best crews in the business. 'The first thing they have is respect. The second thing they have is knowledge. And the third thing they have is a great support staff. You've built up enough humans around you that are that good at what they do that you can concentrate on being fucking great at what you do.'

Along the way, he has become a master at dealing with the varied and frequently ridiculous demands of artists. More than once he's rolled his eyes at requests that are made simply because the artist or their management can. 'One guy was a beauty. In his rider he demanded a Maserati to drive him to the gig. I said to whoever was going to do that, "Get a cassette tape of a Maserati and put it in the machine and put it on – then put him in a Volkswagen – he'll never know. I mean, the guy's blind, right?

'I had to put a handicapped shithouse near the stage for Pavarotti because he's so fucking fat. He couldn't fit on a normal toilet. We also had to split the orchestra seating in two so he could get his motorised scooter up behind his piano where his purpose-built stool was so the fat fucker could look like he was standing. This was a piano, mind you, that I had tuned three times a day and that had flowers all along the front just to cover the blow heaters that were there to warm his legs and hands – but as soon as the fucking blow heaters started, the piano went out of tune, but then he said that he wouldn't perform if it was cold. I love this shit. It's fantastic.'

Some demands seemed ridiculous. One group requested 278 litres of alcoholic beverages – for just 12 people. 'I'd go through the rider and ask them why. I'd ask if they wanted a toilet between the backstage area and the gig because A) if they drank that they would probably be about to burst and B) they would be incapable of playing the actual gig, which would be in breach of their contract.

'It was the Americans and English acts who would always send you these riders, because they do so much touring by bus and all this alcohol was to be taken on the bus afterwards.

'Then you see a rider requesting 240 white bath towels. You don't need 240 white fucking bath towels. You're three minutes from the fucking stage. And ten minutes from the hotel.'

Freeman worked on a James Brown tour once, and says it was all sushi and sashimi and prawns backstage – trays of it. Brown's band didn't get paid a lot. Seven of them were drooling over the lavish food but couldn't touch it, because it was for Brown. They had to wait until he was finished, then they could have what was left.

Freeman and a couple of his crew associates ended up having their own amusement with Brown – but they considered they were simply doing him a favour, assisting with the quality of his performances.

'He was performing like shit, so we snuck into his dressing room and put some speed into his drink. When he sang "I Feel Good", we knew he sure did – but he was so fucked up on angel dust he may not have even noticed.'

If you want to get a rise out of Freeman, just mention a well-known DJ from New York. But he'll also be smiling, because he's been around long enough to see stupidity from so many artists that he just shakes his head. And he knows how to deal with them – quickly, simply and directly.

'Fucking smartarse cunt. The dressing room is three flights up and the cunt is demanding stuff be brought to him. The tour didn't have a lot of money, so I carted leather couches on my back and built his backstage room the way he wanted it. I de-veined prawns and chilled champagne. I'd gone out and bought champagne flutes. All this because the venue wouldn't do it – so I had to. You know, keeping the artist happy.

'I spent six hours getting his room just right. Then this prick goes on and performed really badly, and afterwards smashed up the band room and carried on like an absolute arsehole, and says, "Where's my car? I'm going back to the hotel."

'So I got him out of there, and then I stripped the room and took all the furniture back down where it came from. For the next night I put six milk crates in there, plastic cups, a container of orange juice and some plastic bottles of water. Then I drew a caricature of this guy sticking his head up his own arse, and then wrote the caption: "IS THIS YOU?" That was the third gig of the tour, and after that we didn't have a problem. I had to do that to get the message through to him that he needed to stop taking the piss. To his credit, he did wear it.'

Then there are those in the touring party who aren't even the stars but carry on like complete prats, such is their sense of entitlement. Freeman has a simple test: is your face and name on the posters?

'That's what you tell smartarses on the road when they tell you their donut isn't big enough or that they don't like their seat on the plane. "What's your name? Is that the one I saw on the poster outside the venue? The photo doesn't look much like you. Oh, that's right, it's *not* you – so fuck off! The people on the poster are the reason we all exist.'

There are a thousand Howard Freeman stories. One artist will tell you of times when he and his band would be in hotel swimming pools and Freeman would walk into the water – resplendent in a full dinner suit – carrying a tray bearing drinks and lines of cocaine. All this in front of other guests, mind you.

Then there was the time Jimmy Barnes and his bandmates decided to play a game of golf – inside the singer's room at a resort hotel. They played with proper golf clubs, aiming at glasses above Barnes's bed. Soon there were holes everywhere in the room's walls. Then the participants decided this wasn't challenging enough and that it needed to be wet weather golf. So as each player took their shot, another would douse them with a bucket of water.

Barnes rang Freeman to tell him what was going on, that the room was being destroyed and he'd better come and sort it out. Freeman found one of the resort's golf buggies, fired up the engine and drove it straight through the front door of Barnes's room, glass and door frames going everywhere.

'I hear there's a golf tournament on,' he smiled.

Freeman is one of the real survivors of the road – and he knows it. 'I would figure every one of us on this journey has been slightly fractured. I'm real lucky that I've got the woman I've got. But I know a lot of other people . . . you work so hard that you fall so hard. Your fucking body is broken and if you can't get another gig you're fucked because you've got no super. You've got nothing going on. All you had was the ability to work hard. That's why the suicide rate is so high. Absolutely.

'You look at guys like Pat Pickett, who worked for AC/DC. He was one of the prime sources of humanity in this business, and then he dies in a pub, in a room above the hotel where he lived and wired up the PA there twice a week to pay his fucking rent. All he had was some jeans and a book of poetry. No one embraced him and said, "How you doing?" That's the disappointing thing . . . people who worked on the road not having enough money to live on or survive.'

Freeman knows he's been lucky. Sure, he's extremely good at what he does, but he's been able to develop and expand his skill set while having a stable home base.

'I've got two smart kids and a wife that you wouldn't trade in on any other model,' he says, looking around his home. 'That woman you met today spent six months paying off a $200 coat on lay-by when we were struggling. That was the same price as a gram of blow. I had no problems spending that money on blow. I'd buy a gram of racket and it's gone soon after, and five months later she says, "Look what I've got," and she shows me the coat . . . and I go, "I am fucked." Fortunately, my wife absorbed my selfishness that went with the lifestyle, and got on with raising two children. I've worked with maybe 650 different acts, flown 6 million miles and done 7000 gigs, and in all that time I haven't met anyone better than my wife.'

These days Freeman prefers to point to where the equipment needs to go rather than move it himself – but that's only a comparatively recent change. He's now focusing on imparting his knowledge and experience to a new generation of road crew, and it's something he takes very seriously – both philosophically and practically.

'The thing is that when a 65-year-old guy gets in the truck with a 20-year-old and the 20-year-old isn't really cutting it, then you offer to give him some fucking help and some fucking tips. You show them *how* to lift it up.

'I've loaded trucks – say, in Perth, where there's not a huge body of available humans who've done it before, and so you get a bunch of backpackers. I've had twelve people stand in the back of a truck. "Hands up who's ever unpacked a truck before?" No hands go up. "Hands up who speaks English?" Two hands go up. You drop a 240-kilo case three foot high above your head in a truck – someone is going to get hurt. Probably you and anyone around you. So you've got to embrace and enthuse and teach people, or people are going to get fucking hurt. And then if they do go down, you're the one who's got to call the ambulance and then look after them till someone arrives.'

Part of Freeman's achievement is that he's managed to remain active and relevant in an industry not known for its longevity. It's also one populated by individuals who, in the main, don't like change. Most are stubborn guys, stuck in their ways, and can't conceive that there's any other way to do things than *their* way – so shut up and do what you're told. Freeman has adapted and grown, embracing every change in the world of the roadie.

'The journey has changed,' he says without a hint of nostalgia. 'When I started on the road you had a briefcase and a pad and a list of telephone numbers. Then you'd sit and ring the next town you were going to play in and make sure that everything that needed to happen was going to happen.

'You'd have a telephone number for everyone. I'd be able to call someone at every airport around the world, someone I knew, and discuss seating arrangements and freight and all that stuff. You can't now. Nothing was online – there was no internet, no GPS. You had to actually work on your gig to make it happen. You still do, but it's different. In 1974 I started a book with details on venues, stairs, access, power set-up, all that information . . . I probably stole it from someone like $crooge, like all good ideas are.'

By this stage Freeman has been in full flight for a couple of hours. The phone rings and he leaves the room to take the call. He comes back with a grin on his face. 'I just came out of retirement. I've never done one of these – I'm doing the World Title rematch between Jeff Horn and Manny Pacquiao at Suncorp Stadium in Brisbane. I'm the production guy.' The fight didn't go ahead, but Freeman's excitement about working on it had been palpable.

Why does he keep on going? Surely there's a point where even someone like Freeman has to call time?

'It's nice to know you can still dance. When I finished AC/DC in 2015, I was so physically sore because I'd smashed myself in Perth and ripped the bursa out of my shoulder, so I had no real movement in my arm. Then the other arm went, as I'd been putting more pressure on that for lifting stuff. Then the cartilage in my left ankle went. I can't climb in the back of a truck, and I've always said that as soon as I can't climb in the back of a truck I'm not going to do this shit anymore. Well, to a point, that time has come. It's time to stand at the back of the truck and go, "*You* – take that over there!"

'You live the Peter Pan lifestyle, and you work with young people and it keeps you mentally fresh, your attitude stays fresh. You can't be bitter. If you're bitter and twisted and grumpy, then stay the fuck at home. When you go to work every day, make sure you smile.'

6

D'Arcy

John D'Arcy is a wiry, nasally, pugnacious character. He has been a boxer, and knows how to handle himself. He's a veteran of the Australian road crew world, a reliable, loyal, tough dude who, along with Mick Cox, $crooge Madigan, Nick Campbell and Howard Freeman, is a survivor from the golden era. The fact that all five remain close friends speaks volumes for who they are – and what they were.

D'Arcy grew up having to be tough. His only real friend at school was Chris Flannery, later to become known as Mr Rent-a-Kill. By age 13 D'Arcy was in a boys' home for six months; after being released, he hung out in pool halls and gyms. By 16 he was carrying a gun, and a year later he was living on the streets of Sydney. Things weren't looking all that promising.

One day he was standing on the corner of Darlinghurst Road and William Street in Kings Cross. He saw Billy Thorpe drive by in his Aston Martin. D'Arcy wanted some of what Billy had.

D'Arcy went on to work with Bon Scott and the Valentines, and many other artists. He was there in the very early, rough days of the road. 'We were all in little vans, often Kombi vans, with no mobile phones of course,' he recalls. 'Up and down the Hume Highway and the Pacific Highway. It would take you three days to get from Melbourne to Brisbane. You'd have three or four guys lying on top of the amps in the back. You'd get out at small roadhouses and stagger around and stretch and get something to eat. All those country towns were smaller in those days. And if you broke down ... well, you could spend what seemed like days on the side of the road trying to get help. You'd have to hitchhike into town and then try and organise someone to come out and tow the van or truck and get you into town. These early years were crazy. It's a wonder we survived.'

A wonder indeed. In fact, it remains a significant miracle that many more Australian road crew haven't perished in motor accidents. The fact that most roadies of the era can list on one hand the number of fatalities is a statement of monumental luck, particularly given the manner in which the crews travelled. 'Most of the time we were driving on LSD. We'd be driving along in the middle of the night going, "Did you see that? What's that?" We were off our heads – and the roads were so narrow in those days, with all those small, single-lane concrete bridges.'

D'Arcy started his roadie career with a band called Compulsion, a sort of Jimi Hendrix copy band featuring two Maoris and a white drummer. Manager Michael Browning had brought them across from New Zealand, and they played in Australia before heading to the UK after changing their name. The main feature of the band was the guitarist Reno Tehei, who, according to D'Arcy, channelled Jimi Hendrix 'right down to setting fire to his guitar – the whole trip'.

Compulsion attracted trouble wherever they went in the unenlightened Australia of the mid-1960s. It was a tough intro-duction to the rock'n'roll world for D'Arcy but he was up to the challenge. 'We'd be doing pubs, and as they got more pissed the idiots in the crowd would be calling out things like, "You black cunts" – totally outrageous stuff – at Reno, who was six-foot-four. The drummer and the bass player were cowering in the background, but Reno and I would have to punch our way out of these gigs. He was the one who turned me on to cannabis – and I've smoked it ever since.

'There was this time when we hired 'Swampy' Jarvis, who had one of the first dual-wheel transit vans, to drive us down to Geelong. Anyway, the coppers have pulled us over. They looked at a couple of black dudes with a bunch of long-haired white guys. The cops asked me what I did and I said, "I'm the road manager," and the cop asks me what roads I manage, and I was getting cheeky and going, "All of them." There's actually a bunch of acid and other stuff in the van, and Swampy's freaking out because it's *his* van. The cops went through the van but couldn't find anything, so off we went.

'There was another gig I remember – we were out the back of Box Hill Town Hall. I was with John Swiney. I'm just loading the van and half a dozen dudes come around the corner and they want to punch on with us. John was a big boy. One starts running straight towards him. John took out his false teeth, put them in the van and then swung around and collected this guy with a perfect right. I jumped out of the van with a hammer and said, "Who's next?" Then they just took off.'

When Compulsion eventually imploded, D'Arcy thought his roadie days were over. He returned to boxing, figuring that was where his future was. He had six fights in a three-month period as a 19-year-old flyweight. Then he got a call from his friend Paddy Beach, who had been the drummer in Compulsion. Paddy was now playing with a band called the Valentines, and he wanted D'Arcy to come on board.

D'Arcy was keen, but this was the era of one roadie per band, so after passing an audition with the Valentines at Kew Town Hall, his first job was to tell their existing roadie – the rather formidable Mick Christian – that his services were no longer required.

'Christian used to scare them all off,' D'Arcy says. 'He wasn't so much a roadie as a heavy guy, a security type. Somehow he'd gotten the gig, but he didn't know anything about sound or anything to do with bands. You got a weekly wage, and so you did what you were asked to do. Get guitar strings, sort something out for the drummer and so forth. That was your gig. But Mick just told them to get fucked and said he had things to do. The thing is that the band were shit-scared of him. He was crazy. And he told the band's fans to fuck off too.'

D'Arcy confronted Christian at the end of the Kew gig. There were no blows struck. The new roadie told the now former roadie that he was taking over. The now former roadie told everyone to get fucked, and stormed out of the venue.

Next the Valentines – whose lead singer was the soon-to-be legendary Bon Scott – took to the road. 'It was two years of total madness,' D'Arcy says. 'Sex, drugs and rock'n'roll, the full trip.'

Having started with Compulsion at 18, D'Arcy was a seasoned roadie by the time he turned 21, a milestone he celebrated with Bon Scott and the rest of the band at an infamous house in Centennial Park in Sydney. 'There were these three girls that we knew in Sydney who had a big bluestone house at Centennial Park that overlooked the showgrounds. So any band that came up from Melbourne or down from Brisbane, they all hung with these three girls who were working at the clubs, the two different Caesar's. All the Yank soldiers were around, so these girls' job was that they'd walk the streets and all these Yanks would try and get on them, so they'd take them back to one of these two clubs and start getting them buying drinks.

'All the bands used to stay at their place. They were great chicks. "Curley" [Nick Campbell] moved in there, and it was him and the three chicks and the manager of one of the clubs. I came up with the Valentines. Bon's fallen in love with Carol, who was one of the girls. On my 21st, I pulled the gear out of Caesar's and got back to the house at about 3.30 in the morning, and sitting at the table waiting were Bon and $crooge, who had flown up to surprise me. Vince Lovegrove and Ted Junko and Wyn Milsom from the Valentines were there too. $crooge had bought me a toolbox for my birthday. I still have it in the shed at home. They had a bong out and said they'd been waiting for me to get home.'

D'Arcy also still has the 21st birthday card he received from Scott, who became a close friend. He considers Scott to have been the purest distillation of Australian rock'n'roll of that era. Someone who sang and performed not for a career but because they had no choice. Like D'Arcy, he could probably have donned the gloves and tried to fight his way out of a working-class life – but playing and singing in a rock'n'roll band was a more romantic and potentially lucrative calling.

'It was all he ever wanted to do. Bon was never into the dollars. He never had a suitcase. It was jeans or shorts and a singlet. The Valentines had a teenybopper audience of 12- to 14-year-olds, so Bon used to wear girls' make-up to cover his tattoos. He never had possessions. All he wanted to do was rock'n'roll.'

D'Arcy worked with the Valentines for two and a half years and was paid well. Back in his Compulsion days, he was on an equal split with the guys in the band: if they earned $200, D'Arcy was in for $50. With the Valentines, he was on a wage of $100 a week.

'In the late '60s that was good dollars. There were people working seven days a week at straight jobs and not getting that much – and here I was running around in a pair of moccasins with a torn T-shirt and torn jeans and getting paid a hundred bucks a week.'

When the Valentines disbanded and Scott moved on to the much harder rock-orientated Fraternity, it was time for D'Arcy to find new work. He remained friendly with Scott but started working with a band called Bulldog, and continued the endless round of highways, roadhouses and gigs.

The Australian road crew fraternity of the time were like the proverbial ships in the night, running into each other in remote cafes. 'We'd see each other as we passed on the highway. We'd recognise each other's van, and often pull into a roadhouse together for a bit of a smoke and some food.'

Increasingly at gigs – especially weekend ones – there were bunches of guys hanging around bands and their crew guy, offering to help unload the gear. They thought it would get them into the gig for free, and maybe they'd pick up one of the girls hanging around the band. But help on the way out? Not a chance. They'd be too pissed, and if they hadn't picked up by then they'd cut their losses and disappear. Which was sort of the way the roadie wanted it.

'Sometimes it seemed like a good thing to have a bit of help, but basically they were a hindrance and they didn't know what they were doing. We packed everything up because we did know what we were doing. We knew where everything went – where the leads went, how to pack up the drums. Put them in their cases. And we knew where and how everything fitted together in the van. If these dudes did actually stay around and carry out shit, they'd have no idea how to pack the van. You'd have to supervise everything. You knew where it all went so everything fitted in the van perfectly, and when you got to the next gig it was all packed away the way you wanted it and ready to unload.'

D'Arcy's next move was from Bulldog to Healing Force. The change was simple and easy, as things tended to be in those days. D'Arcy was in Michael Gudinski's office at Consolidated Rock Agency when Bulldog's singer, Mick Rogers, came in to say that he was leaving the band and returning to England to sing with Manfred Mann Chapter Three, which evolved into Manfred Mann's Earth Band. In walked keyboard player Mal Logan, who was starting a new band, Healing Force, and needed a roadie. He and D'Arcy jumped into Logan's car and went back to the house where the band were rehearsing so D'Arcy could check out their gear. It was a roadie's nightmare, as it included a Hammond organ. All the rest of the gear was easy enough to move, but D'Arcy always needed a second pair of hands to get the Hammond in and out of gigs.

A month or so into his tenure with Healing Force, D'Arcy was back in Gudinski's office when the bearded wild man on the move told D'Arcy to 'forget this musician shit' and go with another band who were looking for a roadie. Gudinski thought Healing Force were 'too into the music, man', and lacked commercial viability. He reckoned D'Arcy would have better prospects with this other band.

D'Arcy wasn't keen. Healing Force was his thing. He loved their music. This was real – and good. They sounded like Traffic and other shit that D'Arcy loved. And New Zealand bass player Charlie Tumahai was always dropping trips of LSD. D'Arcy dug that. He saw no reason to move to another band.

Then he thought about his mate $crooge, who was always helping him out with stuff. He told $crooge about this band, and suggested he should get out of the travel agency caper and have some fun on the road. $crooge liked the idea and became the roadie for this new band. They called themselves Daddy Cool.

After Healing Force disbanded, D'Arcy moved on to work with Renée Geyer and her band Sanctuary. That was good for a little while, and then not so good for longer.

'The hangers-on around the band started bringing in the heroin. I'd smoked it a couple of times but that was it. I wasn't into it, but the band were all collapsed everywhere all the time. Renée was losing the plot. I got out but I'd been with her at her best time when she was totally together.'

But D'Arcy kept finding gigs. He was good, and there was no shortage of demand for a good roadie. Next up was a New

Zealand band called Highway, who went through all the trials and mishaps that were typical of a band on the road in that era.

'One night we were driving in the middle of nowhere, on the way to a country town somewhere in the middle of Victoria. We're in a dual-wheel transit and suddenly the lights go off and we're losing power. Luckily it was a full moon, as we opened the sliding door on the van and one of the guys held a torch so we could see where we were going. The van ended up totally breaking down a bit out of the town, so the band ended up pushing it into town with me steering. We ran into all these kids from the gig, who were leaving as they thought the gig was cancelled. So they turned around and we got the van to the hall. I went to load the amps in and they were covered in all this black shit. One of the guys told me he'd knocked his molasses over in the dark. He was a health freak. Ended up dying from a brain tumour, poor bastard.'

Vans – if you didn't have one and know how to drive it, you didn't have work. But they were basic and unreliable beasts, especially given the pounding they took on the road with bands. 'I've just left vans by the side of the road, mate. One time the van broke down in Brisbane, just near the side of the Story Bridge, and we had it towed into the Kangaroo Court Motel, where everyone stayed in those days. We put it in the car park, then we left, and left the van there. Bill Joseph kept asking if I'd sorted out the van and I'd go, "Yeah, yeah, no worries," and then he gets 18 months of parking fines for it. But that was the life, mate. The way we looked at it, you could drive 2000 miles, your van would blow up but if the gig went well, that was all that mattered.'

Eventually D'Arcy decided the smart thing would be to work with some of his mates like Nick Campbell, who were crewing for Ron Blackmore and doing international tours. There was no shortage of those, and D'Arcy worked for a who's who of international artists during the mid-1970s. Some artists, as he recalls, actively socialised with the road crew; others remained aloof and apart from the workers.

'Bad Company were great. There was a reception in Brisbane with three long tables all set up with tablecloths, and there's models and record company people, women all dressed up, guys in suits. Paul Rodgers came in and just went over to one of the tables and pulled the tablecloth out from under it. Then smiled and went to the next table and did the same thing, and then on to the third table. It was crazy, but no one could say anything because he was the star, the main man.

'Then there was Black Sabbath at some gathering in Kings Cross in Sydney. We were all sitting around, and then some chick did something and one of the band picked up a huge bowl of fruit salad and walked up around behind the chick and tipped the whole lot over her. Suddenly all the food was going everywhere. Great days.'

After a few years of working with Ron Blackmore, D'Arcy was starting to tire of the situation and began getting a little more provocative than usual. He didn't like the waste backstage at concerts, and told Blackmore as much. 'They were spending all this money on food backstage and it wasn't getting eaten. Bands were just putting their cigarettes out in it. It was costing about $600 a show, and I said to Blackmore that maybe he should be spending $300 on food and splitting the rest with the crew – but he didn't like that.

'Peter Wilson, the electrician, was unreal. At the end of the gig he'd go around with a rubbish bin and collect all the unused food and drinks. There was no catering for the crew in those days, so that was for us.'

D'Arcy finally split with Blackmore in 1976, and went to work in a factory until 1982. He couldn't get a gig anywhere else. There was also a stint doing security at concerts, including Michael Jackson's 1987 Australian tour. 'After ten years of working on the road with bands, I apparently wasn't qualified to do anything else.'

Eventually he drifted back to music, spending ten years on the road with his son's band, which was called Biscuit in the 1990s but later changed its name to Another Race because of the rising popularity of the American band Limp Bizkit.

Looking back on his roadie years, D'Arcy isn't at all surprised that so many former roadies find themselves in trouble. 'It's a lifestyle, and when you finish it's like you're an alien and you've been to Mars and now you're coming back.'

So does he miss it?

'I miss it, but it's a time that can never be repeated. It was just a special era. We lived what Bon wrote about in AC/DC – it's a long way to the top if you want to rock'n'roll. Bon asked me to go to England with AC/DC, but I'd just had my first kid. I ran into Bon at Bertie's and he asked me but I said I couldn't leave. We had a hug and teared up a bit. Bill Joseph and Michael Browning came out of the office there, and I told them I couldn't do it.

'I come from a broken family. I was worried what would happen to my missus and daughter.'

7

Curley's My Middle Name

Everyone in the road crew community rates Nicky Campbell highly. Jimmy Barnes is not alone in considering him both a friend and one of the 'real deal' guys. He's unpretentious, hardworking, loyal and not one to suffer fools. 'Curley' is actually more than his roadie nickname – he was christened Nicholas Curley Campbell.

Campbell is also one of the smart guys. Before he ventured into roadie work, he'd done a five-year boatbuilding apprenticeship in New Zealand. To earn a bit of extra money in Auckland, he worked behind a 'bar', which served soft drinks to kids who frequented an unlicensed venue where the house band was Larry's Rebels. Campbell hung out with and helped Larry's Rebels, who, along with the La De Das, were becoming big news in New Zealand, winning support spots on tours by international bands. One of those was a tour by The Animals, and through that connection both Larry's Rebels and their roadie, Campbell, met promoter Ron Blackmore.

'He told Larry's Rebels that they should come to Australia and he'd manage them, get them gigs and get them really working,' Campbell remembers. 'They decided they wanted to do that and they invited me to come with them. This was attractive to me as I'd finished my apprenticeship. I knew nothing, really, about being a roadie but someone was offering to pay my fare to Australia. I was 22 by then, so a bit older than most roadies were when they started, but I had the trade to fall back on, so I thought I'd have a bit of fun.'

But in the era of one man, one van, one band, Campbell was at a distinct disadvantage in one key area: he didn't own a van. That problem was solved when Larry's Rebels decided to buy one. After a while, Larry and his Rebels broke up and Campbell drifted into working with a band called The Affair, who also had their own van. He moved to Sydney for a time, before heading back to Melbourne when he picked up a job working with Spectrum, then one of the biggest underground drawcards of Australian music in the late 1960s and early 1970s.

It was with Spectrum that Campbell came of age as a roadie, particularly when Spectrum and Daddy Cool embarked on a huge national tour of universities, and Campbell found himself sharing a truck with $crooge Madigan. 'It was one big truck with all the gear in it, and $crooge and me. It was insane. Just insane. Priceless stuff. We learnt so much just being stuck together going from university to university. $crooge works hard, plays hard and *is* hard. He just has no fear.

'The gear was only little, and the PA systems were tiny and very, very basic. But that was the start of the industry. It was a big learning curve but a great one. And there were a lot of us who swapped information and tricks. You *had* to ask the questions. You couldn't just watch, you had to ask until people got the shits – and then you'd butt out. But there were a lot of people who were prepared to pass information on who had been doing it for longer than you had – people like John Sweeney, who I became very close to.'

It was tough graft. Campbell still recalls the time Spectrum's truck broke down around Albury. The band continued on to

Melbourne on a bus, but Campbell had to stay, sleeping in the truck and keeping an eye on the gear. 'I had no money for a hotel and only a few dollars for food. It was fucking lonely. Eventually a couple of mechanics took pity on me and agreed to watch the truck and gear. I could go and get food. But I had to wait for a motor to come from Melbourne, then have it fitted and then drive to Melbourne, and go straight back into work again.'

After his time with Spectrum, Campbell moved on to work with a succession of classic Australian bands and artists: Renée Geyer, Richard Clapton, TMG, Sherbet and Skyhooks. And with these artists were some of the real greats of Australian road crew: Howard Freeman, John Swiney, Billy McCartney, Jimmy Murrie, Graham Webb, Rocket, Nicky Komous, Alan Anderson and others.

Frequently there were double-billed tours, and Campbell grimaces when he recalls a particular Sherbet/TMG tour. The Sherbet truck kept breaking down.

'It was a real shocker. On those tours the crews for each band would work together and help each other out. And everyone got along. You just had to. The hours were long. The shows hundreds of miles apart. It had to be a team effort. There was no point not being friends. You're travelling together, living together 24/7, so you've *got* to get on. If you don't, then you're not cut out for the job. You had to make it work. If there was friction, it showed in your work. You had to be adaptable.

'And we were close with the bands, too. They trusted us as part of the band. They needed us as much as we needed them. It took the load off them. They'd turn up and know everything was there, set up and ready to go. All they had to do was pick up their guitars and go on. They depended on that – especially because the time between gigs was often so tight. And when the band you were with really fired at a show, you felt part of it. You knew you'd set it all up and done your bit, and then the band did theirs and everyone got what they came to see. No one in their right mind would do what we did – but we did it because we loved it.'

After working with Australian bands, the next stop for Campbell was to crew international tours promoted by the likes of Paul Dainty. Campbell had enjoyed his first taste of working with international artists when his mate Billy McCartney had asked him to lend a hand to load gear for Pink Floyd in Melbourne in 1971, on a tour promoted by Artist Concert Tours (ACT). McCartney continued to give him work in that area because, as Campbell says, 'I was good at what I did.'

And he liked it. 'To me it was the personal contact with the band. We were the first point of contact. You had to be the one who answered the question, "Why isn't this working?" and then it was a case of *getting* it working. That was your fucking job, that was what you were paid to do. You had to always be on the case, and if something stopped working you needed to know how to fix it.'

The money was just a little bit better, which was important for those, like Campbell, who saw crewing as their profession.

'A lot of the guys were only working as roadies at weekends and doing a "real" job during the week. But we were doing it full-time. In the early days we were lucky if we were pulling $40 a week. We were on the bones of our arse. The perks – by which I mean mainly girls – were fantastic, but the pay was shit. But I got to go to places I'd never have seen unless I was working.'

Campbell loved music, too, and this was a golden era. The list of international artists he worked with in the first half of the 1970s is mind-blowing. Just as a sample, try Rod Stewart and Faces, The Rolling Stones, Black Sabbath, Roxy Music, Deep Purple, Slade, Santana, Lou Reed, Paul McCartney and Wings, The Kinks, Kraftwerk, Joe Cocker and James Taylor. Campbell first ventured overseas to work on a 1973 Cat Stevens tour of Japan, along with the pioneering and revered Australian sound guy Bruce Jackson. While there, Campbell teamed up with Dutch band Focus and returned to Australia with them. For the most part, Campbell took these encounters with stardom in his stride but every so often he had a 'pinch me' moment.

'On the Stones tour in 1973, when we were in Perth we all went out to Rottnest Island, and I'm on the boat with Jagger and all the models, and I had a moment of thinking, "Why am I here? This is the top of the fucking ladder." We were treated very well. There weren't too many artists who put you down because you were a roadie. And we were staying in good hotels, and fed better. Catering at venues was only just starting in Australia. Conditions for crew were much better when you worked with international artists, and the money was a lot better.

'Basically, it was a bloody good look if you could get into it. You were learning from the big guys. We were the labourers, pretty much, but what a great way to learn. It was inspiring. These guys – and I mean the overseas crew guys that came out – were working for the best of the best. And they had to keep proving themselves every night.'

Campbell considers working with Paul McCartney and Wings one of the highlights of his career, but if push comes to shove he considers INXS to be the band he'd most like to have worked with. And he would love to have travelled overseas with Skyhooks.

But Campbell did get to work with Cold Chisel. In fact, he was part of the revered 1977 Chisel crew, along with Harry Parsons, Gerry Georgettis, Mark Keegan and Meri Took. 'That was one of *the* best crews, one of the tightest crews I've ever been on. That crew was the cream.'

And of course this was a crew that had to deal with the wild, crazy, unpredictable Chisel, and their more often than not out-of-control lead singer. 'Jimmy was drinking two or three bottles of vodka and doing speed and turning up for gigs in the same clothes he had on the day before. I thought to myself that here was a guy who wasn't going to last. We'd have big lines cut out and waiting for him behind the PA, and he'd come back, have a big snort and then off he went again.

'But this was great. If you got back from your band what you put in, you didn't give a shit what you were paid. You were helping them put on a great show. Of course we wanted more money, but they couldn't give it to you if they didn't have it. And they had a *lot* of expenses – PA hire, lighting hire, truck hire, booking and management commissions and everything else. Often the crew were making more than Chisel in those days.'

Eventually Campbell quit the Cold Chisel crew. 'We were on a long tour and when we got to Tamworth the band decided everyone would have a couple of days off. They told us to drive to the Gold Coast and that they'd pay for our accommodation for a couple of days and we'd have our girlfriends fly up. There were five of us in the hire car, and that fucked things up because I'm always the guy in the middle. Gerry always drove and I was the fucking sucker in the middle. We got to the Gold Coast, had the break and then it was time to drive back, and I quit. I wasn't going to sit in the middle for another five or six hours. Gerry wouldn't let anyone else drive. He liked that seat.' Campbell picked up a gig with The Angels and toured overseas with them.

By 1982, he'd decided he'd had enough. He'd seen too many car and truck accidents, and figured it was only a matter of time before his number came up. 'And I was sick of being away from home and having no time with my wife. I was just sick of being away. It can be very lonely, and it just takes its toll. And I saw too many boys hopping into the truck after too much to drink or smoke and wiping themselves out.'

Campbell got back into boatbuilding, and then into furniture and kitchen manufacture. He still misses aspects of being part of a crack road crew with a good band.

'Everyone had their own job, and without everyone's participation and input it wouldn't happen. And when the show went great, that was a real pat on the back.'

8

Jiva

Jiva didn't work as a roadie for a very long time, but in that period his name became synonymous with the Melbourne scene, and in particular the blues band Chain. In fact, Jiva – who prefers to be known these days by his real name, Clive Lawler – spent just as long editing *Planet*, one of Australia's first music/lifestyle/politics magazines, which was co-founded by Michael Gudinski and Michael Browning. But that's another story.

Growing up in Brisbane, Jiva used to hang around a 'groovy' venue at the time, the rather tiny Red Orb. It was *the* underground hang in the city, the place where many people first heard hip jazz and blues and the music of Jimi Hendrix. Billy Thorpe had played there, as had Lobby Loyde with The Purple Hearts, before they headed south to Sydney and then to Melbourne. Another lesser-known band who played the Red Orb was an outfit called Thursday's Children. Jiva used to go to the club with his girlfriend and dance. He didn't really know anyone in the scene. He just enjoyed the vibe and the music.

This was the 1960s, and for Australian youth all roads led to London. Jiva drove cross-country to Perth, intending to sell his car after the long journey and use the money to get to the United Kingdom. But fate intervened. Jiva arrived in Perth and almost immediately ran into two members of Thursday's Children, who by now had joined The Wild Cherries, a band that had built up a reputation in Melbourne. They were floundering a little: Lobby Loyde – who had left The Purple Hearts to play with them – had just departed.

Two of the surviving members of the band were known as Big Goose (Barry Sullivan) and Little Goose (Barry Harvey). Yes, you may well ask why they weren't Big Barry and Little Barry. Big Goose was a rhythm guitarist who started playing lead when Loyde left, and Little Goose was the drummer. The Gooses invited Jiva back to where they were staying in Perth, and the trio got on famously, bonding over endless joints.

'Big Goose ended up saying to me, "We hate our fucking roadie in Melbourne – would you like to come back and be our roadie?"'

Jiva said yes. England could wait. He sold his car in Perth and bought a transit van, loaded up their gear and drove back to Melbourne. There he met up with the Gooses (who had flown back), and moved into a house with them in South Yarra.

'They were still called The Wild Cherries, but it was really just Big Goose and Little Goose and a bass player called Steve Pristash and a singer, Brian Wilson. They didn't last long because after Lobby left they were a bit rudderless.'

One day Jiva suggested to Big Goose that he should give the guitar away and play bass, as he was really more of a rhythm player. Taking the advice, Big Goose went out and sold his guitar and bought a Fender Jazz and became a bass player. Little Goose, as Jiva recalls, was an amazing drummer, a jazz-trained player. They smoked a lot of hooch and enjoyed themselves. There was lots of laughter. So Jiva and his musician buddies had a good van, a bass player, a drummer – but no gigs.

Then Jiva got offered a job with Chain, who were a different band at this time from what they would become. Guitarist Phil Manning was in Chain, along with Murray Wilkins on bass, Ace Follington on drums, and a blind organ player from New Zealand called Claude Papesch. Wendy Saddington was the singer, but she left to pursue a solo career before Jiva had the opportunity to roadie for her. Eventually this incarnation of Chain broke up.

Phil Manning, with whom Jiva had become close, was at a loose end. He had Warren 'Pig' Morgan as a piano player. Then Jiva suggested that maybe they should get Big Goose and Little Goose, who were just hanging out in South Yarra, to join. Thus, with the addition of Glyn Mason, a singer from New Zealand, the new Chain was formed.

Rock historians and others may suggest that Jiva is giving more emphasis to his role in this amalgam than he should, but that ignores the essential tenet of this world: the roadie is front and centre with anything and everything that happens with their band.

So once again there was one man (Jiva), one van (a transit) and one band (Chain).

This version of Chain began playing regularly around Melbourne, and appeared at the Pilgrimage For Pop festival at Ourimbah, near Sydney. After some attempted studio recordings in Melbourne, it was decided that a live album was the way to capture what Chain was all about. So the five musicians and their roadie went to Newcastle and rehearsed for a month in a big hall, then they headed down to Sydney and recorded the somewhat legendary album *Live Chain* at Caesar's in Haymarket.

'We rented Caesar's on an off night, when it was closed, and brought in a lot of friends and a lot of hooch and the band just played live. It was very rudimentary equipment and we just recorded it as it went down, live in one take. But what a wonderful jam.'

The album credits Jiva as road manager and includes a quote from him: 'It was always a pleasure to keep them supplied.' And towards the end of 'Gertrude Street Blues', you can hear Phil Manning thanking Jiva, 'who kept us in oobliee-doobilees'.

In short succession, Warren Morgan left to play with Billy Thorpe in The Aztecs ('Chain were unhappy,' remembers Jiva), and he was followed by Glyn Mason. Phil Manning said he was going to talk to his friend Matt Taylor about forming a band, and as a result the most famous line-up of Chain came together. The band headed to Brisbane to rehearse, renting the Red Orb by day.

From there it was a drive to Melbourne, where Michael Gudinski was waiting to be their booking agent, manager and eventually record label. 'We took him on,' is how Jiva recalls this connection. 'Michael was a good manager, and we had good fun with him in those days.'

Looking back on his role with Chain at this time, Jiva says he was never particularly close with other roadies of the era. 'I mean, we'd wave at each other but you never really had time for much else as you were so busy. I wasn't a roadie's roadie. I was Chain's mother. I looked after the money and bought all the spare strings and drumsticks – plus I bought the dope and cooked their dinners at home. I was a good cook and most of us lived together, although Matt lived separately. In those days the roadie was part of the family. There was no hierarchy. It was just wonderful. I was the one who handed out the cash. Often after a Saturday I'd have $2000 in my pockets as we were paid in cash. They trusted me and I trusted them.'

Jiva was a strong guy and managed to haul all of Chain's gear in the early days. 'I was surprised by my resilience, particularly being super-stoned all the time.' Legend has it that he always worked barefoot. 'I've heard that too, but I can't remember,' he laughs. 'Maybe it's true. I was raised in Brisbane, and all through the 1950s we were allowed to go to school barefoot. There were no sealed roads in the outer suburbs where I lived, and we lived in shorts most of the year – no singlet, under-pants or shoes.'

Chain's fortunes altered completely when they had big hit records with the songs 'Black and Blue' and then 'Judgement'. Then came the album *Toward the Blues*, the cover of which featured photos taken by Jiva, who'd won $3000 betting on a horse and spent it on camera equipment.

With a heightened profile, Chain's workload increased dramatically; Jiva says the band was doing up to five gigs on a Saturday, starting in the afternoon and finishing at the Thumpin' Tum at 4 am. So he brought in Roger Taylor to assist him.

In between gigs, Chain and Jiva and some other musicians and roadies played cricket, forming a team with another Melbourne blues band, Carson, and their roadies. 'Matt Taylor created this cricket league,' Jiva says. 'We played for the Porpoise Shield, which was a thing he created on an acid trip. He made a proper shield with a porpoise on top. As Matt lived in Northcote Road, we were the Northcote Road Country Club. There was also the Stanley Street Gentleman's Batting and Bowling Association. And there was the Dank Street Desperates – although all of us were really long-haired desperates. We played each other on Sundays. It was mainly musicians and roadies – Carson had three or four roadies hanging around them – but other people were roped in too. I was actually very good at cricket, and so was Matt. Of course we were off our faces for every game.'

By the time Chain started to collapse, Jiva was tiring of being a roadie. Gudinski and Browning offered him the job of editing *Planet* (later *Daily Planet*), their attempt at setting up a competitor for *Go-Set*. Working with a cast of reprobates from the Melbourne music industry, Jiva cobbled together the news-paper for around a year before it collapsed in financial disarray.

Jiva returned to the music scene in the 1980s, becoming a sound engineer. 'There was nothing for roadies to do with sound in the early days. When Matt joined Chain, and because he played harmonica, I had to sometimes turn the volume down so it didn't feed back, but that was about it. There were no real sound engineers in those days. Drummers didn't even have mics on their kits.'

The man now known as Clive Lawler was once one of Australia's best-known roadies. And when music fans of that era see the word Chain, they pretty much immediately think of Jiva. One man, one van, one band.

9

Roger the Roadie

L ook closely at the cover of the cult album *A Product of Broken Reality* by Company Caine from 1971 and you'll see a 'special thanks' credit to Roger the Roadie. It's the second Australian album cover to include a thank you to a roadie – although on Chain's live album from the year before, Jiva is referred to as the band's road manager, so Roger the Roadie may well be able to claim a first.

Company Caine's roadie would become arguably the most successful Australian music business figure ever. After moving on to manage Sherbet, Roger Davies relocated to Los Angeles, where he has been the guiding figure behind such hugely successful artists as Pink, Cher, Joe Cocker, Tony Joe White, Tina Turner, Sade, Olivia Newton-John and Janet Jackson. Davies is very good at what he does. What's more, he does it in a quiet, unassuming, professional manner that is uncommon in the ego-driven music industry.

Growing up in Melbourne, Davies was obsessed by music from an early age, subscribing to English magazines *New Musical Express*, *Melody Maker* and *Disc and Music Echo* in the late 1960s. Frustrated at waiting for overseas albums to be released locally in Australia, and annoyed that often the lavish packaging was truncated, he began importing them, initially paying for them with money earnt on his paper rounds, and not long after by selling copies to other similarly inclined kids at school. Against his parents' wishes, he also tried his hand at playing in a band, as well as writing reviews of the records he was importing.

Next Davies began organising concerts at his university, Monash; he also continued writing reviews, and came to the realisation that his band wasn't going anywhere. In his spare time, as well as doing paper rounds, he was also working at a petrol station, eventually stockpiling enough cash to buy an old Ford transit van. Davies was now a student by day and a roadie by night, working for up-and-coming bands. Have van, will roadie.

After working for a band called Pig Face, he was asked if he'd help out Company Caine. He did that for a week, and then the band, who soon shortened their name to Co. Caine, told Davies they were moving to Sydney – and said he should come too.

'I thought this was a way I could get out of Melbourne and get away from my parents, so I said okay, and we drove to Sydney in my battered old white transit van. The band moved into a house on Ocean Street in Edgecliff. It was connected to a church and had about ten bedrooms. I moved my mattress into one of the rooms, put it on the floor and that was Sydney.'

For Davies and Co. Caine, day-to-day life was that of all aspiring bands at the time. Lots and lots of gigs, and hours on the road travelling between cities. Band and roadie together. One man. One van. One band.

'We'd overnight between Sydney and Melbourne all the time, and I'd be the one driving the whole way. Maybe I'd have some diet pills or something to try and stay awake. I also mixed the sound from a four-channel desk. We had a couple of lights, and we had a Hammond organ too. It was typical stuff. If we were in Melbourne, there'd be a pub show in the afternoon and then three gigs at night – Q Club, Bertie's, Sebastian's or maybe the Thumpin' Tum. I remember very clearly lugging a Hammond into gigs at 1 am for a 2 am gig. It was such a thriving scene.

'In those days the roadie picked up the money at the end of the gig. Everything was in cash. We just paid for the petrol and divided everything else up. There was no flash accounting. But I learnt how the business worked with Co. Caine. You had to learn quickly in those days.'

In Sydney in late 1971, Davies soon moved into the orbit of Michael Chugg – the two having met in Melbourne. Chugg was opening a management and booking agency office there. Like Davies, industry heavyweights such as Chugg and Michael Gudinski have all done brief stints in the formative years of their careers plugging in cords and packing vans with gear.

'It was a stepping stone,' Chugg says. 'Just a way to learn about everything. There was no training. I ran a dance in Launceston and that's how I got into it. And when I moved to Melbourne I had a band called Ida May Mack, and I was doing roadie work with them and helping Gudinski run dances, and it just went from there. Then I got a job as a poster boy at Consolidated Rock and that was that. Why be a roadie? That work was too hard.'

Slowly, Davies graduated from being the office boy to a junior booking agent. With Chugg increasingly away with his bands, Davies took the reins and started booking the bands on their roster. Eventually he gave away the job of being roadie for Co. Caine, as it was getting too hard. There was too much booking work for him to concentrate on. So almost before it began, Davies's career as a roadie was over. Roger the Roadie became Roger the Booking Agent, and soon Roger the Manager of One of Australia's Most Popular Bands.

For some time, one of Sherbet's roadies, Graham Webb, had been calling Davies and urging him to come and see this band called Sherbet, arguing that he and Chugg should represent them. Davies kept declining; they were running a *serious* rock agency, and Sherbet was a pop band.

Eventually Webb's persistence wore Davies down and he went to see them at Chequers nightclub. The band was playing three sets that night, and Davies had a light-bulb moment. He began booking them, and a year later became their manager. Sherbet became one of the two biggest Australian bands of the era – the other being Skyhooks.

Through the ranks of the Sherbet organisation came a roll-call of Australian road crew legends. Graham Webb did the sound. Howard Freeman was a tour manager and also worked with Davies in his office in Spring Street, Bondi Junction. Then there was Ray Maguire, who once bit the head off a cane toad during a Sherbet tour – but we'll get to that story a little later. Jim Murrie was in charge of lighting and pyrotechnics. 'He was very big on pyro,' Davies says, 'and of course no one really had any idea what we were doing in those days. There were no health and safety regulations back then. Ray was really creative . . .' Throw in 'Swampy' Jarvis, and it's clear Sherbet World was home to some of the greats.

Towards the end of the 1970s, Davies moved to Los Angeles, taking Sherbet's singer, Daryl Braithwaite, with him. From there he built his management empire.

Throughout his time at the top of the industry, Davies has always prided himself on being as involved as possible with the road crew who work with his management clients.

'I'm never too far removed from them,' he says. 'That's where I came from.'

10

P-p-p-peter Wilson

Peter Wilson has a pronounced stutter. There's a famous road crew story that Wilson – the best-known electrician cum lighting guy to ever work in an Australian crew – was up a ladder sorting out a lighting issue. He yelled down to Ray Maguire, the tour manager, asking him to get something.

'S-s-s-sure, P-p-p-peter,' Maguire said.

Wilson climbed down immediately and laid into Maguire. What he didn't know was that Maguire was also a stutterer, and was not having a go at him over his speech issues.

Wilson is famous in road crew and promoter circles. He's *the* sparky – the go-to guy. The man who's been dealing with electrical issues at shows and on tours since the 1960s. In many ways he's a throwback to those days. In 2017 he finally bought a cheap mobile phone – his first.

Now in his mid-70s, Wilson has stories about every major – and not so major – tour of this country, usually because he worked on it. If the Stones come to town, Wilson is there. Ask him about the 1973 tour for promoter Paul Dainty, for whom he's worked a lot, and off he goes.

'It was a three-week tour, almost a month. We started in Auckland and then went to Brisbane. It fucking rained in Brisbane, poured, we got fucking soaked. It was Milton Park tennis courts, three inches of rain in a couple of hours. They put all the seats on the grass and they just sank into the ground. Then we went to Melbourne for the show at Kooyong, which was stinking hot, and then Sydney, and then to Perth, with Adelaide and Memorial Drive in between, and they flew home from there. In Perth the stage was built on 44-gallon drums. They put the stage on top of them. We once did a gig on boards over a swimming pool in Perth.'

Wilson was a key part of Dainty's production crew for more than 15 years. Aside from the Stones, he can rattle off an impressive list of names that he worked with: Fleetwood Mac, The Jackson 5, Leon Russell, Slade, Uriah Heep, Focus, Neil Diamond, among many more.

Wilson moved between two jobs. His day job was for an electrical contractor, and then he'd take time off to go on the road with bands. Paul Dainty was the dominant Australian concert promoter; Dainty did a tour every five or six weeks, most of them pretty successful.

And Wilson recalls them all, often in minute detail. A prompt on Dutch band Focus immediately has him railing against the road crew they brought with them. 'They were fucking lazy. Such a lazy road crew. Eventually they were sent home – but via a bus trip from Melbourne to Perth. The promoter found the slowest and cheapest way to send them home, and then the Australian crew took over for the rest of the tour.'

It was a hand-to-mouth existence in the early days, but Wilson was nothing if not pragmatic. 'You never knew where the next gig was coming from – but if you want to survive in rock'n'roll, there's one thing I recommend: don't take loans.'

Wilson worked with The Bee Gees back in the 1960s. 'In those days you could put everything in the boot of a car – drums, guitars and a couple of amps. That was The Bee Gees. Now you need ten fucking semis for a band like that.'

Then there was a set-up with the young AC/DC at Festival Hall in Melbourne. It was a Sunday afternoon show, and Wilson was exhausted after a long and late Saturday night. 'I had my road box onstage. We'd been flat-chat working the night before, so at one stage before the show, once I'd done my stuff, I curled up on top of my road box and had a sleep. What did the cunts do? Rolled me out onstage and put me there as a bloody stage prop, didn't they!'

Wilson also worked alongside all the great characters in the early days of Australian road crews – and has stories about them all. 'There was a famous roadie, and one day we were doing a load-in at Festival Hall. He sees a bus full of women coming past and decides to do a brown eye, doesn't he. A few minutes later the bus comes back. There were 43 female police officers in that bus.'

Wilson went on to work for Jands, combining his rock'n'roll sparky work with two decades working in a hospital. He's been blown across stages sorting out wiring at an ABBA concert, and had all sorts of adventures.

Michael Chugg still recalls the ABBA incident very clearly. 'Peter went to hook up the power in the towers in the rain at the Showgrounds. The next thing we see is this blue flash going up the pole. Eric Robinson and I ran over going, "Where's fucking Peter?" And he wasn't where he was supposed to be – he had been thrown about 25 metres away, and when we got to him he just looked up at us and said: "D-d-d-did you f-f-f-fucking see th-th-th-that?"'

Wilson remembers it all too well. 'They had thunderstorms, didn't they,' he says matter-of-factly. 'I went up to sort something out, and the next minute *fucking bang*. I didn't get hurt so much, just blown out because of the air pressure. When the lightning hits the tower it warms the air up. Down the bottom it's fucking cold and it rises up – it's like blowing a piece of confetti around.'

Over the years, Wilson has worked on a lot more than just rock'n'roll shows. He worked with Pope John Paul II (as you do) at the Melbourne Cricket Ground and Flemington Racecourse. From that tour comes a terrific roadie's story, where the crew person in question may have been Wilson. Before the Pope's appearance, a roadie was on his knees rolling up electrical cords. The Pope arrived at the venue, saw him on his knees, walked to where he was, looked down and said, 'Bless you, my son.'

Wilson was also there in the early days of World Series Cricket, and was involved in the process of working out what colour ball would be best under the night lighting. He has done stints with the Dalai Lama, and at Phillip Island Raceway. He laughs ruefully at mention of the Bicentennial celebrations in 1988. 'We were dealing with five different voltages – 100, 120, 200, 230 and 400 volts. And you had to know *exactly* what you were doing. I still have all the technical folders that I had to go through for that one.'

Wilson exudes a quintessential Australian spirit. He's a hardworking, irreverent, highly skilled electrician with a dry sense of humour. Nothing much fazes him.

'I see crews rocking up in jeans and sandshoes. I always wore protective boots and overalls. Then at night before the show you'd change into your blacks and be part of the crew.'

Part of his old-world attitude has been his stoic refusal to embrace the digital revolution. 'Only the younger guys picked it up,' he says of the move to digital lighting. 'Not the old guys. I am from the old school – I did not wish to know about it. I'm 75. Why would I want to learn that stuff, even when it came in? If someone says a power point isn't working, I fix it. It's that simple.

'I learnt the hard way. When I was an apprentice, we did five years, and to become an electrical engineer I went to night school for seven years. *Then* I got involved in rock'n'roll and thought, "Fuck it, I'll make more out of rock'n'roll," and I enjoyed it. So I stuck with what I know.'

And what Wilson knows is a lot. It's made him indispensible to Australian promoters for decades now. He's pulled them out of all sorts of jams – some of them extremely dangerous ones.

'I have had some hair-raising moments,' he says. 'One night at the Hordern Pavilion in Sydney, a driver drove a truck through the overhead mains. This was during set-up for the show. Boy, did that guy get a roasting. I needed to put a set of live mains back in the mains box. So we got cardboard boxes and laid cardboard all along the ground, got some steps and a small ute and put cardboard all over that, and I got up on it with gloves and a face mask and I connected it all back again.'

Wilson is one of those crew guys who's been smart with his money. Of course he also had other work to fall back on. 'I was talking to a Sydney guy a while back – Squirt – and he was telling me how he'd just bought a house. He thanked me for the advice I'd given him. It's what I told all the young guys: whatever you make, put half in the bank and spend half on yourself. Most of them didn't listen.'

Electrical work and crewing is in Wilson's blood. When we chatted, he arrived pushing a walking frame and was less than two weeks out of hospital after heart surgery. Naively, I asked when he gave the concert and lighting business away. He looked at me like I was speaking a foreign language.

'I worked the fucking Harvest Festival recently,' he said. 'I've kept all my licences up – first aid, public liability and so forth – so while I keep them, they'll keep getting me to do things.'

Peter Wilson is a road crew lifer. It's hard to imagine him wanting it any other way.

11

Elvis, The Stones, Lynyrd Skynyrd . . . and Lou Reed

Not many people can be at the end of a three-hour conversation about their life in rock'n'roll and just throw in – almost as an afterthought – the line, 'I managed Lou Reed for a little while.' Bill McCartney can. He worked on the road with Elvis Presley, was the Australian production manager for The Rolling Stones on their 1973 tour, just avoided being on the plane that crashed and killed the key members of Lynyrd Skynyrd, and did a stint in New York trying to look after the notoriously difficult-to-manage Lou Reed. Not bad for a guy who started as a roadie with bands around Melbourne in 1967.

McCartney grew up in Glenroy, part of a migrant family. He recalls that Angry Anderson (who at the time had shoulder-length hair) and his band used to rehearse nearby, while Joe Camilleri was around the corner – something he remembers because 'Joe had a very attractive sister'.

It was while doing an apprenticeship as a mechanic that McCartney came into the orbit of music and bands, and for a number of years he did roadie work as well as learning a trade.

'With mechanics in those days you learnt everything,' he says. 'They made actual parts and didn't just replace parts. These were skills that helped me a lot later on.'

One of the other mechanics was the drummer for The Chessmen, the band that backed the then rock'n'roll and later country singer Johnny Chester. The band had an impressive claim to fame: they'd supported The Beatles on their Australian tour.

McCartney went along to a few gigs with them and 'caught the bug', starting to cart gear around for them and other bands, such as The Nova Express, on the fringe of the Melbourne scene. Things evolved from there. 'For some reason I seemed to find myself doing all the pop groups that no one else wanted to do, bands like Zoot and later The Mixtures. I didn't mind this, because they made money and could pay their bills, which therefore meant paying me. And with the pop bands it was easier, as they usually didn't have things like Hammond organs.

Before working with those bands, McCartney owned the truck, but he wasn't getting paid because there wasn't enough money coming in. 'But it was an adventure. And a busy one, particularly with a very popular band like Zoot, who played constant gigs.

'It could easily be four gigs in a day. That might start with a show at the ice-skating rink at Ringwood at one o'clock in the afternoon, then we'd go to Mentone for an early session at the drive-in, then we'd drive to Werribee and be the opening act for a gig down there, and then to Q Club to do a spot, and then maybe something later in the city. That sort of work schedule really made you close with the band, because if you weren't really on top of everything, then things didn't happen.'

McCartney quickly became part of the family of Melbourne roadies. It was a comparatively small band of guys, and everyone knew and helped each other out. 'Usually on a Sunday everyone would go to Bertie's and hang out and help whoever was working load-out. If you were there, that was the done thing – you helped out. You didn't even think about it. And that attitude stayed right through when I started working with international acts.'

By 1970 McCartney had finished his apprenticeship. As well as road crew work, he was doing a spot of earthmoving to bring in some money. Then he was offered work on some early international tours, including one by the American bubblegum pop band 1910 Fruitgum Company. The support bands included Zoot and The Mixtures; McCartney thinks they were offered shows so the headliner could use their gear. The tour was being partially sponsored by TAA airlines, so there was a lot of loading in and out of planes around the country.

After that, McCartney found himself being offered an array of astonishing work opportunities, including the early 1970s Australian tour by Pink Floyd. There was Manfred Mann, again with Spectrum on the bill – more for the use of their equipment than the need to sell extra tickets. Throw in Free, Deep Purple and the like.

There were lots of shows at Festival Hall – which McCartney refers to as Festering Hall. 'The venue had the most basic of equipment, very rudimentary. The sound system was designed for boxing, and the ring for that was in the middle of the room, so they weren't in any way designed for concerts.'

The tours kept rolling along. Cliff Richard, Cat Stevens, Rod Stewart and The Faces – as well as the cream of them all in that era, The Rolling Stones. McCartney was the production manager. In those days the Stones were far less aloof than today, and McCartney was not alone among the crews on that tour who had a lot of interaction with the band.

'In Perth, I'm sitting there mixing the support act and Charlie Watts is over my shoulder watching and listening. Mick and Charlie, in particular, were very approachable. They were just lads having fun.'

This was the tour when, according to McCartney, Mick Jagger – although some claim it was Keith Richards – came up to legendary electrician and stutterer Peter Wilson and asked about the weather. Wilson famously replied, 'M-m-m-might r-r-r-rain, m-m-m-might n-n-n-n-not.'

Looking back, McCartney recalls all these tours as fun – lots of fun – and, obviously, hard work. 'You were doing things you'd never done before. That was the whole attraction. The hard work was just what you did.'

In early 1974 McCartney went to Asia with Rod Stewart and The Faces, playing shows in Hong Kong and Tokyo. He'd been invited to work on that tour by the pioneering and hugely innovative sound guy Bruce Jackson, among other things the founder of Jands. While in Tokyo, Jackson asked McCartney if he wanted to continue on to the States and do some work with him on a few Elvis Presley dates. 'They were very short tours, maybe 20 shows in 18 days. But that was the longest tour Elvis ever did. And I did a shorter one with him too.'

The fist gig was at Oral Roberts University. Oral Roberts was a preacher who had built a university from the donations he'd solicited, and Elvis was playing the campus auditorium. 'I almost got into serous trouble at this gig because we'd been told not to get up on the stage. Anyway, one of Elvis's microphones stopped working during the show and I didn't even think. My way of doing things in Australia just came to the fore and I hopped up onstage to fix it. I looked up and there's Elvis looking at me. So I fixed the mic and came back to the side of the stage, and had shit poured on me from all the people around Elvis. I went home from the venue that night really pissed off. I mean, you didn't exactly have a surplus of microphones in those days. When we pulled in to the next gig, everyone's being very nice to me, and I couldn't understand why. Then finally someone told me that Elvis had liked what I'd done and so it was all okay. But I made sure I never got up onstage with him again.'

McCartney had the briefest of contact with Elvis on the tours. 'He shook my hand at the start of the tour and shook it again at the end.'

There were many upsides to working with Elvis, not just the money. 'I put a truck on its side in a ditch in Pennsylvania. Basically I fell asleep. Eventually a state trooper came over, and as soon as he saw I was with Elvis he flagged down another truck, got it to turn around and come back and pulled me out. I handed him a few souvenirs from the truck. That happened a few times. I got pulled over for speeding once, but again, as soon as they found out I was with Elvis – *and* Australian – they let me go. A lot of servicemen who had been in Australia during the Vietnam War and had been treated well were now with the police force.'

Aside from these perks and bits of luck, the pay working for Elvis was something McCartney had never experienced in Australia: $100 a gig – and in American dollars. That was huge, crazy money by Australian standards: $2000 American dollars for a short tour.

After Elvis, McCartney – who was still only 25 – travelled to the United Kingdom and worked with the likes of Procol Harum, The Faces again and, well, anything. He was doing okay but didn't have any real savings, so he had to keep the money coming in.

Then McCartney started working with Peter Rudge, the man tour-managing the Stones in 1973 and whose clients now included Lynyrd Skynyrd and the 16-year-old Tanya Tucker. McCartney had played Rudge the Australian country rock band The Dingoes, who subsequently joined Rudge's roster.

McCartney also looked after Lynyrd Skynyrd on their first European tour, and continued working with them in the States. There were always visa issues, and McCartney was careful about never overstaying his. He recalls a bus driver for Lynyrd Skynyrd going into Canada and being stopped on the way back into North America because of an outstanding warrant. McCartney tried to start the tour bus but couldn't get it in reverse due to the heavy snow and sleet. Eventually he went back into the customs and immigration people and persuaded them to briefly bring out the arrested bus driver to show him how to get the vehicle into reverse, after which McCartney somehow managed to drive to the next gig.

With The Dingoes' star on the ascendancy, McCartney toured with them through the latter part of 1977, before they were to join Lynyrd Skynyrd as their support act. McCartney arrived in Austin, Texas, two days before that leg began.

'I drove into Austin and was setting The Dingoes' gear up, as they had a gig there. I'd done a lot of gigs with Southern acts and people in Austin knew me. I was doing my stuff and noticed that everyone was really quiet, and I asked what was wrong. Someone asked if I'd heard the news, which I obviously hadn't. They told me that the Lynyrd Skynyrd plane had gone down that morning.

'The Dingoes just came to a screaming halt in America after that, because most of the tour was supporting Lynyrd Skynyrd. But boy, I was just lucky. If I hadn't gone on ahead, I probably would have travelled on the plane with Ronnie Van Zant and the others, as we hadn't seen each other for a year or so, and since I'd last worked with them they'd become big stars.'

McCartney also worked on Skyhooks' tentative and ultimately unsuccessful foray into America. Australian crew member Michael Oberg came with them and was doing lights, but McCartney recalls that the rest of a skeleton crew was picked up in America.

'I got into trouble with management after I cancelled a show. We were opening for someone and we were given such a small part of the stage to perform on, and it was a very high stage. What use was a singer with a broken leg or worse, as Shirley Strachan moved around a lot. So I pulled the show. Michael

Gudinski wasn't happy but as far as I was concerned, I was the production manager and the safety of the band and crew was my responsibility.'

Next McCartney found himself in New York City managing Lou Reed, a relationship that went back a few years to when McCartney had worked on Reed's first Australian tour. This was the period when Reed was being particularly difficult. He'd recorded *Metal Machine Music*, the double album of electronic noise made to piss off his record company. It had done just that, as well as alienating his diminishing fan base.

'It was just severe babysitting,' McCartney recalls of this period. 'I was stuck in the Gramercy Park Hotel, which wasn't what it is today, doing it by myself. He was living with his transgender partner, Rachel, who I got on fantastically with, although I was well aware of the rather long flick knife she carried with her. But I had to go. I could see the end of the money coming. There was enough to keep Lou going, but I had to tell his lawyers, who I was working with, that it was pointless. He wasn't about to go back into the studio.'

McCartney returned to Australia, before going on to forge an extremely successful career in Asia, working on shows like David Bowie's Serious Moonlight Tour, and then moving into event-styled shows both there and in Europe. He was involved in building stages and roofs throughout Asia in locations that didn't have them, and where it wasn't practical to freight them in and out.

After this, McCartney moved to work on David Copperfield's productions, which he did for many years, taking in seasons in South Africa, Egypt, Israel, Cyprus, Greece, China and Russia. He would still be doing it if he hadn't come back to Australia to look after his ailing parents. McCartney still cares for his 98-year-old father.

'I loved it, but on the other hand you do get sick of living out of a suitcase. I've been away from home and by myself most of my life. A lot of the time I was wondering where the next meal was coming from – and a lot of the time I was doing very well. I never got married. Never grew up. I was a gypsy. A lot of us in the industry were like Peter Pan. It was very much like running away to join the circus. This was the allure even when I was an apprentice. This other world was beckoning. You didn't know what it was, but you wanted it.

'And I've been lucky. I've always worked, in the main, around good and talented people. I've been very lucky in that way. For a little migrant boy, I've done okay. I always told my parents I wanted to travel and see the world. They encouraged me, and I ended up doing exactly that – and for the last 20 years, when I was on the road I was travelling first-class and getting paid to do it.'

12

Tooth

Dentistry, or the absence of it, means that Noel Jefferson is better known as 'Tooth', or sometimes 'Noel the Tooth'. The world of roadies is full of eccentrics. It's just the way it is. It's a universe that welcomes an array of weird, wonderful and extreme characters. Noel Jefferson is one of them.

Now in his late 70s, Jefferson is a great character, and an inspired and fanciful raconteur who – if you sit with him for a few hours – turns out to have been front and centre at a myriad of great rock'n'roll moments. And he's rarely anything other than highly entertaining.

Jefferson tells of being around The Rolling Stones when they toured Australia in the 1960s. He refers to Brian Jones as both 'BJ' and 'Jonesy'. He says that in 1964 he was working with Big Norm Miller, who was touted as Australia's answer to Roy Orbison. Apparently, Miller was on the same bill as Orbison during an Australian tour, and the American said to the Australian, 'You're better than I am.' That's how Jefferson recalls it anyway.

Jefferson became addicted to the rock'n'roll world when, as an 18-year-old, he saw Buddy Holly perform at Cloudlands in Brisbane, on a bill that also included Jerry Lee Lewis, Paul Anka, Jodie Sands and Johnny O'Keefe. Jefferson ended up hanging out with Buddy Holly's drummer, and later began working with an array of fledgling Brisbane bands. Exactly what he was doing is lost to history, but he's certain that right from the start he was fulfilling one of the basic duties of the roadie: scoring drugs. 'I was really like a messenger boy for them. If they wanted drugs, I'd go off and buy them an ounce for $30.'

Jefferson's major roadie stint was with Johnny O'Keefe, which he says was a relationship that started back in 1961. 'I was 21. In fact for my 21st we had a Coke and a hamburger. That was the year he had the breakdown, and Menzies was prime minister.'

There are a myriad of JOK stories in Jefferson's head, and some seem to jumble into one another. Life on the road – and decades of retelling – can do that. During a stint working in Canberra at the Bureau of Census and Statistics, Jefferson once again encountered JOK, who was driving from Canberra to Sydney when his car broke down. Tooth assisted the singer to get back to Canberra and onto a plane to Sydney.

After moving to Sydney in the early 1970s, Jefferson needed a job. He went to JOK's office in Double Bay and told him that he was good at what he did and wanted a job. According to O'Keefe's manager during this period, John Hansen, this was a time when the singer had decided to do more touring. With a band, a truck and plenty of equipment, he had to bolster his existing road crew, so Jefferson was given the job.

Jefferson, though, remembers things a little differently. He insists that he was the audio engineer for JOK, and was also entrusted with other significant responsibilities. 'He said to me one day, "Tooth, here's a cheque – go out and buy a truck," so I bought a dual transit van. I used to put the whole band and gear in there, with a mattress so they could sleep when we were going to Melbourne, Adelaide, Perth and so forth.'

Jefferson says JOK was difficult to work with – 'he was a prick' – but they managed to get on, and the roadie kept his job. 'I called him Boss and took the piss out of him. One day he gave me a cheque and told me to go and pay for tickets for him and me and the band to go to New Zealand. That was the particular day that Mr Brown robbed Qantas, so I'm there and there's coppers running everywhere, there's fucking guns and everything.'

Eventually, Jefferson says, he tired of working for JOK, and couldn't cope with the singer's erratic behaviour. 'He was never ready. I'd go and pick him up and he'd be on his third double scotch. I'd get to a club and the first thing he'd do was demand I get him drinks. Sometimes I'd have to drive him and his Firebird back from a gig because he was too pissed – and one of the crew would have to drive the truck.'

Jefferson moonlighted on other tours, helping out on Frank Sinatra's 1974 Australian tour. Tooth happily rattles off a multitude of names he worked with: Ram Jam, Suzi Quatro, Joe Cocker, Jimmy Barnes, Nathan Cavaleri, Art Garfunkel, John Wayne, Farrah Fawcett, Ronnie Wood, Queen, Sherbet, Madonna, the Easybeats.

There's an old adage that you should never let the facts get in the way of a good story. Noel Jefferson is living proof of that. His stories may be embellished sometimes, but one thing is for certain: Noel the Tooth is one of the larger-than-life characters in the pantheon of Australian road crew.

13

In the Air with Tangerine Dream

If you need to get a touring international band and their equipment – and their wives and partners – from Adelaide to Perth in a day in the midst of a national plane strike brought on by unhappy air hostesses, then Adrian Anderson is your guy.

It's March 1975 and German electronic band Tangerine Dream are on their first Australian tour. Things are going fine until Sir Reginald Ansett decided to describe his airline's cabin crew as a 'batch of old boilers'. Suggesting that they're little more than glorified waitresses doesn't help matters either. In fact, the air hostesses want increased pay, the right to fly during the first trimester of pregnancy, and an increase in their 'retirement' age, which is just 45. The dispute escalates, and there is a national strike, so all Ansett and TAA flights are grounded – giving a massive headache to thousands of Australian travellers, not to mention some very unhappy tour promoters, road crew and bands.

Tangerine Dream got caught up in the drama – as did promoters Michael Gudinski and Ray Evans. The problem came on top of a slew of equipment issues that had to be sorted out by the road crew and paid for by the promoters.

One of the crew working on this tour was the very experienced Anderson. Like so many road crew of the era, Anderson had drifted into the work. He'd been running dances in a church hall in Elsternwick, in Melbourne. At the age of 18 he enlisted in the Army, joining the Citizen Military Forces. He also studied printing technology before moving into surveying. Unlike a lot of his friends though, Anderson wasn't sent to Vietnam. He was also doing a graphic arts apprenticeship, and one of the guys he worked with, a sculptor named David Tucker, was managing a band called Sunshine. The year was 1968.

'David asked if I could give them a lift as he thought I had a car. I told them that no, I didn't, but that I could borrow the car from my mother and we could put a pack rack on it, and with a tow bar we'd just need a trailer.' Soon after this the manager decided he'd had enough, so Anderson took over picking up the band and driving them to rehearsals and gigs. He was now their roadie.

Still living at home, Anderson dragged the family phone into his room at nights so he could work for Sunshine, and went out putting up gig posters – all while holding down a day job. One night a week and at weekends, he fulfilled his Army commitments.

During his days, Anderson worked through his lunch break so he could finish early and then head to the offices of Australian Entertainment Exchange (AEE), the people who booked gigs for Sunshine and many other Melbourne bands. Sunshine was a 'progressive blues band', which essentially meant they did cover versions of blues songs, giving them a Sunshine tweak. The band members all had day jobs, and eventually they were able to purchase a truck and PA equipment.

When Anderson was away doing Army work, he organised a stand-in roadie, Dennis Dickie, for the band. Tragedy struck when Dickie was killed while driving his motorbike to a gig.

As he went on, Anderson was mentored by more experienced roadies, who gave him basic but important advice. Bill McCartney was the first to tell him he needed a box for all his leads. 'He told me I couldn't keep just throwing them in the truck, so I went to an Army disposal store and got a box.'

Anderson often slept on a mattress in the back of the van. 'I'd get home and just fall asleep. The next thing I'd hear would be a *tap, tap, tap*, and it'd be Dad on his way to work, telling me to wake up and get out of the van and get a proper sleep.'

As was the custom at the time, if Anderson wasn't working he would help out mates with other bands. One was his buddy Ian 'Piggy' Peel, who was working with Ariel. He was babysitting PAs owned by other bands, helping other roadies and generally assisting to make sure all the gigs around Melbourne went as smoothly as possible.

When the first Sunbury Festival was organised, Anderson was dispatched to the site and told to help promoter John Fowler out with whatever he needed. Then Anderson had a period living in Sydney, basing himself at the Astor Hotel, where he met Split Enz in the lift one day. As he recalls it, the whole band, their wives and partners, and their roadies were sharing one room. 'They were using the same beds in the room in shifts. The roadies would sleep in the beds during the day and the band and wives would take over at night, and the roadies would go out and walk around town.'

A number of people take credit for convincing Split Enz to relocate to Melbourne. Skyhooks member Red Symons has said he took Michael Gudinski to see them play in Sydney, and then told them to go south. Anderson's version of the story has him asking Split Enz to give him a tape of their music, which he listened to in his room. Then he called Gudinski and said he should advance the band the money for petrol so they could drive to Melbourne.

By this time, Sunshine had faded into obscurity and Anderson was busy working on international tours – which brings us back to Tangerine Dream.

Anderson had just finished working on the first Australian Blues Festival Tour with Freddie King, Hound Dog Taylor, Alexis Korner, Duster Bennett, Sonny Terry, Brownie McGhee and others. He went straight to Ray Evans's house in Toorak to meet Tangerine Dream. Among other things, the pioneering German band wanted a quadrophonic PA system, which involved setting up speakers in four corners of each venue.

This PA was new and cumbersome, and prone to causing all sorts of issues. It also took seven hours to set up and test before each show. 'It was operated by a computer system the size of a car. There was some issue with the power in Brisbane, and it blew up. We got it on a plane back to Melbourne for the next show.'

At this point they ran into the airline strike. After Tangerine Dream played a third show at Dallas Brooks Hall in Melbourne, Anderson agreed to drive the band straight over to Adelaide. The roadie was exhausted. It had already been a long, stressful tour. He put a deposit on some blankets and pillows from the Melbourne hotel they had stayed at so the band would have some basic comforts on the drive. He got out of the car at Border Town and had a cold shower at a petrol station with his clothes still on so he would stay awake before hopping back into the car dripping wet and continuing on. After Adelaide, there was the issue of how to get the band and their gear to Perth for two shows at Winthrop Hall.

Evans and Gudinski had mixed feelings about the Perth leg of the tour. At one stage they were prepared to cancel the two shows, but they decided they had to go ahead; presumably there was a financial imperative. Also, the band was flying out from there. So they had to work out a way to get across the Nullarbor.

The phone rang at the Adelaide venue at 11.25 pm, just as Tangerine Dream was finishing its show. On a long lead, it was bought to Anderson. The caller was Evans, saying that he and Gudinski had talked and they were to drive from Adelaide to Perth. The plan was to move the shows in that city back a day or two to allow for this.

Anderson's response was to tell Evans to get fucked. If the band and crew were going to Perth, it would be via air . . . somehow.

Ian 'Smithy' Smith was also working on the tour. He and Anderson went to work at the Travelodge. They tore a phone book in half and started ringing all the charter airlines they could find. In the early hours of the morning they hit pay dirt. In a moment of inspiration, Smith suggested calling a guy from Opal Air who flew miners to Coober Pedy. The Opal Air pilot was in. He said that he could off-load his passengers with someone else and that he'd meet Tangerine Dream, Smith and Anderson at Adelaide Airport at 3 am. He would fly them to Perth in his twin-engine Cessna, which had long-range fuel tanks on the wings. The cost was $2000, a lot of money at the time. Anderson guaranteed the payment, and said he'd sort it out with Evans and Gudinski later.

For Tangerine Dream, the prospect of travelling in such a tiny plane – which held just eight passengers and the pilot – was a bit of a mind fuck. The smallest they'd been in previously was a Fokker Friendship. 'I had to push them in the door. It was a bit like getting horses into a float. My briefcase went in the wing locker. The amps were in the nose cone. There was stuff and people stacked everywhere inside.'

The heavy equipment was already on its way to Perth on a pre-booked freight plane. Anderson and Smith had begged to put seats on that plane for the band, but were told that wasn't an option. So Tangerine Dream and sundry crew were in the air for a nine-hour flight from Adelaide to Perth.

'We took off and the plane seemed to be flying so slowly. The first stop was Ceduna, which was really just a dirt strip. The pilot had to buzz around to get rid of the sheep before we could land. There was a little outdoor dunny and a petrol bowser. The keys were left somewhere. We managed to refuel by dragging the hose to the wing and putting in 27 and a half gallons of fuel.

'Then we went to Forrest and landed on an old F-111 concrete strip in the middle of the desert. They came out with an aviation drum on a front-end loader and literally poured the fuel into the wing. Tangerine Dream had never seen anything like it.

'By the time we got to Kalgoorlie everyone was pretty hungry. All we had was a Tupperware box of barley sugar under the dashboard. We had no food. So while we were refuelling there I borrowed a car and drove around town. I threw money on a counter and got fish and chips and hamburgers – and beer.'

One version of this saga, as recounted on a Tangerine Dream blog, adds that the plane's radar system fell off during the flight, but whether or not this is true, the plane, band and crew made it to Perth, did the shows and flew on to London. There they played a sold-out show at the Royal Albert Hall, which would have been cancelled if they hadn't made it to Perth. For his troubles, Anderson received a thank you on a subsequent album by band member Edgar Froese.

Anderson went on to work with a number of other bands, including extended stints overseas with The Cobbers Bush Band and then Air Supply. Today, Anderson is a key figure in the Australian Road Crew Association, and a mine of information about the history of Australian road crew and other music industry figures. But really his place in roadie history was secured when he got Tangerine Dream onto that tiny plane and saw them to Perth. That's as good an example of road crew ingenuity as you'll find.

14

From Roadie to Driving the Mogul

From 1999 until 2016, Geoff Lloyd was a driver. That was his job. If his boss was hanging at a rock'n'roll gig or at Crown Casino at 5 am, Lloyd would be sitting in the Jaguar outside, waiting. If there was a trip to the airport at 2 pm, guess who would be loading the bags and their owner? A meeting in the city at 4 pm, dinner in Richmond at 7 pm and then a concert at Rod Laver Arena? Easy. Pretty much 24 hours a day for 17 years, Lloyd was there in Melbourne whenever Michael Gudinski needed to go somewhere. It was a job that took every bit of the patience, smarts and good humour that had carried Lloyd through his earlier working life.

Even Lloyd sometimes has difficulty remembering that he had a life in the years BG – Before Gudinski. But he did. These days he's a man of comparative leisure on a country property outside Melbourne. But back then Lloyd was one of the most tireless, hardworking, smart and downright amusing guys working on the road.

Lloyd started working as a roadie with Chain back when they were at the peak of their popularity, doing three or four shows a day at weekends. He was the third guy on their crew, working with the legendary Jiva, who by then had taken on a second roadie, Roger Taylor. Then Lloyd did a bit of work with the band Friends, before moving to Perth and working with The Dave Hole Band and others.

While in Perth, Lloyd did a short stint as a guest of Her Majesty, having been busted in 1970 for a block of hash the size of his thumb. 'Perth at that time was fucking straight,' he recalls. 'If you think they're straight over there now, imagine what it was like in 1970. I went to court with the guy who imported the hash. The judge just saw the two of us and couldn't separate us in his mind, so I got six months.'

After being released Lloyd moved back to Victoria and lived in the country. He didn't do a lot for a while. By the mid-1970s he was back in Melbourne, 'just selling pot and delivering stuff. And one of the [people] I delivered pot to was a roadie, and he asked if I wanted to come and work with the band Last Chance Café, which I did for a couple of years.'

Like most at the time, Lloyd had no training. 'You just learnt stuff, like how to set up a light show. There was no "lighting guy". There was just everything in the truck. You set up everything – band equipment and lights. There were maybe ten lamps in those days, and a switchboard, so you turned them on and off and made the show a little prettier. There were no faders or anything. No three-phase power. It just came out of the wall. Good basic stuff.

'With guitars, you just grabbed a guitar and a tuner and worked it out. I learnt how to tune drums. You just watched how other people did it, saw how they stretched the skins and then you did it. I learnt how to solder. It wasn't that hard. If something's not working, what use is it? So you go and fix it.'

When Last Chance's sax and piano player, Billy Rogers, was invited to join Dragon early in 1979, that was the end of that band. By now Lloyd was a fixture on the Melbourne roadie scene. He knew people who knew people, and he wouldn't be out of work for long. The demand for really good road crew was like that in those days. Everyone's band played with everyone else's. Friendships were forged. It was common knowledge who was a good crew guy – and who wasn't. If a good guy became available, you nabbed him.

'Last Chance broke up on Tuesday and almost immediately – it might have actually been the next day – a Ranger truck came backing down the dead-end street where I lived and the Jo Jo Zep & The Falcons crew jumped out and said they'd heard that Last Chance had broken up and that I should come with them as they were going overseas. They said – and this is funny – that they'd get Joe Camilleri to like me.'

Lloyd had little idea that he would work with Jo Jo Zep & The Falcons for the next half-decade. They were well managed by Michael Gudinski and Michael Roberts, who called themselves Loud & Clear Management. 'Gudinski was the loud part, Roberts was the clear bit,' Lloyd laughs.

In a rarity in those days, the band's crew was paid a retainer when the band was off the road – but that was usually only for a couple of months a year. In his downtime, Lloyd picked up work with the likes of Skyhooks and The Jim Keays Band.

These were the golden days for Australian rock'n'roll bands and their crews. Everyone was continually working and on the road. 'It was trucks and crew running all over the country. Dozens and dozens of us – and everybody knew each other. There were real servos then – Golden Fleece servos that would give you a good feed at any time of the day or night. You'd pull into one of those and there'd be three or four crews all together heading to one town or another.

'And there was a real "the show must go on" mentality. Often I think that the crew had more of that than some of the acts they worked for. Some of the lengths that crews went to get shows up and running were amazing, and they'd only tell the bands afterwards what they'd had to do and what had happened.

'The camaraderie was immense. Everyone was just in this beautiful world of rock'n'roll. At gigs you'd do all the work, the running around, the "check one, two, check one, two," then the lights would go down and you'd hear the intro tape and you knew exactly where you were and what you had to do. Then after the show there'd be four guys, maybe five, maybe ten if there were a few bands playing, and you're in this unified struggle to get everything back into the truck and out of there.'

Lloyd gets quietly reflective when he thinks back to crew guys he worked with in those days, particularly those who did lights. Some are still around, but many are not. 'Some of the early lighting guys were sheer fucking geniuses with what they did with lights. It was uncharted territory, and incredibly creative for those guys who were really into it. You always knew the lighting guys in a crew You just felt it. They strode to a different beat.'

People liked Lloyd. He was good at what he did, and fun to have around. Eventually he graduated from working with Australian bands to a stint on a Moody Blues tour that Kevin Jacobsen was promoting. 'John Winchcomb really liked me, and he was the head production guy for Jacobsen then. I must have done a good job on that, as four months later I'm on the 1985 Bruce Springsteen tour as the Australian promoter's rep.'

From the outside, you would imagine that this was an enormous responsibility: Springsteen at peak popularity and on his first Australian tour. And you'd be right. It was a huge responsibility – if you were actually called upon to do anything.

'It was pretty easy,' Lloyd laughs. 'Springsteen's people were so well set up. They booked all the accommodation and stuff that I would have been expected to do. I was really just there in case something went wrong. If the nosebleed happened, I had the hanky. It was a nursemaid job.'

After this experience, Lloyd moved to America and found himself a job as a caterer working on . . . Bruce Springsteen shows. 'There was one show and I looked through the meshed wire fence and I see Gudinski – it was just like we were at Sunbury. He was having trouble getting into the concert, so I whipped out my world pass and gave it to him. I said I'd get another one and pick this one up from him when I was back in Melbourne.'

Lloyd continued to work as a crew guy, doing a stint with the multi-instrumentalist David Lindley and his band El Rayo-X. 'That and working with The Falcons are my career highlights.' He also did some work with Divinyls when they toured in America as the opening act on an Aerosmith tour. 'That was one of *the* worst tours I've ever done. The rest of the crew hated me, because for whatever reason the usual guitar tech didn't get to come on the tour and they resented me being there.'

Then Lloyd met the musicians who would become Crowded House at a Midnight Oil party in Los Angeles. He played them the new Black Sorrows record, which Joe Camilleri had just sent him, and they in turn played Lloyd some new songs. 'They were still The Mullanes and were over in the States doing their first record. I had no green card and I really needed work – and I wanted to work with them. I begged and begged to be their roadie.

'Neil [Finn] told me they were sorted, and that Paul Taylor was going to be their crew guy. So I went to my home and waited till it was the right time in Australia and called Paul and asked if he was going for the job. He said that he wasn't and that he was sick. So I went around to where the band were staying and said, "He's not going to do it, he's not going to do it." But they made me wait till they all came back to Australia and sorted out who was going to be their manager. I just kept begging them – and Paul Hester liked me. I could make a good cup of tea and roll a good joint.'

Lloyd worked with Crowded House until the early 1990s, when he'd had enough and started doing less pressurised work, driving vehicles on international tours and working on the production side as a runner. Eventually he decided to move back to his farm and do nothing. But doing nothing wasn't as easy in the '90s as it had been in the '70s, and soon Lloyd needed a job. One day, while doing a delivery job, he ran into Michael Gudinski, who said, 'Give me a call – I might need a driver.'

Lloyd has reflected on his days on the road – the good parts and the not so good. 'There's always the night where the band hits the first chords and something like the lights die. Your head spins, your stomach churns. Everyone had disasters in those days. You were always trying that little bit harder to be that much more special. Pushing the PA and lights to make the band sound bigger and better. I can't stress how lucky I was. Completely arsey, to get that gig with Last Chance and then to push it out to the world that I really liked the work, and then to be with the Falcons . . . I mean, we worked *really* fucking hard. As did every band at the time.

'The work has changed, but there's still basic stuff that has to be done every day for the sake of the show. But there's nothing like the feel of everyone being there, totally in the moment for a show and when everything's going just right.

'Part of the attraction was that we were like cowboys. We were taking drugs. We had different women in every town. The thing with girls is that we weren't going to be there tomorrow. That was the great thing about us. And the only people who talked about it was them and their friends. No one else needed to know that they had snuck off with a dirty roadie.

'You'd look forward to getting into new cities or towns. We'd pull into town and everyone was against us – so the crews became really close. And very loyal. It was band and crew. To this day, if someone says to me the name Daddy Cool, I'll go "That was $crooge's band."

'And it was a problem-solving lifestyle. *Nothing* was ever as the rider said it would be. You'd get to the venue and the stage size would be smaller than you'd been told, or the load-in was more difficult, or – worse still – the drinks weren't there. Problem-solving is a big part of it. And that was also the buzz of it. You were as free as a bird out there doing it. It was fucking hard work, but that was your job.

'Being a roadie is just one of the greatest things I've done with my life.'

15

Shine a Light

Shane Scully was working as a roadie and lighting operator for The Church at the Tivoli in Sydney in the early 1980s when he nearly broke his back after someone dropped a speaker box during a load-in.

The Tivoli was a notoriously tough load-in for crews, up three flights of stairs. And if it was tough on the way in, it could be lethal on the way out, with spilt beer, glasses, cans and other rubbish littering the stairs. Scully was on the comparatively easier load-in – but you always had to watch inexperienced crew supplied by support bands. They often had no clue how to move heavy gear. This was one of those days, and Scully was in a world of pain.

The band's then manager, Michael Chugg, had Scully lifted into a car driven by one of his employees, who was told to take the roadie to a well-known osteopath in Newport Beach. Not a quick drive. Chugg opened the car door just before it left and threw a joint in Scully's direction. 'Get stuck in to that,' he said. 'That'll sort you out for the drive to Newport.' It did, and so did the osteopathy, and Scully survived to load and light another gig.

He worked during the halcyon days of the late 1970s and 1980s, with bands such as INXS, The Church, Australian Crawl and Crowded House. The pub circuit was at its zenith, and Australian bands regularly played six or seven nights a week in their home city, before venturing on the road for seemingly endless interstate tours. Often the road crews thought these tours had been booked by agents who used a dartboard rather than a map, so crazily long and illogical were the drives.

Sure, the crews were bigger in those days. But so were the PAs and lights, and the trucks they needed to be loaded into. The drugs and booze were pretty much the same. There was a lot of drinking, a lot of pot, tonnes of speed. And still no RBTs. That changed in December 1982, but a million miles had been driven by road crews before then. It was a tough working life, and work and life rolled along together.

Scully started out as a drummer, having a knack for timing – something he would ultimately parlay into a career doing lights. In the 1970s he was in one garage band and his mate was in another. The other band started getting a few supports with bigger bands around the St George area in Sydney. Scully went along to watch them, and soon they needed someone to do lights for them.

'The lighting guy from the main band would show you which six switches you could use. There were 24 faders and you'd get six. You had no back lighting, just the front lights. I said to myself that if I ever got to be in that position, I was never going to do that to a support band. And I didn't. I would take special effects and highlights out but I would always give them enough front and back lights so they could have a decent show. I didn't think it was fair to them otherwise.'

As his rapid trajectory through the world of lighting and road crewing gathered pace, Scully found himself doing lights with The Eyes, a bunch of Darlinghurst squatters with no money who had a minor hit with their song 'Traffic Lights'. But The Eyes had a savvy manager and ended up getting supports for touring international artists such as The Cure, XTC and Magazine. In 1980 they even supported the first Australian tour by KISS. Seeing these international acts and the lighting they used changed Scully's approach to his craft and inspired him to keep at it – and to do it better and more inventively.

'They had all these creative lighting guys. I realised it wasn't all rock'n'roll fingers of God stuff by going flash, flash, flash as I had been. My lighting became more theatrical and subtle and I started experimenting with projections. That's how things started to change for me. I think Chris Murphy must have seen what I was doing, and he told me he was managing this band who had just changed their name to INXS.'

When Scully started working with them in 1979, The Farriss Brothers had three crew, but that soon went to four as the band became INXS and their following increased. It was tough work. A typical gig at the time saw the headline band finishing at midnight, although it was frequently much later. After INXS walked offstage, it was at least three hours before the crew, who had been on the go since midday, could close the truck door.

There was an average of eight shows a week. Saturday was usually a double show. INXS would perform at Campbelltown Leagues at 9 pm and Selina's in Coogee at midnight. The crew would set up at Selina's on Saturday morning around midday with their own PA, lights and monitors, but no stage gear. They'd be finished by 3 pm and would drive to Campbelltown with the stage gear, while a second crew was setting up there. INXS would do the first gig and then the crew would get the stage gear, load it in a small truck or tie it down in the big truck. They'd get to Selina's by about 11 pm, set up the stage gear there, and the band would go onstage at midnight. After finishing about 1.30 am, the crew would start packing up and loading everything out. If everything went well, they'd be out of the venue by 4 am.

If it was a city gig, the crew would then head back to the hotel and relax. If they were doing a run of country dates, though, they'd get some sleep before getting up at 8 am to do another four-hour drive to the next town. Repeat night after night after night.

'And you're not going back to the hotel to read the in-room Bible,' Scully smiles. 'There's always a couple of stiff drinks and a few joints to mellow you out.'

And more often than not these motels and hotels were somewhere between the minus and one-star level. It was very common throughout this era for bands and crews to stay in separate hotels to maybe save $10 a room per person or twin share – the latter being the most common. The crew would be sharing a room at a dive down the road, while the band would head off to the maybe one-and-a-half-star luxury accommodation where the cockroaches at least knocked first.

Scully worked with INXS for three years from 1979 till 1981, starting when they were still The Farriss Brothers. These were rudimentary days for both band and crew. 'INXS were pretty good with the way they treated the crew,' Scully recalls. 'We used to stay at Macy's in Melbourne, for instance – all of us, ten in a room.' Yes, that means Michael Hutchence, the rest of the band and the crew all bunked down together in stretcher beds in a single room. Their manager, of course, had his own room.

'Macy's was rough,' Scully says. 'It was like a dormitory room with the ten beds. It was pretty noisy and uncomfortable because by the time the crew got back, the band had been back for a few hours, so they're wanting to sleep – or they're still partying and you want to sleep.'

Scully and the crew did over 200 shows a year with INXS. He always enjoyed their tours up and around the North Coast of New South Wales and into Queensland. They often used Music Farm Studios in Byron Bay as a base – where they were still ten to a room – and would roam to do gigs in Grafton, Kempsey, Lismore and surrounding towns.

'It was funny,' he recalls. 'The hippies would all come out of the hills and make mushroom soup for the band and everyone would be absolutely flying. There was a lot of free love going on then. Not a lot of bras being worn and girls just climbing into bed with you. It was just like you would imagine – or fantasise. The early 1980s hippies up the North Coast were legendary.'

At that time Scully was being paid $200 a week. It was hardly retirement money – but it was twice as much as the band themselves were getting in those early years. 'The band were getting $100 a week, so every so often I'd buy a bread stick and six bananas and feed the band lunch if things were a bit tough.'

It was common in the late 1970s and early 1980s for Australian road crews to be earning more than the bands they worked for. The crew would be on a fixed weekly salary, while the band would divide up whatever was left after all their commitments – crew, truck hires, PA costs and so on – were paid. What the bands had that the crew didn't have was the long-term earning potential, the brand name, the merchandising income, and the record and publishing royalties. The long game for the band was usually better – unless, of course, they didn't get anywhere and broke up.

INXS were savvy operators, and when they found talented crew they wanted to keep them. In this case, they had Scully, the highly rated Col Ellis on sound, and two others. They were a tight unit, and the band didn't want to lose them.

If the group took a few months off to record an album, their management would get the crew gigs with other performers – perhaps a Hee Bee Gee Bees theatre run, or a Norman Gunston tour – so they had a regular income and would still be around when INXS needed them back. A lot of those shows were in theatres, and the audiences would be seated, so it gave the roadies a break from the mayhem of INXS tours. And they could stay in one place for a few nights instead of dashing to a different town every night.

The rock'n'roll world in those days was every bit as crazy as the mythology held it to be. Scully still gets a little poignantly reflective while he talks about the audience responses he witnessed at shows. But with the fun and excitement came many risks to life and limb.

'I've come off a few ladders and been blown across stages after plugging in dodgy three-phases that have been busted or buggerised. I was once thrown ten feet across the stage and nearly had a heart attack after being electrocuted. All your joints ache after that. It's not a lot of fun.

'Coming off a ladder was usually the result of putting your hand in the back of a lighting can and loosing focus because when you get zapped you throw yourself off the ladder. So there's been a few injuries. Broken fingers from trying to get trusses joined together. In venues power points were always mistreated. Back in those days there was no tagging or testing of electricals as there is today. Imagine some of the dodgy pubs around Australia with everyone pulling out their leads and kicking power points. A lot of things didn't work and there were constant power issues.'

In the world of crewing, Scully almost became known as the lighting guy who killed Crowded House – or at least Neil Finn. At any pub gig or bigger concert there's a lot of equipment surrounding and above a band. Everyone hopes it stays where it's meant to, and does what it's meant to do. But that doesn't always happen. Scully stills sweats at the thought of his involvement in an incident at a show at the Jet Club in Coolangatta.

In those days Scully was known in Australian lighting circles for his use of a grey cyclorama, a contraption which, when lit up, looked like a screen; when it wasn't lit up, it was a full black screen. He could do projections on it and create all sorts of effects. With The Church he'd projected their *Seance* album cover and all sorts of ghostly images. It was one of the things that set him apart from a lot of other Australian lighting guys at the time.

On this occasion there was a mezzanine above the stage, and the leads were coming down to some dimmers. Scully was watching the show and said to someone next to him that something didn't look quite right. But he couldn't work out what it was.

'The next thing that happened was that the whole back truss fell, and the screen covered Paul Hester. The cans stopped less than a foot above Neil Finn's head. I looked up at the mezzanine and I could see some guys running. They'd obviously snuck up there for a better look at the show, but no one was meant to be there. They must have tripped over the leads and that caused the trees and truss to fall.'

The leads from the dimmers must have halted the fall, otherwise Finn would surely have been killed. The show was stopped and the crew pulled the truss back up and secured it before the performance resumed. But Scully remained in shock all night. 'The band knew how lucky they were. It scared the hell out of me, and that was when I started to think that I'd had enough, and that it was time to stop before I really did kill someone.'

After INXS, Scully had done stints with Sunnyboys, Australian Crawl, The Church and Divinyls – all bands he loved. With each, he'd do a different style of lighting that he thought augmented the music of the band. There was funky shit for INXS, weird atmospherics for The Church, and simple old-fashioned *flash, flash, flash* for more basic bands that Scully didn't particularly care for.

Like most crew guys, he did brief stints with bands whose music he didn't particularly like. But these would usually be for short bridging tours to pay the bills. Lighting guys, in particular, have to learn whole new sets of songs – and quickly. Most people have a threshold. 'I did The Choirboys briefly, and I quickly got to the point where I didn't want to hear "Run to Paradise" one more time.'

There was also pressure to stay at the top of your game. 'There were usually other crew guys at shows checking out what you were doing. There was a lot of peer group pressure. Management were keeping an eye on you, plus there was your own personal sense of pride. Plus there were the fans who would get to know you. In every city there'd be 30 or 40 guys and girls who knew you. They'd be at every show. But the pressure you put on yourself to maintain a certain level was the biggest thing for me.'

The physical and mental wear and tear on crews of this era was phenomenal. Regardless of how aware they were of their own physical and mental wellbeing, their health took a massive beating. For starters, most were rarely off the road for any length of time, meaning they rarely took time to rest and recuperate. The work was plentiful and the comparatively low wages meant that they needed to jump from one job to another.

Scully estimates that during his time on the road, he rarely had more than one or two weeks off a year. 'Of course there were always things to keep you going, but usually they weren't things that were good for you. It was drinking, smoking pot and doing speed. They were the three things. And by the early 1980s the bands were just starting to delve into coke. Your heath did suffer, so you tried to invigorate yourself if you had a few days off and eat good food – or at least try and eat better food – and ease off going to the Manzil Room and Benny's.

'A few of us were fairly healthy by standards. Me, Jock Bain, Neil Thompson and Joe Newendyke all lived together at one stage in a terrace house in Paddington that we called Boys Town. Neil was INXS's tour manager, Joe was doing Divinyls,

I was doing Aussie Crawl, and Jock was Midnight Oil monitors.
We had four of the biggest bands in the country represented in
that house via their roadies. We had dinners, red wine, lots of
girls coming around. No one had permanent girlfriends. Maybe
you'd have a girl for a month, and then you'd go away for six
months and by the time you got back she's gone. There was
no real maintaining of relationships. But I did meet someone
and got married during my time with Australian Crawl. In
fact I left Australian Crawl when I got married but went back
to working with them, and then Crowded House came along.'

Part of the problem with maintaining relationships – or the
lure of not being tied down – was the constant flow of women.
'You always knew a couple of girls in every town,' Scully smiles.
'There were groupies everywhere, as well as fans of the band
who you wouldn't classify as groupies – they just wanted to be
with you. Then there were the hardcore groupies who would
fuck anything. Some really dreadful lowlife.

'Oh, there were some famous ones. The Lithgow Leaper was
before my time, but in Shepparton, for instance, there were two
girls called Slash and Gash who used to sort the crew out in the
back of the semi. I never partook in that but it was funny: "I'm
Gash and she's Slash." This was well before Guns N' Roses.
Then there were a group of girls in Melbourne known as the
Car Parkers. They were famous down there. There were certain
girls who just really dug crew guys, and you got to know quite
a few like that. They weren't interested in being with the band,
but they knew all the crew that came through town.

'There's that famous crew T-shirt: "It's OK, I'm With the
Band." With some girls it was a case of the band being untouch-
able and the next best thing was the crew. The thing about
crew is that we were down-to-earth and not rock stars. Most
of the crew guys were pretty grounded and just did their job.
They were good guys. We worked hard, played hard – and we
knew the band. The band would all have the most glamorous

ones, and the second tier would be with the crew. And make no mistake, the second tier was pretty cool too.'

In the early days before he got married Scully had girls in Melbourne and Perth, but 'never been laid in Adelaide' was a saying of his. His Melbourne girl would follow his band's progress around via gig guides, and at the first load-in at the Frankston Pier she'd be there. She'd have taken time off work for the time the band was in town. 'If she wasn't at the load-in or soundcheck, you could bet that once the show was just about to start you'd get a tap on the shoulder and there she was. Then she'd stay with you – or you with her – for the whole week. It was a good set-up. Having a regular girl in each town was actually more comfortable than having a girl every night – not that that wasn't okay too, but with long-term girls you could go back to their place for a shower, and you'd eat better food.'

Once Scully started working with The Church, he graduated bigtime in the 'girl on the road' stakes, much to the bemusement and envy of the guys in the band and the rest of the crew. Yes, Shane Scully was officially hanging out with a Penthouse Pet of the Month. She was September 1981, in case you're wondering. 'I got so much grief from the band as I was "just the lighting guy". She was a friend of a friend in Sydney. We were introduced up here and then she moved to Melbourne. And in those days The Church would do a week in Melbourne every month. They were on fire. And then she'd come back up to Sydney with me.'

This was an era where, more often than not, good crews travelled as a well-established unit. Personal differences – unless they were massive and confrontational – were generally put to one side. That was the way it had to be. 'You put up with little idiosyncrasies. You just had to. It was head down, go hard and get it done. You were pretty much a team. It was pretty high-pressure stuff – getting set up and ready and then the band coming on and then everything you had to do afterwards. And crews had their own language, their own banter. I think sometimes it was something that only we understood.'

Scully believes that most bands had a good attitude to their crew. They understood how much work was involved to get them onstage, and they appreciated that. More importantly, they knew that the crew were looking out for them. If any shit went down, the crew would be there for them. Musicians also knew that their crew were working to make the band look good.

Crews in the early 1980s punished themselves after gigs, and then more often than not stepped into a vehicle, either as a passenger or – worse – as the driver. Scully is another former crew member who is staggered that there weren't more serious road accidents. 'After the show there would invariably be a bottle of scotch and a bong. Some of the crew would be in the truck and others in the crew car, if you'd graduated to having two vehicles on the road. Thank God there was no RBT. Because you were doing it all the time, you became pretty good at it. But there were a few crew who decided not to drive because they didn't trust themselves.'

Scully liked to drive, and did a lot of it. He considers that he was a bit more together than some of his cohorts. Certainly, he had a Class 3 licence, which meant he could drive a truck, but he'd also drive the crew car or the Tarago, which was a rather unsafe vehicle prone to rolling. Over the years he had a few incidents, but nothing he'd classify as major. And he's still around to talk about it.

'I fell asleep once heading to Cairns with ten tonnes of gear in the truck. It was about 4 am. That drive is 14 or 15 hours, without a break or anything going wrong. It was an old Bedford truck, so maybe an even longer drive. I'd left Surfers after a show, and we had a day and a half to get to Cairns and set up for the next show. Insane stuff. There were three guys in the front of the truck, so we each took turns at driving.'

Scully knows they were lucky, and over the years had many narrow escapes. Some became legendary. One guy rolled a Cold Chisel truck on the Cahill Expressway in Sydney just before peak hour. He closed down the whole Harbour Bridge for a few hours. 'He never lived that one down,' Scully says.

Then there was the violence. Nothing had really changed since the torrid world the crews inhabited in the 1970s. The aggro and plain stupid behaviour from audience members continued. 'I've copped many a full can of beer in the back of the head. They bloody hurt. I've split my head open many times. It's usually just the local dickheads up the back of the venue pissed off because the girls are hanging around the sound or lighting desk. Violence was a big part of being a crew guy back then. Crews were targeted a lot – especially after the show. You'd be packing up and loading out when they came for you.

'I remember one night at the Goulburn Workers Club with The Church. The crew that night was me, Tony Wilde, Gerry Georgettis and Greg Thompson, doing monitors. Hippo and Gerry were big guys, and they were in the truck packing while Tony, Tommo and I were running up and down bringing the gear out, down the stairs. I had a monitor box on my shoulder when I get king-hit from behind by some dickhead from the local football club, who wasn't happy because he thought all the girls were looking at the crew and the band.

'These guys – they're pissed and jealous, and so they waited for the three smallest guys while the two big guys were in the truck. Then they launch into the smallest of the small guys – and while he's got a monitor on his shoulder and on the stairs. That's real hero stuff. And there's the rest of the football club cheering him on. Real shit like that was what we had to put up with.'

The small-town violence was still raging too. 'Violence was more common in country towns. Bathurst, Goulburn and places like that, where the local footy teams and guys in general felt like they were being ignored by the girls. But you didn't miss out in the capital cities either. Melbourne was a bloodbath in the '80s. There was always an all-in at those suburban beer barns like the Frankston Pier. Every night. You knew if you were going to specific venues that something would happen. Traralgon, Moorabbin, those places – you knew that there was always going to be a brawl with ten or 20 guys going for it.'

In Sydney, Scully knew to expect trouble at places like the Family Inn in Rydalmere or the Comb & Cutter in Blacktown. At those venues, he'd tell the management he wanted a security guard for the load-out, and at the back of the sound and lighting desk during the show. 'It wasn't so much to look after us but to look after the equipment, because if something happens to that, it fucks up a tour. You can't replace a sound or lighting desk if you have a show booked every night. You don't have a spare in the truck.'

Idiots spilling drinks around the desk was a constant threat. 'You'd tell them, "Listen, it's a fucking desk – if you spill a drink over it, then it's fucked."' But cordoning off the desk would piss off the venue management because it was taking up space that could otherwise be used to squeeze in more punters.

'The band's girlfriends would often come in there around the desk for protection and sit on the road cases with the sound and lights guys – and of course that makes you a target because all the drunks are jealous that you have all these good-looking women around you. They forget that they're the band's girl-friends, not yours. Occasionally other girls would have a go at the girls with us. "So, you're Tim Farriss's girlfriend, are you?" That sort of thing.'

Then there were the idiots who thought it was a good idea to run onto the stage. 'With a band like The Church, you've got 16 guitars on the side of the stage. I remember seeing their stage guy, Tony Wilde, trying to deal with all the guitars, keeping them in tune and staying on top of guitar changes, and then there's some dickhead trying to get onstage while he's doing all that.'

Despite the rigours, the long hours, the violence and the other hard aspects of the lifestyle, Scully loved it. Maybe he has the rose-coloured glasses on, but he recalls the excitement he'd feel at watching audiences going crazy for the band.

'House lights down before the show starts – that's the biggest buzz for the lighting guy. And the call from backstage saying the band are ready. Then they ask if you're ready, and then, as the lighting guy, you get to call house lights down and the crowd goes wild and the hairs on your arms rise up. Then the lights come up and away you go. It's that amazing buzz. Anticipation and excitement. Everyone is there to see their favourite band. You get to pick up on all that, being out front as the lighting guy. You pick up on all that energy. Every night. That was the hardest thing about giving it away.'

The end came for Scully when he was working with Crowded House. It was an emotional time. The band was on a rapid upward trajectory, and heading to America. Scully could have gone with them. He wanted to go with them. But he had a nine-month-old child, and he knew he couldn't be a good dad *and* travel the world with rock'n'roll bands. 'I think I was getting close to the end. I was tired after many, many years of night after night after night. There were the back injuries, the shoulder injuries, the electrocutions.'

Does he miss it? Thirty years after his last show with a major Australian touring band, Scully says he'd still like to be doing it. There's a sadness to that observation – along with a reminder of the lure of the life and world of the road crew. 'It's the best thing I've ever done. I still get told to shut up by my wife every now and then. She says it's in the past and that it's what I *used* to do. But I say to her that I was passionate then and I haven't been as passionate about anything since. Everything I've done since has been work.

'I'm not saying it was like climbing Everest, but it was enjoyable, satisfying, challenging and addictive. It's an adrenaline thing. House lights down, the band walks on ... it's a drug. You can't get away from that. So many years later, and I can still feel that.'

16

Wall-to-wall Hookers

Greg Little was the epitome of the Australian roadie in the 1980s. Hardworking, reliable, talented, making it up as he went along, and doing the best possible job he could for the artists he worked with. It was a decade that provided both the most work *and* the hardest work for roadies.

In the 1980s the touring circuit around Australia was relentless. Bands lived on the road, honing their performance skills so that they gained a reputation for being among the finest live acts on the planet. With them for all of that were the legions of road crew.

Little came into the industry the tried and true way – by accident. He was 17 years old, just out of school and did not know what he wanted to do. A mate who was a roadie asked Little to give him a hand.

This was the late 1970s, and Little and his mate were working for a Sydney-based quasi-punk band called The Press, who had an album called *Fodder for the Critics*. Initially they played mainly on the weekend. Then they ascended to the level of doing a tour. Little and his mate set off in a truck with the band, their stage gear and some lighting. The tour was a disaster. That was it, they all thought – the end of The Press.

At the time, Little believed his short-lived experience as a roadie – there was no way he thought of it as a career – was over. He got one of those things called a real job, selling spare parts. He hated it. 'It was the same desk, the same four walls, the same people every day. It was the tedium of going to the same place, catching the same train, getting the same seat, then everyone at work doing their repetitious thing. I was watching the clock every day, waiting for the end of the day.' Soon it became too much. Now he knew there was an alternative that suited his temperament: road crew work.

After getting in touch with Now Studios, Little began loading gear in and out for any band that needed it. One day he was asked if he knew anything about doing lighting. He didn't, but he was willing to learn. Before long he was doing lights for the QVs, learning more and more as he went on. Gradually the bands he worked with became bigger, and his work included a lengthy stint with Jenny Morris's band QED, followed by work with DD Smash, Machinations and Gang Gajang. There were gigs everywhere; it was the golden age for roadies. It was hard work, but also invigorating and compelling.

'The average gig in those days had the crew leaving the venue at 3 or 4 am. Then you'd go home or back to the hotel, then there'd be at least a two-to-four-hour drive, usually more, if you were on tour. You'd aim to be at the venue by 2 pm, allow four hours for set-up and then grab some dinner before it was show time. You got into the momentum of it pretty quickly. The first couple of days were hard but after that it was all good.'

Like all crew guys, Little loved and embraced the rush of the work and had trouble dealing with the comedown at the end of a tour. He thinks of one of the last episodes of that old TV show *21 Jump Street*: it was all about the rush, the thrill of the chase, the excitement of the hunt. 'Then it was all about what you do when the excitement stops,' he muses. 'You fall flat, the party is over.'

Little also contends that pretty much every roadie is a rabid music fan – not so much a failed musician (a common misconception) but a music obsessive. 'I always had this underlying drum beat in my head as I set everything up. Others may have had different things, but we all had something musical going through us. And there was that tingle going up the spine as the show was about to start. I worked on the Australian Made tour, and in Perth there was this amazing Mexican wave that the crowd did. It was just this perfect example of everyone acting in unison. It still thrills me every time I think about it.'

Eventually Little had had enough of the day-to-day grind (and fun) of touring Australian bands. He wanted to work on bigger shows. He wanted more vibe, more rush, more excitement. Where did an Australian roadie in the 1980s go to find that? The same place they had the previous decade: Jands.

'With bands, if you or they took a week or two off, it could take a month to get back the momentum of playing and working, but with Jands you could just keep going and going and going. Maybe take the occasional day off if you felt like it.' Of course, Little immediately encountered the near mythical Jands figure of Eric Robinson. 'Personally, he scared the crap out of me,' he laughs. But Little, like so many crew guys of the era, had some memorable experiences at Jands. He was on the crew for the Bob Dylan/Tom Petty & The Heartbreakers Australasian tour in 1986. He wasn't the top dog, but he was there.

'I was the newbie, but that was okay,' he says. 'They ended up getting rid of the main lighting guy who came out with Dylan. He was the guy who had been involved in that incident when Michael Jackson's hair caught fire during a video shoot. He kept carrying on about that. Initially, there was this crazily over-the-top lighting set-up for Dylan. It was total overkill.

Then a new guy came in and got rid of most of the lights and
kept it nice and simple.'

For the international tours during the 1980s, there were
usually two weeks of preparation before the show hit the road.
The crews were much smaller than they are now. And there
was much less equipment being road-freighted between gigs.

Little and his fellow crew were paid directly by Jands. They
shared rooms on tour – two to a room – received a per diem
of $30 to cover incidentals like food, and got a weekly wage
of $600, less tax. 'It wasn't great,' he says. 'I mean, it wasn't
bad either – it was okay.'

I travelled on the Dylan/Petty tour as a journalist and
remarked to Little that I was amazed at how many drugs were
around, particularly at the shows in New Zealand. This was
an era when customs in that country were renowned for their
vigilance when it came to stopping drug importation.

Little just smiles. 'They'd be put in drawer cases and road
cases. They'd be put in with tools and buried somewhere back in
the trucks or freight. Of course they'd be relying on customs not
taking all the gear apart, but everyone was very blasé back then.
It's different now. Back then they were advertising customs agents'
jobs in the newspaper. Think about it. And cops and customs
had to be pretty keen to get a crew to unpack a whole truck.

'Whenever a tour was going through Adelaide, you'd put
some empty packing cases in the back of the truck. That's
where you got the best pot. And if someone needed something
desperately, there was always the Shure microphone case which
you'd fly to a gig.'

Little left Jands towards the end of the decade, after a memorable tour with a Texan band. 'That was possibly *the* best tour
ever to work on. A local act were supporting, and most of the
shows were outdoors.'

What made it so memorable for Little was both the music
and an incident in Perth at the end of the tour. 'I was backstage,

and I walked down a passageway and opened a door to a back room and inside it was wall-to-wall hookers. It was near the end of the show and they'd been put in a back room and asked to wait there till after the show had finished. They were all dressed up – or undressed up – maybe 30 or 40 of them. We did the bump-out of the gear, and towards the end the production manager told us that no one was going anywhere. It was an end-of-tour party and all the crew were invited.'

Next, Little worked with Skyhooks on their reformation tour in 1991. 'That tour covered 22,500 kilometres, and there were shows five nights a week. The band and the crew all drove, but the crew would always leave before the band. We decided that it was better to leave straight after the gig and get to the next town. It was preferable to drive through the night and then get to the next town and go to the hotel and sleep, and go to the gig in the afternoon. There's less traffic – it's a much better time to be on the road.'

During his time on the road Little has experienced some pretty horrific things, including pulling people out of a car wreck south of Kempsey on a known death zone on the highway.

Cows on the road feature in one of Little's road stories – vehicles weren't the only hazard. 'We were coming back from Cairns, driving to Sydney. That's a two-day drive. We're screaming down the road at about 120 kilometres an hour, but on a good road and in a vehicle that could handle it. We came around an S-bend down to a creek and there's a cow in the middle of the road. I hit the anchor and blow the horn. The cow starts to run away as we slide in, but the front left bumper bar sort of scoops him up so his bum is leaving a trail as we slide down to a stop. Eventually the cow just flipped up over the roof – it breaks the windscreen and ended up coming down at the back of the van.'

Little, along with many roadies from that era, moved to the corporate circuit. It was different work. 'Stuff you could get away with at rock venues you couldn't at these things. There couldn't be any loose and visible cords, and the sound needed to be precise. The work can still be as rigorous as rock'n'roll. You're still starting really early and getting out pretty late. There's just not as much travelling and there is not the same buzz.'

Then came a stint in the film industry, setting up lighting for studios, before Little gravitated towards concert rigging. That's what he continues to do to this day, along with basic lugging.

Towards the end of 2017, when I was in Wollongong watching the build and set-up for an Elton John concert, one of the crew loading the stage gear saw me and wandered over with a big smile to say hello. It was Little. You can't keep him away from the scene. 'Crewing's addictive. You really do get addicted.'

17

Girl on a Mixing Desk

Louise Le Raux laughs when I ask her what name I should use for her. Back in the day, when she worked as mixer and crew person in Newcastle, she was known as Karen McLean. But there were other names.

'People will know me as "Dimples", or "that chick from Jands", or "that girl from McLean's", or "Mike Emerson's girl". And if you asked one manager of a very well-known Australian band of the 1980s, I was "just a groupie". Then there was the band who considered it part of my employment for me to change into my schoolgirl uniform and dance while they played "Wild Thing" during their encore. Their crew called me "jailbait".'

Le Raux started young and saw everything in the heady days of 1980s Australian pub rock. She was the '80s equivalent of a pioneering figure like Tana Douglas – a woman mixing (literally and figuratively) in the machismo-saturated boys' culture of the time, and holding her head up high.

Asked when she started in the sound and production business, Le Raux doesn't hesitate when she says she was six years of age. 'My father had a sound and lighting business in Newcastle, and he used to get me to make mirror balls while I was watching Disneyland. That was my Sunday-evening task. I'd sit there with that really heady glue and stick the mirrors on to the balls. Now they're made in China, but not back then.'

This was the early 1970s, and Le Raux's father, Neville McLean, was well established in the Newcastle music scene. He'd had his own independent record label (MGM Sound Recordings), and had done sound for The Bee Gees when they played Newcastle. Le Raux believes he may have been the first person to make a mixer with tone controls.

'They used to only have volume but he added treble and bass. This was just before the Queen's visit in 1956, so the sound for her visit had treble and bass, as well as volume going up and down.'

Eventually Neville started McLean's Sound & Lighting, hiring gear to local bands. His daughter hung around and soaked it all up. 'It was in my blood. I became hooked very early on, and I loved the technical side of it. It's giving me goosebumps just thinking about it. I really couldn't get enough of it. But that was a big part of the problem – trying to have a career as a girl. People wouldn't accept that a girl would be interested in doing that work, and especially one so young.'

Le Raux was working in the music business midway through her 15th year. Prior to that she'd moved to Caboolture, in Queensland, where she went to school with Keith Urban. She moved back to live with her father in Newcastle when she was in Year 11, and he pretty much put her straight to work.

'I was working three nights a week at Newcastle Workers Club and one night a week at Belmont 16 Footers. I was doing follow spots and sound. I could work a mixing desk before I had my learner's permit. Most of what I did at 15 and 16 was front-of-house sound. I did my first official tour as a sound operator when I was 16. That was with a local Newcastle band called The House Rockers.'

Naturally, a 16-year-old schoolgirl mixing rock'n'roll bands – in licensed premises – raised, shall we say, some issues. One band member told Le Raux that the guys in his band were fighting over who would 'have' her. 'All the guys were at least ten or 12 years older than me. So that dynamic was really interesting.'

In the '80s, getting into venues underage was pretty simple. No one seemed to care – and even if they pretended to, there was fake ID. All Le Raux's friends went to pubs to drink and party. She herself went to work, and fended off her friends' regular requests to add their names on the door at gigs.

Newcastle had a busy rock'n'roll scene at the time. There were lots of local bands who played a thriving pub and club culture. As well, Sydney-based bands would use Newcastle as a testing ground for new material. And at the middle of it all was Le Raux, blissfully ignorant of the impact she was making.

'I used to turn up at the venues in my school uniform. I'd go from school, straight to the venue to see if the bands needed anything – this was before mobile phones, of course. I had to get turnbuckles to hold up part of the stage for Orchestral Manoeuvres in the Dark. Iron Maiden need sparkling Evian water, and in Newcastle in the 1980s that wasn't easy to find. I might have failed there. I had to find a valve amp for Jimmy Barnes. Sometimes I was just replacing a blown light or getting gaffer tape, but I was constantly there.'

Le Raux had gone to Perth for her 16th birthday, and while she was there her uncle took her to see Mondo Rock. Soon after, they played in Newcastle and Le Raux was working with the support band. It was there that she met their sound guy, Mike Emerson. They hit it off and became boyfriend and girlfriend.

'I had no real training but Mike took me seriously and taught me how to tune a room by ear. Before digital sound came in, everything was analogue and much more reliant on the sound person's skills than it was on technology. He taught me the skills. It got to the point where I knew frequencies by ear – and I'm only 16. I used to stay up all night with him talking about the theory of sound.'

Unlike most of those around her, Le Raux wasn't into drugs, and witnessed the negative influence they could have on people. 'There was a lot of speed, and it scared me. And when I got my licence, bands got me to drive because I wasn't out of it. I ended up doing tours from Melbourne to Cairns and back again, just because bands knew they could rely on me.'

Eventually it all caught up with Le Raux. She got glandular fever and was chronically fatigued and had to repeat Year 11. But she kept working, doing gigs and also working in the hire department of her father's business.

'I don't think my father saw me as a daughter – I think he just saw me as labour,' Le Raux says without a trace of irony. 'But I used to set everything up at gigs, so I learnt about electricity, wattage and ampage and voltage. How to load a circuit, patching in three-phase and generally making sure everything on the technical side was good.'

In the end the taunts of the male road crew and musicians got the better of Le Raux. She was sick of being treated like a novelty, not to mention a potential sex object. She also resented the suggestion that she was only doing sound because her father couldn't find anyone else. 'That's when I got into doing lights. It was easier to believe a girl doing lights rather than sound. Because lights were more "creative". One of the first lighting gigs I did was for John Paul Young at the Cambridge Hotel. I got the gig as his regular lighting guy didn't turn up. It was a packed venue, and afterwards I went to get paid and the manager refused to pay me. He said I should be thankful for the experience. He paid everyone else, though. That still hurts.'

Then there was her encounter with INXS's management. The band were playing in Newcastle at the 1700-capacity Civic Theatre. Le Raux, who was by now an established figure on the lighting and sound scene in the city, had been with the band and crew all afternoon helping sort out various aspects of their equipment for the show, but at the end of the afternoon the manager refused to give her a pass to see the show. He told her she was 'just a groupie'. As she points out, that wouldn't have happened if she was a guy.

Come 1984, and Le Raux remembers working 64 days straight, including 49 nights of shows with the likes of The Angels, Models and Rose Tattoo – all while she repeated Year 11. 'I was usually in bed by 5.30 am and then up soon after 6 am to go to school. I spent my 17th birthday with Goanna when they were in Newcastle.

'You fall in love with this job. It wasn't for the money, and you're not fazed by the bands and the star stuff. It's all about the technical side of it, and your own expression through sound and lights. Crew members who went on to have proper careers loved what they do.'

There were tours, more gigs, tours. Le Raux did some significant damage to her back while helping lug a PA into a venue in Coolangatta. Increasingly she found herself working on the production-hire side of things. When she was 18, Mike Emerson left her for a 19-year-old, but she quickly got over that. After three and a half years working in Newcastle, she moved to Sydney and took a job with Jands in 1987.

Then Le Raux fell pregnant and had a baby. Her last gig was on the Skyhooks reunion tour in 1991, when she was six months pregnant. She walked away from the industry to care for her baby, and a few years later, when she tried to return, things had changed so much it was pretty much impossible. 'The digital stuff had come in,' she says. 'Three years after I was working with them, a band like INXS was using a 96-channel desk with a CD in it. It was crazy how fast the technology changed – and it made me obsolete. I had no chance just because of the technology.'

As far as Le Raux is concerned, digital was all about programming. What was lost in the transition, she feels, was the interaction between the band, the sound and lighting person, and the crew, which wasn't the same as it used to be. 'Bands used to rely on the crew – now they were relying on technology.'

Le Raux saw lots of crew fall by the wayside with the changes, but many did make the transition. 'A lot of them *had* to. They'd been working for 15 years or so, were in their mid- to late 30s, and had families and needed to keep working.' She saw too many crew working when they physically shouldn't have been. 'Everything on the road was hard, and now for many of them, through a lack of money, lack of attention along the way and lack of support, they end up sick *and* broke. In many cases a band's career went on an incline and the crew often went on a decline.

'Most crew guys are on their second or third wives – they've had multiple relationships. And look at the impact on the kids. Dad's always away, and Dad is missing so much of his kids growing up. "Where's Dad?" "He's on tour with some famous band." If you don't know the lifestyle, then that seems exciting, but people who don't live in that world have no understanding of what road crews do for a living and how unglamorous it really is.

'Often crews don't get the recognition and treatment they deserve. Everything centres around the band. Of course no one would be at the show without the band, but on the night of the show that ratio reverses. If all that behind-the-scenes produc-tion stuff doesn't happen seamlessly, then the show seems like rubbish. The audience can't hear the singer, they can't see the band if the follow spot operator isn't on their game, and people walk away disappointed. So much of the success of the show is dependent on the crew – but they go to second-rate hotels after they finish work and get maybe an hour or two's sleep before the next set-up.

'It was all about the band and needing to get to the next gig. And a lot of managers were not looking at the important things, like the physical toll on the crew. It was always a case of "Oh, the crew will take care of it," and not being aware of the personal pressure that was put on them. More often than not the crew managed what they had to do with alcohol and drugs. It was like an iceberg. You saw the tip of what crews were doing but a lot of managers only saw the tip. They had no idea or concern about what was below the surface. Often bands got a rider and the crew were left to go down the road and get a hamburger or a Chiko Roll. How hard was it to give them a plate of food that was hot and didn't come from the service station?

'In my day I had to share rooms with other guys in the crew. There were no separate rooms for female crew. So little personal stuff was taken into consideration by management – the need to sleep, to eat, to do laundry. There was virtually no information given about individual venues. Just realising that one venue could have easy access and lifts so the load-in would take three hours, and that another would have 800 steps, bad access and take six hours. That stuff compounds. Most crew accidents came from exhaustion.

'Crews are meant to be big, strong guys working with rock stars, but no one realised how vulnerable many of them were. And how so many of them were pushed to the limit. They were performing very skilled tasks every night, but a lot of them were vulnerable and with no one to talk to. Maybe they sometimes talked to each other, but more often than not they kept it to themselves.

'Bands' needs were taken care of, but no one really thought of what crews needed. No attention was paid to them. Two guys working 18 hours a day and then having to share a personal space with other guys in a hotel room. Sure, it's economy, but when you're on the road for months . . . and some of the places you were staying. I mean, hotel rooms back then were like $35 a night. Sell an extra few tickets and get them their own rooms like the band. A lot of the hotels were disgusting. Often single beds in tiny rooms. There was no personal space and crews never seemed to have the time and space to unwind.'

Le Raux got out of the business as she headed towards her mid-20s. 'I went from seeing rock stars shooting up and running around naked to raising three kids and reading bedtime stories.' But she doesn't look back on her time working as part of road crews with regret. 'For a long time it was great. I lived history. My normal night would be like a lifetime pinnacle for a lot of my friends. It just happened that my work was with famous people.'

18

Blondie, Merle Haggard, LRB and Little Rock Connie

Noel Bennett has seen and done a lot since he began working as a roadie back in 1976. He's an old-school guy who has successfully moved through many facets of the business and is still working. Along the way there have been work and encounters with some of the almost mythical figures of the music world, some of them artists, others not. But were it not for fate – and a federal election – Bennett would never have become a roadie. He would be flying planes.

'I was training to be a navy pilot. But the 1973 Defence budget cuts by Whitlam, who was my hero, put paid to that. I'd left school after fourth form and joined the navy at 15. They sent me to Perth to finish school, and someone there suggested I could be a pilot. I was one hour of training away from flying jets and was heading to flying helicopters, but then they scrapped the HMAS *Melbourne*, sold the Skyhawk fighters to New Zealand, and squadron pilots were cut from 40 hours a month to four hours, and from ten guys on the course only two were retained, and I wasn't one of them, so that was that.'

Bennett needed work. And, well, if you can't fly, you can always lug gear and learn to mix sound, right?

Like most crew, it all started in a pretty straightforward way. Bennett began with Hugh McLean Sound in Melbourne, before touring with Australian folk (with a hint of rock'n'roll) band The Cobbers.

In those days the workload was typically extreme. Bennett recalls regularly doing up to three gigs in a day. Once there was a 7 am load-in for a Wednesday residency at a pub in Melbourne, then he flew to Sydney for a lunchtime gig at a university, then got on a plane back to Melbourne to do that pub gig, which finished at 10 pm. After leaving two crew members to load out the gear, he headed to Malvern Town Hall to do a late set for a teachers' college ball with hired production. Nothing unusual there.

Bennett honed his skills after receiving solid but basic training with McLean. 'I started with him doing free entertainment in the parks for Melbourne City Council. That's the best grounding anyone could ever have for doing sound, because you never knew what was coming next. We'd do jazz artists, pop, country, old-time dance, rock – it was a different genre all the time, so I learnt all the different styles. Hugh told me how to stack a PA, how to plug it all in, and then one day he told me to have a go at mixing sound, and then corrected me on what I'd done.'

Quickly Bennett moved to working on international tours, in between Cobbers gigs. The first Blondie tour of Australia, in November 1977, was a tough gig for Bennett, brought on by a set of unforeseen problems – mainly because the drug supply in Australia at the time was much better than what was available in many other parts of the world.

'One of the guys in their crew just couldn't cope as the heroin in Australia was way stronger than what he was used to in the States. He just ended up sitting in the corner in a stupor, so they sent him home. It was the same problem Steve Earle had a few years later.

'So because of that I got promoted. Barney Deutscher was meant to be doing monitors but ended up doing front-of-house, and I got promoted to monitors, which was way above my skill set at the time. I wasn't ready for it, and the band weren't happy with me. The drummer, Clem Burke, wanted to punch me as he walked offstage at the Palais. Debbie Harry loathed me. I did that Melbourne gig and then the Adelaide and Albury shows, but when we got to Sydney I got subbed off and went to work on a John Denver tour.

'On my last day with Blondie I saw Debbie Harry in the hotel foyer and she apologised to me. She must have felt bad for the pressure they put on me. I grabbed a piece of paper and wrote my telephone number on it and handed it to her. She asked what it was, and I told her it was my telephone number and that the next time she and the band came to Australia not to call it. Then I walked off.'

Fourteen years later, Bennett would encounter Debbie Harry again. He was tour-managing David Essex and she was in the midst of a solo tour. Both were in Brisbane at the same time, and staying at the same hotel.

'She was staring at me one day like she remembered me from somewhere, and I went over and said, "Still got that piece of paper – the one with the number you weren't meant to call?" She knew who I was then. It was okay – she called me an arsehole, but it was good-humoured.'

Bennett's working life continued with Johnny Chester, a major country music attraction who toured endlessly, before he moved to Hobart to work for a sound company there. After moving back to Melbourne in 1986, Bennett was back on the road with tour after tour with artists such as Charley Pride, Midnight Oil, Glen Campbell, The Shadows, Shirley Bassey, INXS, Gene Pitney and Jimmy Barnes. Bennett can say on his

CV that he's done sound monitors for the Pope *and* systems-
teching for Torvill and Dean.

Most tours have been predominantly enjoyable, but there
are always exceptions – like travelling the country with the
legendary but notoriously cantankerous Merle Haggard.

'Right from the start I knew that this one was going to be
bad,' he laughs. 'I met him in Sydney, and knowing that he was
a bit like Willie Nelson, I handed him an ounce of pot. And he
looks at me and goes, "An ounce? I need a fucking pound!" I
told him I'd give him a phone number to ring but there was no
way I was going to buy him a fucking pound.'

When the tour reached Townsville for the first show, Haggard
and his wife had a terrible argument at the airport. Among the
crowd who witnessed the whole thing were Chris Isaak and
promoter Michael Chugg.

Bennett recalls how unreliable Haggard's performances were.
'We were told his show was going to run for 90 minutes plus an
encore, and I had all the production set and loaders booked to
get the gear out when the show finished. So he goes and plays
for two and a half hours, and I've got all these guys sitting
around getting paid by the hour doing nothing. The next night,
in Sydney, he did 55 minutes and told the audience he'd been
told he played too long the night before so he was finishing
early. He was just an arsehole.'

By the early 1990s Bennett was divorced and had moved to
Adelaide to be closer to his kids. There wasn't enough work there
so he moved back to Melbourne, picking up regular gigs including
sound for Little River Band. He ended up touring overseas with
them until 2000. 'Mixing that band in front of 250,000 people
in St Louis on July 4 under the Freedom Arch is something you
don't forget. And to be mixing a band that does a 75-minute
show that is just one hit after the other is just amazing.'

With LRB, Bennett encountered one of the world's most
legendary groupies, Little Rock Connie (real name Connie

Hamzy). Check her out on Wikipedia if you're in any doubt about her status. Bennett has a photo of himself with Connie outside LRB's tour bus. She's grabbing his genitals. 'Connie flew back in from Miami after the Stones had taken her out for a week for old times' sake,' he smiles. 'She found out which hotel we were at and came over to say hello . . .'

Bennett finished with LRB but stayed on the road until 2013, when he suffered major kidney failure. While being cared for in hospital, he died and was revived three times. 'I had ten days' sleep in intensive care. I have no front teeth as they broke them keeping me breathing in the ambulance. I've lost 65 kilos in the past two and a half years. I was a big guy until I came off the road and gave up cigarettes and cocaine.'

These days, Bennett concentrates on sound production work at the Palms in Melbourne's Crown Casino. He likes the work and needs to put a roof over his head. But it's clear part of him misses the old days, as he easily recites the type of schedule he once did with the likes of Johnny Chester. He can reel it off without missing a beat – or a town.

'You'd do Wednesday, Thursday, Friday, Saturday and Sunday in Melbourne, and then an overnighter to Bourke. Monday night was off in Bourke, which is a wonderful town for a party on a Monday night. Tuesday night you'd play Bourke, Wednesday in Charleville, Thursday in Longreach, Friday in Cloncurry. Saturday was Mount Isa, Sunday Tennant Creek, and Monday you're sitting in Darwin.'

19

Lippold

Most people don't use Michael Lippold's first name. He's just Lippold. And most people in the music and roadie community aren't in any danger of being confused. There is only one Lippold.

In his classic book *Strict Rules*, Andrew McMillan talks of Lippold as being a veteran of the celebrated 'old school' of roadies. Starting as Midnight Oil's stage manager in 1980, he signed on when, as drummer Rob Hirst says, 'We desperately needed someone who wasn't about to sit down and have an intelligent conversation with some drunk punter who was going to slam a beer glass into his face. He'd just knock 'em over the head with his wombat basher and that'd be it.'

McMillan goes on to say that Lippold – who also often worked as Peter Garrett's minder during his Senate campaign – has a fierce reputation 'for dealing with problems by punching walls, kicking trees, punching telephones and loudly abusing people. Later in the piece, when he's simmered down, he'll usually apologise while making it clear that whatever transgression it was that offended him should never be repeated. But by that stage, it's often too late. Around him, people – even his crews – tend to walk on eggshells.'

Lippold grew up on the meaner streets of Melbourne. His older brother Tony was a roadie working with various bands around Melbourne including The Bootleg Family Band, and Peace Power and Purity, a band that was fronted by Angry Anderson before he joined Buster Brown and Rose Tattoo.

'Tony was a bit of a ratbag,' Lippold says. 'His main thing was being a roadie. But we once got arrested by three coppers who were drunker than Tony and I were for consorting with a known criminal. Lippold was a really bad name to have in those days.'

The younger brother drifted into working with mates' bands – 'parties on Saturday nights in people's living rooms with a band playing. I was just into music – my bedroom wall was covered with posters from *Go-Set*.'

For a real job, Lippold followed his father and worked on the waterfront. It was meant to be a job for life. More importantly, it had a culture that taught Lippold about hard work and being tough. 'I started at 7 am and worked seven days a week there. You got paid a fortune on the waterfront. But I wasn't cocky, and I had a strong work ethic. You couldn't go and study rock'n'roll in those days – you just went to gigs.'

After a few years on the waterfront, brother Tony suggested Lippold come and help him crew for Broderick Smith's Big Combo, a band managed by Howard Freeman. This was a hardworking group who often played a dozen gigs a week in and around Melbourne or when touring interstate.

'I was *really* lucky to come into it at the later part of the 1970s, working with people the likes of $crooge (probably the baddest of the bad), Howard, Russell Kidner, John Brewster and Pat Pickett. It could have been frightening but I was brought up in Fawkner and violence was normal to me. Contrary to popular belief, I'm not a violent person. I'm not comfortable with it, but I *was* used to it. They were really violent days.'

Lippold worked not only with Big Combo but with many other bands based in or coming through Melbourne, plus some international artists such as Canned Heat.

'After Broderick, I just did loading work, which you did anyway between tours. That's how you made a living.'

Fate intervened after a big night at Bananas nightclub. Lippold was living in South Melbourne, his brother in St Kilda. Following tradition, when the night out ended they continued on at Tony's place. The next morning Lippold woke up early stretched out half under the coffee table. He could hear his brother's half of a telephone conversation: 'Yeah, I know someone who can do that.'

The call had been from someone involved with a Sydney band called Midnight Oil. They needed a stage guy for a single gig at the Prospect Hill Hotel. Lippold had no idea who they were. This was in 1980, and Midnight Oil was a very long way from being a household name.

'For some reason I got it into my head that it was Mental as Anything,' Lippold laughs. 'I'd only been to Sydney a few times with Broderick, so I didn't really know much about the bands there. But I knew Mentals and I'm thinking "'The Nips Are Getting Bigger' – that's who it is!" Boy, was I in for a fucking surprise. I went to the venue at 11 am to meet the truck coming from Canberra. Chris Grant was the sound guy and Mark Edwards was doing monitors. He told me he was only going to show me once, and then I was on my own because he had his own job to do. That was how you learnt. It really was. If anyone asked if you could do something, you said yes. If you fucked up once that was fine; but if you fucked up twice on the same thing . . . duck. It was: "Come to the back of the truck with me." That's where people had things *explained* or *taught* to them without anyone else seeing.'

Lippold notes that while he might make a lot of noise and bluster, he's really not that aggressive. But if he asks you to come for a walk, look out.

'I'm always joking around with people I work with, and I say, "How many people have you seen me hit?" The answer is usually none or one. But they remind me that I go for a lot of walks. I tell them that's different. There's no witnesses. Two people go out for a walk. Whoever comes back was right. How I was brought up was that you didn't get belted because you fucked up – you got belted because you didn't ask. I learnt that way.'

When he got to the Prospect Hill Hotel, Lippold discovered that the band wasn't there for a soundcheck, so he was none the wiser about their identity. But he did get suspicious it wasn't the Mentals when the crew guys started putting nails through the rubbers in the cymbal and high-hat stands, and used sandbags to weigh things down. When he asked what they were doing, they knowingly said, 'You'll see.'

'And when Mark stood on a case to tune the singer's microphone, I asked again, and again I was told, "You'll see." I thought it must have had something to do with ambience, having the microphone set that high.

'After the set-up the punters came in, and when the Oils hit that fucking stage and erupted – they just destroyed it. The place was packed. Those were the days when a room that should have had 300 in it had 700 people jammed in, and that was only because 701 didn't turn up.

'At the end of the gig, someone said that the Oils had a few more weeks to go on the tour, and that they were going to Adelaide next, and did I want to come? It was that simple. It wasn't much money but I went to Adelaide with them. And then they said they'd like to pay me a $100 retainer to make myself available when they went out next. That was unheard of at the time.'

Lippold started working with Midnight Oil at the end of 1980, and that would be his gig for the next 13 years. He started as a stage roadie and watched as the Oils went through a lot of crew guys. But he stayed, eventually becoming their production manager.

His first show in that role was a tour warm-up gig in Jindabyne. A new crew guy came up to Lippold and said, 'I can't do this.' When Lippold asked him why, the guy said it was too intense. Wrong thing to say. 'I said, "What do you fucking expect? It's Midnight Oil. What were you expecting? Simon and fucking Garfunkel?"'

It was during the 1980s that Midnight Oil exploded as a band, in Australia and internationally. Lippold was mission control for every night of every tour, soaking up incredible pressure. 'I was a nervous wreck. It was like being at war. I have amazing peripheral vision now. I'm aware of every fucking thing around me. It's all because I had to watch so much on- and offstage.

'As a stage guy, I had the best gig. The stress and tension was what it was all about. Forty-five minutes to an hour before a show I'd be pacing to get myself in the space to concentrate. We smoked copious amounts of pot in the early days, but you couldn't be stoned with the Oils. There was a cut-off point with the Oils where I had to be *totally* there. I couldn't do it on speed, either. I just needed to be totally straight. They've said to me many times that they fed off me too when they needed a lift. They'd invent problems to watch me run out and do stuff.'

Fascinating footage shot by filmmaker Ray Argall of Midnight Oil's 1984 tour – finally commercially released in May 2018 – shows Lippold and the band in full flight. The roadie had a rat's tail haircut (which now embarrasses him) and the shortest denim shorts. It's only now that he realises that he's famous in roadie and band circles for those shorts. 'We didn't have any money, so your jeans became your shorts.

Michael Kerr, one of the band's roadies, started cutting them –
and I didn't realise he was cutting them shorter and shorter.'

Midnight Oil was well known for constant touring of
regional areas of Australia. Lippold was there for all of it. 'On
those tours we were known as the Leyland Brothers, because in
the crew there was Mal, Mark and Mike in the truck together.
We'd pull the truck up in the morning and walk into the hotel
and say, "Hey, we're the Leyland Brothers – he's Mal, he's
Mark and I'm Mike."

'With a lot of the crew guys you didn't know many people's
real names. We had a lighting guy called Wormie. I did four or
five Oils tours with him and didn't know his real name. Maybe
it was Ron something. Everyone had nicknames, and you usually
didn't need to know their real names. When you needed to
organise passports, you're calling people you've worked with
for years going, "Hey, what's your name? No, I mean your *real*
name – this is legal shit."'

And there were the hijinks and shenanigans of an Oils tour –
and a ferocious determination not to be messed with.

'We were at a pub in Broken Hill during the "Beds Are
Burning" era. We had this stuffed dingo and kangaroo as part
of the set. Our dingo got knocked off. It took a week and we
were in another part of Australia, but I fucking got it back.
The word went out. I had no shame.'

Lippold worked closely with many of the now departed
members of the Australian road crew fraternity, such as Jock Bain.

'Again, we were in Broken Hill. The thing you have to
remember is that in country towns the crew were part of the
entertainment for the local guys. We were a threat to their
girlfriends. It was as simple as that.

'So we're packing up. Remember how the disco used to start
straight after the band finished? Anway, all the chicks are on
the dance floor, and all the guys are standing around glaring
at them – and us. And there's Jock on a road case, with two

chicks – one at each end – spinning the road case around in the middle of the dance floor. Jock's got his shlong out – and he was seriously fucking hung and he didn't mind showing it off – so he's doing his famous helicopter with it on top of this road case. The birds in this pub are just worshipping him as he spins around, and the rest of the crew go, "Fuck, we're in for it tonight."'

Then there was Pat Pickett, a charismatic figure who worked with AC/DC, Models, *The Rocky Horror Show* and many other acts. Andrew McMillan once described him on a Midnight Oil tour as a 'walking billboard, covered in tattoos and adorned in an obnoxious pair of red pants and a brilliant blue jacket'.

Lippold had known and worked with Pickett, a brilliant road crew person and astonishing character, 'forever'. His death still makes Lippold bristle. 'He wasn't one of the ones who suicided, but he might as well have. Pat didn't die of cancer, he died of poverty. He knew he was sick. You know your body.'

When this revered roadie died, he was living alone in a small room above a hotel on Sydney's Parramatta Road, paying his way by wiring up and keeping an eye on the pub's PA.

Lippold has been comparatively lucky, but he also lived the life and has paid the price that comes with it. It's a lifestyle that others can find almost impossible to comprehend.

'It was so common to work 18-hour days. You'd finish at 2 am and start again at 8 am. People might say we should have gone straight to bed and got six hours' sleep, but to that I say, "Do you finish work at 5 pm and go straight to to bed? Do you have 20,000 or 30,000 people jumping up and down and screaming while you're at your desk at five minutes to five before you finish for the day?" In this work it's very hard to just go home and relax.'

The end with Midnight Oil came during a European tour in 1993, when Lippold's health finally gave way. He was increasingly unwell in Germany, and then travelled to London. He saw a doctor, who told him he'd be dead in two weeks if he didn't get off the road. His immune system had shut down. It was the cumulative effect of those 18-hour days and overall bad living.

It took Lippold 18 months to recover. He could function for three hours a day and then needed to sleep, suffering from what is now recognised as chronic fatigue syndrome. Eventually Lippold needed to go back to work. He was living in a cabin he'd built in the bush. He says a lot of people thought he was well-off, but the reality was that he was struggling financially.

Lippold applied for a job in the audio-visual world, and despite having never had a job interview before, he got the gig. From there he moved on to have a relatively successful career in the corporate world. He's still not well-off but he gets by.

These days it seems Lippold has a love/hate relationship with Midnight Oil and his days with them. 'They were a big part of my life. But I don't like to be defined by Midnight Oil. I've done much more, but they will not go out of my life and are a recurring feature when anyone talks about what I've done. I was lucky. I grew up among some serious tough heads in the business. Serious people. And you're not treated as a youngster, you're treated as an equal in a road crew. That's one of the great things about it.'

As Lippold sees it, the crew were a bunch of individuals like a family, coming together for one purpose. 'And it went off perfectly every time. It had to. In the early days of a tour, if there was conflict maybe you punched each other in the mouth, but it was sorted after that. And then you were gaffering cables together next to that guy.

'But there was a downside to it. As soon as you locked the truck after the last show, that was it. And for the two weeks before the end of the tour, there could be a bit of tension because you were all chasing the same jobs and you'd realise that you'd spent all your money and you needed another job.

'We were a bunch of ratbag blokes who made shit up. There are a lot of skill sets you learn from being a roadie. And the key one is dealing with people. You get to meet every level of society. We're chameleons. We can be whatever a situation needs us to be.'

20

It Was All Going So Well...

In 2017 Midnight Oil re-formed for their Great Circle world tour. Over the course of the tour they played 77 concerts in 16 countries on five continents to an audience of more than 500,000 people.

Midnight Oil had the same core road crew with them for the entire tour. If they were going to pull this off they needed a tight-knit inner circle of band, crew and management. There was no time or logical reason for changing the road crew from country to country.

These seven key crew individuals started the tour in Australia in April and ended it in Australia many months later with a run of concerts in November. They were: Colin Ellis (sound), Steve Granville (lights), Paul 'Kenno' Kennedy (monitors), Pat Meyer (stage tech), Ben Lyons (stage tech) and Clem Ryan (drum tech). Working alongside and overseeing them all was production manager Alex Grant.

By the conclusion of the tour this was – if you'll excuse the obvious pun – a very well-oiled machine. Band and crew as one. All knowing their jobs and doing them to the best of their abilities.

So by the final weeks of the tour everyone knows exactly what needs to be done each night. It's a bit like flying a plane: once you know how to do it it's a pretty straightforward exercise. You only find out how good you are when something goes catastrophically wrong.

Towards the end of the second of two nights at Melbourne's Sidney Myer Music Bowl, as the band could see the finishing line of the world tour – Wednesday, 8 November to be precise – Midnight Oil have their version of a mid-flight engine failure, the musical equivalent of one of the engines on an A380 shutting down a half-hour before the scheduled landing.

As the band reach the conclusion of 'King of the Mountain', the final song before the encore, guitarist and keyboardist Jim Moginie slips and takes what seems momentarily to be an unfortunate but not-major tumble. A split second later that all changes.

A twist, a sudden snap – a *loud* snap – and Moginie has torn a hamstring right off the bone. He's in agony. He momentarily loses consciousness.

The band are stunned. The audience aren't really sure what's going on. While Moginie is treated by paramedics in attendance at the concert, the other members of the band return to the stage in bewilderment. The planned triple slam of an encore – 'Short Memory' into 'Power and the Passion' and then 'Best of Both Worlds' – is shelved as they perform an acoustic version of 'One Country' before leaving the stage to check on Moginie.

This is bad news. Very bad news. On all sorts of levels.

In three nights' time – Saturday, 11 November (the date has been picked deliberately) – Midnight Oil are due to perform at Sydney's Domain, then do it again the Friday after at the same venue. The basic staging will be in place between those shows. In between the two Sydney shows there's an indoor show in Wollongong and a return to the Sidney Myer Music Bowl. All shows have pretty much sold out.

When the full state of Moginie's injury is revealed there is – to put it mildly – massive consternation in the touring camp.

Prior to this occurring I'd been given permission by the band and its management to observe the concert stage build, soundchecks and all the background to the show for the book you're reading. I wanted to see the Midnight Oil crew in action, observe the way they worked after such a long tour.

By Friday, tension in the camp is palpable. I'm within a whisker of being told I can't be around. The word on Moginie is not good. One doctor says immediate surgery, another says he can wait till after the remaining concerts. Whichever way you look at it he's in a massive amount of pain – and he certainly can't walk or stand.

Alternative dates for the Domain have been canvassed and March 2018 is the next date available. And that's four months away. If that happens the band will have lost match fitness. Many of the crew have accepted other work. There is nothing to like about this.

On Friday, 10 November the final phases of the stage construction are being done, lights and sound and video screens loaded, semitrailers of gear moved into the backstage area and onto the stage. No one's saying much. It's a methodical, almost by-numbers approach. Everyone knows what has to be done.

No one knows if they're doing it for nothing. In the back of their minds is the awareness that at any moment the announcement of a show postponement might come through and everything will need to be dismantled and put back in the trucks.

Moginie is in enormous pain and on crutches. The band had planned an early Friday evening soundcheck but I'm told this isn't going to happen.

It's times like this when a great road crew come into their own. Production manager Alex Grant is affable but business-like. Whatever he may be thinking he's keeping it to himself as he directs everyone in his charge. The Scotsman has done a *lot* of touring – much of it with John Butler Trio and other big-crowd-drawing Australian bands – and knows what he's doing. For this tour he has four semitrailers full of gear to deal with and a big crew of people.

Following the news about Moginie, it's been a particularly busy time for Grant. Aside from everything else, he has to work out how Moginie – if he can even get through the pain barrier – can sit onstage and play his guitar and keyboards.

By the time I grab a few minutes to talk with him, Grant has worked on five possible options for positioning Moginie onstage. No one wants these shows to not go ahead on schedule.

If Moginie is even remotely up for performing, all options have been canvassed – including a special ramp to wheel him safely on and off the stage if need be.

On stand-by are a Zimmer frame, a swivel chair that can be locked and unlocked to move positions, a wheelchair and an orthopaedic chair – if it can be put on a stage and a musician can sit in it and play guitar and keyboards then Grant has considered it and knows where to get it *very* quickly.

At about 5 pm – seemingly to the surprise of most people – a white van pulls through the backstage gates and drives right up to the stage area. Now there is a definite stillness. A tension in the air. No one is talking. In a wheelchair Moginie is lowered to the ground and pushed onto the stage. There for the next half-hour he experiments with different seating arrangements, finally finding one that he's both comfortable in *and* able to perform from.

The soundcheck that wasn't going to happen takes place. Moginie's stage tech moves gear this way and that. Grant oversees it all, standing with the band's manager John Watson as they weigh up the viability of Moginie performing in these conditions. Eventually everyone onstage appears comfortable. Moginie says it can work. It's now a definite – the Saturday night show will go ahead.

There's no high fives from the band and crew. No grins. Maybe just deep sighs of relief that the show will go on as scheduled. No one really wanted to think about the reality of the alternatives, even though it was impossible not to.

Soundcheck over, Moginie is wheeled back to the van and driven away. The rest of the band head off. The crew guys keep tinkering with onstage equipment for another half-hour before they hop into vans that will take them to their accommodation.

That was a high-stress day. But tomorrow is show day and with it comes a whole new set of challenges, some of them known. Others will just happen and the crew will deal with them as they arise.

That's what they do.

21

It's All About Loving Your Band

Ted Gardner thinks there's one thing that separates Australian road crew from their counterparts in the rest of the world. It's called – wait for it – love.

'Here we *loved* our bands. If you worked for Cold Chisel, you worked *for* Chisel, you were part of Chisel. If you worked for Men at Work, you *were* Men at Work. No one could say anything nasty about them. If anyone got on their stage while they're playing, you'd smash them.'

In America, Gardner explains, that attitude doesn't exist. An American crew are hired hands, and the crew guy simply does his job. He gets three meals a day, he can only be made to work a certain number of hours each day, he has a tour bus he can sleep on, and he has a shower at least every second day. 'It blew my mind when I got over there – three meals! I get breakfast, lunch and dinner, *plus* I'm getting a per diem of $30 a day on top of that. I was saving the per diem and just eating at the venues.'

Before moving to America – where he ended up working on Frank Zappa's crew, managing Jane's Addiction, and co-founding the Lollapalooza festival in 1991 with that band's members and booking agency – Gardner had worked his way through the ranks in Australia as a young roadie.

Gardner left home in 1967 and headed to Coolangatta, where his intention was to surf for the rest of his life. Pretty quickly, reality collided with that idea, and he realised he needed to earn money. So he became a band equipment loader at the Tallebudgera Playroom on the Gold Coast. 'Someone like Johnny O'Keefe would come to play a gig and I'd assist a couple of the crew guys. I showed them where the equipment was, how it worked and so forth.'

After 18 months of doing that, Gardner moved to Melbourne but found it hard to get work with bands, so he became a fencing contractor for a couple of years before drifting into being a security guard/bouncer. Eventually he managed a couple of clubs after falling in with industry figures Michael Gudinski, Ray Evans and Michael Roberts.

It was while Gardner was booking bands at the Bottom Line Club that a guy called Chris Plimmer persuaded him to relocate to Sydney to work as a booking agent for the Nucleus Agency. 'He gave me Midnight Oil to book – how hard was that to sell? Not hard at all.' Gardner was also booking a band named Matt Finish, and eventually left Nucleus to join them. 'I drove them around, helped set up gear, collected money – a tour manager without actually having that title.'

From there he drifted into a job with Men at Work. It was then that he first encountered one of the hardest-nosed guys in the business, Michael Lippold, who was in his early days with Midnight Oil. Around 1982, the Oils and Men at Work were doing a show together at the Music Bowl in Melbourne. Men at Work were opening the show, and Lippold made sure the openers were using as little of the stage space as possible so his own band could set up around them and look more impressive when they played on the full stage.

'I said to Lippold, "Don't give me any shit about only having six feet for my band to play on. This is meant to be a co-head-lining gig – you're just on last." He said I was the only person he'd do this for, so he moved the drum kit back ten feet from where it was set up, nailed the fucking kit to the floor, looked at me and said, "Have you got enough room now?" I told him he was a cunt and that I hated him – which I didn't, but he did piss off a lot of support bands.

'But that was just what we were like in that day and age. I was the same with Men at Work – "You're the support band, here's your six feet, make it work, don't talk to me – I'm busy." That's just the way it was. Colin Hay used to tell me I was treating support bands badly, and I said to him, "You're the headliner – they're just filling in time."'

Gardner has observed many eras of roadies. He feels that the younger crews these days have an entirely different perspective on the work and lifestyle. 'They don't really comprehend the conditions we worked in, or what we got up to, all of which was part of the job. They can't really imagine gigs like the Manly Vale Hotel, where we had to get everything up three flights of stairs. You're lugging a big Soundcraft desk up there, and then at the end of the night we're loading it back out through broken glass and blood, and when we're finished all we wanted to do is go to the Manzil Room. Then we'd sit around, do copious amounts of speed, drink ridiculous amounts, and then the next day we'd turn around and do it all again.'

The Manzil Room was the Sydney venue where all the crews got together. Other cities had similar hangs, but nothing quite like the Manzil.

'There was no real antagonism between crews, no real anger or animosity. Everyone was respectful of each other. You were mates. If someone was new, you embraced them and said, "See you next run." Mind you, away from the Manzil Room when we were out on the road it was a different thing as you'd be telling people from other crews that this was all the stage area they were getting, or that they were only getting a certain number of lights and things like that, so people did start to get their backs up. But it was, "Take it or leave it – what do you want to do?"'

Gardner went to America as the road manager for Men at Work and ended up staying there for two and a half decades. 'Men at Work took all their crew to America, including the rigger, which was something they didn't need to do. Everyone flew first-class to America – band and crew. We all stayed at the same hotels. But that changed a bit when we got on the road and they got more popular as everyone wanted a piece of them.'

And Gardner made the most of this world, looking after himself and the rest of the crew in the time-honoured tradition. 'Men at Work were headlining and had their own catering budgets, so it was my *duty* at the end of the gig . . . the band would disappear slowly and then I would swoop into the backstage area like a magpie and clear everything up – all the leftover, untouched food, all the booze. It *all* went on the bus for the crew. Nothing like that would happen in Australia. The budgets just weren't there – and no one thought of it. Feed the band? Sure. But feed the crew? That was not going to happen.'

Gardner noticed that the difference between Australian and American road crew was their work ethic, and in the Australians' more varied skill sets – simply because they'd worked their way through the roadie ranks, learning a bit about everything.

'When we – see, I talk like I'm part of the band! – when Men at Work were opening for Fleetwood Mac in America, Mick Fleetwood came over one day when I was putting the drums together and he asked if I was the drum tech. I told him I wasn't, I was just the roadie/tour manager guy, but that if something needed doing you just got it done. Seriously, he was flabbergasted.

'When I went to work for Zappa, he had a full crew of Americans and they were amazed that I could do a little bit of sound, a little bit of lights, a little bit of monitors, and that I could put all the gear together and set the stage if need be, if someone was busy elsewhere or sick. They all asked where I got to learn that, and I explained that it's what we do in Australia. The only way you can survive as crew is by being able to do bits of everything.

'When it came to Lollapalooza, I worked with the riggers at 6 am, learning from them and the lighting guys. I just wanted to keep learning. I'd watch the sound guys and what they were doing. For me it was an ongoing learning process. I wanted to know what was changing, and be able to keep up with what was happening.'

Gardner believes he worked in the best eras of music – and with the finest crews. And he still thinks there's something that makes Australian crews different.

'It was a fantastic era of music, the 1980s in particular. The bands who played it were fantastic, and they had crews that were incredibly determined that their band was going to be seen to look and sound the best. Australian crews *love* their band. American crews don't love their band. American crew work for their band and are loyal to their band, but they don't love them like Australian crews love their bands.'

22

Kerry Fucking Cunningham

Kerry Cunningham is one of the true legends of the Australian road crew world. Stories involving his exploits on the road could fill this and several other volumes. Cunningham is a tough guy. An enforcer when necessary, with a mythical take-no-prisoners attitude when it comes to a sense of fair play with his fellow road crew or the bands he worked for.

And like most of the really tough guys in the business, he doesn't look all that formidable physically. Ask anyone about him, though, and they'll tell you that you underestimate Cunningham at your peril.

'He's mellowed a little over the past couple of decades,' recalled one long-term crew guy when I mentioned Cunningham's name, 'but boy, could I tell you stories!'

Cunningham's days in and around the Sydney music scene go way back, and provide a fascinating snapshot of the nascent music scene in that city. As a member of a sharpie gang from Paddington, Cunningham used to go to gigs at Paddington Town Hall put on by a young promoter named Michael Chugg.

'My gang didn't pay to go into any gigs,' Cunningham says. 'And I had to tell Chuggie that. I told him that if he let my boys in, he didn't need to get any security, and if he didn't let us in, then it was going to be bad for his security, because we were probably going to have to beat his security guys up as they'd want us to pay to come into the gig.

'Initially he didn't listen. All we wanted to do was to come in and see the La De Das – without paying. But he told us everyone had to pay, so we beat up his security guards and walked in. After three gigs of this, I said again, "Work with me here," but he ignored me and kept hiring bigger and better security guys. And we kept beating them up. We were a pretty savage little mob. We could fight – and finally he learnt.'

Then Chugg opened a music venue at the Doncaster Theatre in Anzac Parade in Kensington, which he called the Green Elephant. He took out all the seats and put in beanbags and big, heavy poufs.

'Me and my gang came along and said we were coming in. Chugg was there with Ray Arnold, who knew me because I was a pretty heavy dude around town, and so was he. And they'd brought in this other heavy dude, Leno Forensio, to do security. They thought they'd show us. But I walked in and said, "Hi Leno," and he said, "Oh, it's you, Gorilla," as that was my nickname at the time. I went *whack* – I hit him and he dropped down. I stood on his neck as I walked in and said to Chugg and Ray Arnold, "Here we are, boys."'

'But they kept on trying to stop us. So one night I saw the Sherbet guys loading the gear in. This was before Daryl Braithwaite joined. I asked them if they'd like a hand and they said yes, so my gang and I loaded the gear in and we were inside the venue.

'Chugg had hired this guy called Fred Vella who was this karate expert. He'd just chopped down a house with his bare hands or something like that. He had sixteen of his best karate disciples with him – but thanks to the Sherbet guys we were already inside the venue.

Graham Webb leaning against Bill McCartney's Dodge van at the Wallacia festival. (Courtesy author's collection)

Tana Douglas with Francis Rossi from Status Quo. (Courtesy author's collection)

Bill McCartney standing against the Nova Express van. 'One of those skins could buy a lot of petrol.' (Courtesy author's collection)

A classic Australian road crew from the 1970s. (Courtesy author's collection)

Bill McCartney becomes Lou Reed's manager. Back (*left to right*): Rachel, RCA's Annie Wright, Bill McCartney. Front: 2SM radio's Mike Drayson and Lou Reed. (Courtesy author's collection)

Andy Rayson unloads a van. (Courtesy author's collection)

Road crew legends. Back (*left to right*): John Swiney, Eric Robinson and Vagn Stenvei. Front: Howard Page (*left*), Eddie Robinson. (Courtesy author's collection)

Michael Coppel and Eric Robinson. (Courtesy author's collection)

Left to right: Mark Keegan, Gerry Georgettis, Jimmy Barnes, $crooge Madigan, Don Walker, Shirley Strachan. (Courtesy author's collection)

Nick Campbell (*left*), and Mark Keegan. (Courtesy author's collection)

Pat Pickett – a candid shot. (Courtesy author's collection)

Left to right: Peter Wilson, Tony Wilde and Norbert Probst. (Courtesy author's collection)

Gerry Georgettis. (Courtesy author's collection)

Left to right: Steve 'Pineapple' Alberts, Gregory 'Bear' Horrocks, Ray Maguire and Grahame 'Yogi' Harrison. (Courtesy author's collection)

Janson Bond (*left*),
and Howard Freeman.
(Courtesy author's
collection)

Sophie Kirov (*left*), and artist K. Flay (Photo courtesy Jordan Galvan)

'Without Fred and his crew noticing we took all these heavy poufs upstairs. There was a spot selling pies and drinks, so I told my guys to go and get all the tomato sauce bottles from the stand. Then I told someone to start a fight with this Fred Vella guy – I had two karate experts in my team, and I told them to get him under the mezzanine and when they did we started propelling all the poufs over the side – and they were *really* heavy. Then out of the dark we attacked and squirted them with sauce containers. Half his guys ran away and when Chugg walked past he saw all these guys laid out on the floor covered with tomato sauce. It looked like a massacre.'

Not long afterwards, Cunningham made peace with Chugg, and he and a mate started working for the promoter. 'We'd get drunk, drink a bottle of Jack Daniels and take some mandrax, and go out and hang posters for him. That's really how I started to get into the music game.'

Then he started working for the rock band Buffalo. 'My mate Timmy Palmer was their main guy. None of us had truck licences, but that didn't matter so much in those days. You always got asked for your logbook, so we had four logbooks in the name of Tim Palmer.'

Cunningham's world was the gritty Sydney music scene in the first half of the 1970s. His turf included legendary venues such as the Bondi Lifesaver, the epicentre at the time for all things sex, drugs and rock'n'roll.

Close to the centre of this was Ray Arnold, a larger-than-life individual who was ever-present, even though to this day no one seems to know exactly what he did. Some say he was AC/DC's first roadie. Others say he was their manager. 'Ray was a legend,' is Cunningham's take. 'He originally started with AC/DC. We'd go and pick them up in his car. He used to call them his band of midgets because they were all pretty short guys.

'Ray lived around the corner from the Bondi Lifesaver, in Hollywood Avenue. On his lounge you'd find Jimmy Barnes, Swanee . . . a whole lot of people lived on his couches, including his crew of people. He had a couple of PAs down the back in his garage. We'd all work at the Lifesaver when we weren't doing gigs. Swanee was the cook in the kitchen, and at one stage Angry Anderson was the DJ. I was a doorman, Howard Freeman was the assistant manager.

'Bon Scott used to be there all the time. He rode this Triumph motorbike, and I remember one day he pulled up with this silly look on his face and a tooth missing. He got off the bike and he was off his head. He fell one way and the bike fell the other way. AC/DC were about to go on tour and I said, "This is no good," and I said to the other guys, "We need to get rid of this fucking motorbike or he'll kill himself." So we stole it, took it up to Ray's place and put it in the garage behind some PA gear and boxes. Bon came out and said, "Can you believe it? Someone stole my fucking bike," and Ray said, "Don't worry about it – I know all the bikies in town. I'll see if I can get it back for you. They probably stole it for parts." When Bon returned to Sydney, Ray said, "Found your motorbike – I got it back for you." And Bon went, "You fucking legend!"

'They were about to go on tour again a couple of months later, so we steal the motorbike again and hide it. Bon comes in: "You wouldn't fucking believe it – someone stole the fucking bike again," and Ray goes, "Fucking bikies! Don't worry, Bon, I'll find it for you." So, sure enough, Bon goes and does his tour and comes back, and Ray rings and tells him he's got the motorbike back. Bon goes, "Fucking legend!"

'When we stole it the third time, Bon comes up to Ray and goes, "You're not going to believe it but the fucking bike's gone again – but you know what, I'm not even worried, because I know you'll get it back for me." And sure enough when Bon gets back from the tour Ray's found the bike again.'

Arnold was forever the facilitator. A man with contacts, an anything-is-possible attitude to life, and an ability to think quickly on his feet. Take, for instance, the time that Cunningham and Arnold both needed truck licences. They came up with the most harebrained scheme, even if it was ultimately successful.

'I didn't want to do the test and all that stuff,' Cunningham recalls, 'so Ray rings these bikies. We go see one of them, hand him $50 and he asks if I want a licence to drive a truck, a semitrailer or just a car. Then he gives us an Army licence each. Mine said Lance-Corporal Cunningham and Ray's was Lance-Corporal Arnold. The bikie told us to go down to the Department of Motor Transport and tell them that we weren't in the Army anymore and that we want to change our Army licences to civilian licences.

'So Ray and I go to the Department of Motor Transport and hand over the Army licences to the guy behind the counter, and he starts doing all the paperwork. We both had long hair, and at one stage he looks up at us and goes, "Hang on, if you guys just got out of the Army, how come you've both got long hair?" I'm about to do a runner, but Ray doesn't miss a beat and goes, "Special Services – mind your own business."'

Now armed with a real licence, Cunningham went on to work with some of the most iconic – and uncompromising – bands of the era: Buffalo, Dragon and Rose Tattoo.

'In those days, when you started you were basically a loader. You did everything. I reckon 90 per cent of the guys came from being loaders, and then you just learnt everything as you went along. There was no real pay packet in the very early days . . . you did it for the chicks and the lifestyle.' The crew and bands became close. 'I did around 15 years with Rose Tattoo, and Angry is like family. He's like a brother. Same with Marc Hunter before he died.'

Lack of money meant that many roadies of Cunningham's era resorted to all manner of ruses to improve their finances. Some of them involved criminal activity. In the 1980s Cunningham had some canvas covers made, which just happened to be exactly the right size to cover a cigarette machine or a *Space Invaders* game.

You can guess the rest. After a gig in some country town, the last thing loaded into the truck at the end of the night would be hidden under one of these covers. 'No one was usually around, and if they were they certainly weren't paying attention to us, as they'd just want us to be finished so they could close up and go home. So we'd just unplug the cigarette machines or whatever else we could get and put them in the truck.' Later, the coins inside the machine would be liberated – 'that would put diesel in the truck' – and if it was a cigarette machine, the crew now had smokes for the next leg of the tour.

A favourite place for jettisoning the now useless machines was a hill near the Oaks milkbar near Newcastle, a popular spot for road crews to stop for a break. 'I think about it every time I drive up that way,' Cunningham smiles. 'There's this one place where we'd stop and have a joint as we smashed open the machine, and then down the hill it would go. There's a graveyard of machines at the bottom of that hill and a few other places in the area.'

Of course there were guns too. Lots of guns. Sometimes the crew and band had them; at other times it was the audience with the firearms. Cunningham recalls shows with Rose Tattoo when band and crew were given police escorts out of regional towns.

In Port Kembla one night, there'd been an altercation after the gig. Cunningham and Angry Anderson started chasing one guy who'd come at them outside the venue. 'He heads to his car and I see him getting his key out and putting it in the boot. The lid pops up and he reaches in and pulls out a shotgun. Angry backed off, and I said, "Dude, you better have some shells in that thing because I'm coming at you." I kept walking straight up to him, grabbed the gun, cracked it open and there was nothing in there, so I just beat the fuck out of him with it.

'People always had guns. But you just bought them from gun shops – you didn't need a licence. I remember someone stole a truck we were using for a John Paul Young tour. We were more worried about the guns that were in there than the gear. There were about four rifles and a handgun in the truck. We were really worried that whoever stole the truck would kill themselves, because there was one gun that backfired when you shot it. It was a motherfucker. We ended up getting the truck back. They took the gear and dumped the truck without realising the guns were behind the seats in the sleeper compartment.'

There were also lots of girls in Cunningham's world. 'There were a lot of really good band moles, which was great. They could supply us with our mandrax and stuff like that. At the Lifesaver there was a woman known as the mandy queen. All the girls would go down to Cocaine Corner, and she would be doling out the pills to all the other girls. She knew all their tolerances and doses to get them nicely stoned: "Pammy, three for you . . . Susie, you're a four." She was in charge of the groupies and sorted them out: "You're going home with Ted Mulry tonight . . . and you're with the guitarist." That sort of thing.

'And in Melbourne there were the Car Park Girls. There was Marcia, Debbie, Carol . . . about five of them. They were amazingly resourceful. We'd be leaving Melbourne and they'd tell us they'd see us in Sydney. When we pulled into the hotel in Sydney, they'd already be there waiting for us. We'd ask them how they managed it and they'd say semitrailer truck drivers were much faster than us. They'd say, "We just give them a blow job and off they go." They were quite legendary. It helped keep us all together and was part of living on the road.'

And living on the road was tough. Most crew guys couldn't deal with it straight. According to Cunningham, the more out if it you were, the better it was. You were numbed.

Cunningham's own days on the road ended in 1987, when his first child was born. 'This game ruins relationships. You've got one family or the other, and you need to choose some-times.' But Cunningham didn't retire; finances and the fact that crewing is in his blood made sure of that. He simply moved to another line of work, as a production runner for big concerts in Sydney. 'You're still a problem-solver. If an amp goes down in the middle of a show, I know what to do and how to get it sorted. That's what I do.'

And in that world Cunningham is still in high demand, often weighing up three or more shows and tour offers at one time. When we spoke, he was about to head off and solve whatever problems arose at a Foo Fighters concert that night in Sydney. Not bad for a guy who was kicked out of school for bashing up his music teacher.

'I wish he was around these days,' he laughs, 'so I could say, "I'm still working in the music industry, you fucker."'

23

Is the Real Jerome Swinbourne II in the Building?

Ross Ferguson doesn't really have a problem with his birth name. He's used to it and accepts it. But he does have a penchant for creating and assuming the identities of fictional characters. Ferguson, one of the most experienced and respected of Australian road crew, knows all too well that to survive in the roadie business, you need a strong sense of humour and an ability to amuse both yourself and the artists you work with.

Ferguson is – unsurprisingly – best known to most people in the road crew world as 'Fergie'. But over the years he has had many other identities. And whenever he created a new persona for himself, he took on the whole character – even refusing to answer to anyone who called him by his real name.

'It was just to keep the work interesting and fun. When we were doing one INXS tour I decided that Fergie was going on holidays and Eddie Munster would be taking over for a while. So I dyed my hair black, got all the clothes and dressed the part. As the tour began, someone announced to the band and crew that Fergie wouldn't be with them this time. Michael Hutchence was particularly upset. Then I walked into the room all dressed up and told them I was Eddie Munster, and that they had to call me that. I kept it up for the whole tour.'

But Eddie Munster just wouldn't do for the major American awards ceremony INXS was rehearsing for, so Ferguson retired him and created the more authoritative persona of Jerome Swinbourne II to deal with the people planning the television event.

'INXS hadn't been around for the early part of the set-up, but when they arrived for the rehearsal everyone was telling them how great Jerome Swinbourne II was. Confused, they asked who this guy was. When they were told that Jerome Swinbourne II was their crew and production representative, Hutch just put his head down and grinned. It was like, "Here we go again."

'Then I figured that Jerome Swinbourne II wasn't the sort of person who could load trucks and move gear, so I invented Jerry Swinbourne Jnr, the filthy drug-taking slut. I got a Metallica T-shirt and cut the sleeves off it and swore at everyone. One night Kirk Pengilly came offstage, and as he did I spat on the stage just where he was about to step. Kirk fired Jerry Swinbourne Jnr that night but kept Fergie on.'

For a while Fergie was also known as Mr Dog Vomit; he wore a jacket with a dog wearing sunglasses on the back. He wouldn't answer to Dog Vomit – it had to be *Mr* Dog Vomit. 'You'd be surprised how many people have come backstage at INXS shows over the years hoping to get access and asked for Eddie Munster or Mr Dog Vomit.'

Ferguson, who is now 64, started in the roadie world when he was 17. He'd been a drummer but had no talent in that area. But he did have a driver's licence and a van – one with peace signs painted on the sides and surfboard racks on the top, although he never used them as he was afraid of sharks.

A friend had a band called Pagan, which was entering a Battle of the Bands competition. They needed a van, so Ferguson drove them. And then he did it again and again.

The year 1971 was a big one for Ferguson, aged 17. He'd married his first girlfriend, had a child, bought a house and was running a business – Ferguson Handmade Leather Goods – with a small factory and half a shop. And he smoked lots of pot. Yes, he was 17.

After Pagan he became a roadie for Crazy Otto, and when Rabbit poached Crazy Otto's lead singer Ferguson threw his lot in with him and moved too. When Rabbit went out on tour with the Ted Mulry Gang, Ferguson became friends with their crew, in particular Billy McCartney and Nicky Campbell. They schooled him in the ways of the road and how to deal with artists.

'They taught me to give it your all – that if someone wants their tea at 37 degrees, you give it to them at 37 degrees. It's not being a suckarse, it's just doing your job. Iva Davies always wanted packets of chewing gum at gigs – one packet unwrapped, one half-unwrapped, the other wrapped. I didn't give a shit about that – if that's how he wanted it, then I made sure that was what he had.'

Touring with TMG taught the young Ferguson about how hard road crews worked. From what he remembers, the tour included 75 gigs in 71 days. There were seven crew travelling in a campervan and Ferguson driving the truck on his own. Show after show after show. It was a tour he didn't see out, but not because he didn't want to. In Darwin he succumbed to the disease pericarditis. He'd previously had a similar incident in Bangkok with Sherbet.

'On some legs of that tour we were doing 450 miles on dirt roads between gigs. The van was destroyed. The toilets and show areas ended up being used for storage for extra fuel. Robert Green and Squirt from the crew shot the windscreen out with their rifles on the tour. They had been shooting them out windows, but something happened and we hit a bump and out went the windscreen.'

There's not much Ferguson hasn't seen or experienced on the road. He once fell off a ladder when he was setting up some lighting simply because he fell asleep. He's been in a number of car accidents when others have fallen asleep. There was another heart attack in Bangkok during a tour with Sherbet.

'I did all sorts of things that were potentially dangerous. The relatively small number of crew road deaths is a miracle. Once I drove the Nullarbor on my own on the TMG tour. I remember sitting in the truck with my feet up on the dashboard. I had a cassette playing things like "The Faith Healer" by The Sensational Alex Harvey Band, a brick on the accelerator and I was smoking a joint as I drove into the sunset. I was thinking that this was shit, but it was pretty cool shit.

'I told everyone I worked with over the years who worked on crews with me that it was going to be hard work. I made sure they realised that there'd be overnighters after gigs, so lots of travelling through the night, and that the money was shit and that I didn't blame anyone for not wanting to do it. But if they did decide to do the work, then *shut the fuck up* because you know what you signed on for, so get to it and do the fucking work. Of course the hours are hard. Don't take the job and then walk around moaning.'

Ferguson moved on to work with Sherbet, who were going to take him to America with them. When they didn't it broke his heart. Then he fell in love again, decided to leave the road, worked for a stint at BHP and helped out local Newcastle bands. But before long Ferguson found himself drifting back to the world of the roadie. A mate invited him to check out a gig by The Sports. 'I went, and I'll never forget looking at the black road cases. It was like the way a junkie looks at smack. Crew work is really like an addiction.' Ferguson joined The Sports' crew, then moved on to Mondo Rock, doing periods of work with Richard Clapton and others along the way.

Like so many musicians and crew of the time, Ferguson – a non-drinker who only took drugs to stay awake – fell into the world of heroin. 'They used to call us the sewing club as there were so many of us using needles,' he says. Somewhere along the line was a stint with Jimmy Barnes. 'I can't remember when but I have a platinum album from Jimmy.'

A clean Ferguson went to America with the John Farnham-era Little River Band, and also with Models. Then, when INXS needed a guitar tech for Kirk Pengilly, Ferguson found himself working for INXS. 'I really gelled with them – Hutch in particular. I loved Hutch. In the end I was the only Australian crew guy they kept. They had Prince's lighting guy, The Cars' guitar tech, Neil Young's drum tech, The Rolling Stones' sound engineer, Paul McCartney's monitor engineer, and me.'

Ferguson also did six years with Tina Turner. 'Every night she'd come up this set of stairs to start the show. I'd be there as I'd just handed a guitar to one of the band members, and I'd say, "Tina, welcome to Rock Ridge," and she'd said, "Hi Fergie." Rock Ridge is a place from the Mel Brooks film *Blazing Saddles*, but she obviously hadn't seen the film. Not once on the tour did she ever ask where Rock Ridge was – or tell me that she knew we weren't in Rock Ridge.'

Tricks and games and shenanigans. Sometimes it was just little things, silly things to keep the crew fresh and the band on their toes. During an Australian Crawl tour, Fergie insisted one night that all the crew work in flannelette pyjamas. When the band asked why, the answer was simple: 'We're tired and we want to go home and sleep.' For part of the tour everyone on the crew spoke to each other in a new language called Elf – gibberish only vaguely understandable even to the participants.

Ferguson was always quick to exploit a phobia in a band member. Australian Crawl's guitarist Simon Binks hated fish. Before the final date of a tour in Perth, Ferguson and a couple of the crew guys went to a fish market and traded four good tickets for the band's concert at the Entertainment Centre for three tubs of fish. When the band went offstage before their encore, the crew worked quickly by torchlight. 'There were fish *everywhere*. On his pedal board, all over the stage. We even had some attached to fishing lines so we could manoeuvre them around the stage. When the band came on they were slithering everywhere.'

Despite such antics, Ferguson was never short of work. Crowded House came along, and that morphed into years with Elton John and his band, with whom Ferguson traversed the globe. He returned to Australia after his sister was murdered in April 1988. Eventually he worked again, doing an extended run with The Beastie Boys.

Ferguson still keeps his hand in, and is coming up for his 20th year managing the main stage at the annual Byron Bay Bluesfest. He's good at it, and knows how to deal with people. 'There's two ways to get people to work for you – by fear or by respect. If it's fear, then the moment you walk away, they don't give a shit.'

And Ferguson is still making up names and trying to bring a bit of levity to his work. A few years back at Bluesfest, the American band Little Feat came backstage and started introducing themselves to him.

'I told them I'd never remember all their names, so why didn't everyone just be Fuckhead? They were all Fuckhead, and I was Fuckhead. It was like, "Fuckhead, can you move that amp?" "Sure, Fuckhead." "Good, now, Fuckhead, can you do this . . ." It keeps things friendly and amusing.'

24

Are You Ready Yet, Axl?

Jon Pope admits that he's been lucky. He has been front and centre at some truly notable rock'n'roll moments. Many of them have been stressful and damn hard work, and a lot of them have been hilariously funny. But they've all been memorable – and, let's be honest, the sort of experiences most people don't get to have.

One particularly pinch-yourself moment was the time he was flying over 72,000 people at Eastern Creek in Sydney in a helicopter with Axl Rose, looking down at the bonfires that had been lit by the crowd. Pope and the notoriously difficult Guns N' Roses singer had flown from Mascot after a limousine had raced them from the Ritz Carlton at Double Bay to the helipad.

By this stage, tour manager Pope had smoked a whole packet of cigarettes in the loading dock at the hotel as he waited for Rose to decide if he was ready to go to the concert. Promoters Michael Gudinski and Michael Chugg had been ringing Pope every 15 minutes, checking if the singer was on his way. They were nervous. The crowd at Eastern Creek was getting restless because of the wait, and they were petrified that Rose – who had form in the not-turning-up-for-concerts stakes – would decide he didn't feel like doing the show.

Eventually the tension got to Pope. Gudinski called again and Pope explained the situation bluntly. 'I said, "Michael, you know I'm the fucking guy that if you want me to go up there and knock on the door and tell him to come and get in the fucking helicopter, I will. Do you want me to do that?" He said no, as they didn't want to piss Axl off. Eventually Axl came down and off we went.'

The memorable moments continued after the show. Within three minutes of Guns N' Roses' performance finishing, Pope and Rose were stepping into the helicopter for the ride back to the city. 'The view was amazing – and it was the same in Melbourne. Just looking down at the highways as Chugg and Gudinski had organised to make all lanes of traffic inbound immediately after the concerts so that all the traffic could be quickly cleared. There are six lanes of red taillights, 70,000 people, 40,000 cars.'

Pope almost seems blasé when he talks about his experiences in planes and helicopters with famous rock'n'roll stars. He estimates he's been in more than 20 privates planes with the likes of Bob Dylan, Red Hot Chili Peppers and Metallica. These are artists who don't think twice about playing a show in Sydney and leaving straight afterwards because they feel like sleeping or partying on the Gold Coast that night. Or flying from Sydney to Adelaide, doing a concert and coming straight back to their Sydney hotel. It's much simpler, really: no need to check out of the hotel and pack your luggage again.

There was the time Billy Joel was doing multiple shows in Australia on his Storm Front tour. A final Melbourne show was added to a ridiculously long run of dates, but Joel and his entourage didn't feel like checking out of the Park Hyatt in Sydney. 'We just flew down in a small jet, did the show and flew back,' Pope says.

The next minute he's telling a yarn about being in America doing advance preparations for Coldplay's Viva la Vida tour. The band had a 57-seat private plane, so plenty of room for wives, partners, kids and friends. 'When I was there they were basing themselves in Miami and then flying out to do shows and then back. After that, they were moving to another hub and doing the same thing.'

This high-flying world is a long way from where Pope started in the music caper in the late 1970s, helping out a few school-friends in a Christian band. They introduced him to some other guys, Ali Emmett and Dave West. West, who would be best man at Pope's wedding years later, did lighting ('I saw him put up 96 lights on his own, on three trusses'), while Emmett did sound. By this stage Pope had invested in a little PA system of his own. Emmett had taught him all about audio: how to tune a PA, and the best equipment to buy.

In the early 1980s Pope became more involved with the Sydney independent band scene and with ska revival band The Allniters and proto-pop/punk band Spy vs Spy, who were using his PA equipment. Pope also worked with Julius Grafton, who ran a successful small business hiring equipment to bands. Eventually The Allniters offered Pope a salary and he went on the road with them, doing their sound and providing their equipment. It was a hard slog. The Allniters toured a lot, and in the process his PA system was run into the ground.

'It costs the bands $350 a night – which was the cost of me, the truck and the PA. And then to keep up to date, you needed a new effects rack, which would cost you $1000. And then before you knew it there'd be something that was meant to be better than what you'd just bought, and that would be $1200. Lighting is still like that.'

In Pope's opinion – and he's not alone – the 1980s was the great era for roadies. 'The real art of being a roadie died after this period. Bands like The Allniters would headline on a Thursday, Friday, Saturday and maybe Sunday night, and on Monday, Tuesday and Wednesday you'd be out on a bill with bigger bands. There'd always be three, sometimes four bands on a bill, so you'd watch how other crew laid out their cables onstage and set their stuff up. It was like a university, and you learnt from everyone, right down to how they put their lighting trees in the truck. It was all about watching and learning and doing stuff, and then working out what worked for you. It was real on-the-job training.

'I think that's why Australian crews that came through that era are so good. They knew *everything*. These days on big tours, lighting and sound are kept right apart from each other, but in those days you learnt a lot about both. Everyone loaded and unloaded trucks together. As production got bigger, things got separated – "Oh, that's lighting, that's *his* job" – but in the '80s everyone worked with everyone else. It was a gelled unit of people from all different backgrounds who worked together. Occasionally a guy would be a dickhead and he'd have to go, but not that often.'

Having his own PA meant that Pope worked with an extremely diverse array of bands and music. 'It was not unusual to be with an American gospel group one night, a standard pub rock band the next, a punk rock band after that and then a ska band. And of course the shows would usually be at different venues every night.'

Pope was mentored by some significant figures in the road crew business. Wayne 'Swampy' Jarvis was one who took Pope under his wing. 'He taught me a lot of what to do – and what not to do,' Pope smiles. And because of Spy vs Spy's connection through shared management with Midnight Oil, Pope became close with their main roadie of that era, Michael Lippold.

Towards the end of the 1980s, Pope saw a significant change in the Australian rock'n'roll landscape, which also meant a change in the roadie world. 'The crews had gradually gotten bigger. The core used to be front-of-house, lights, stage and monitors – a tight four-man crew. Then when bands like The Angels graduated to two trucks, they'd have what was called the fifth man, who didn't do anything except look after the trucks and the packing up and loading of them. That's when crews expanded to five, and then six and then more.

'That early '80s era changed when the big pub bands like The Church, INXS, Sunnyboys and Hunters & Collectors and so forth moved from pubs to places like the Hordern Pavilion, and a lot of them went overseas. That left a gap below them that wasn't really filled, and there was less work for local crews.'

Pope decided to move with the times, and joined the Frontier Touring Company as a combination front-of-house/tour manager, before graduating in 1992 to tour-managing only.

One of the earliest things Pope did was go around the world with Australian dance/pop band Indecent Obsession, which became one of the first Western acts to tour South Africa in the post-apartheid era. 'It was funny playing to 36 people one night at a venue in North Sydney, and them going to three shows in Johannesburg Arena soon after with 8000 people a night.'

The first international artist's tour Pope did for Frontier was the American rap artist Tone Loc. And that's where he was working the night another of Frontier's tour managers, Ian Saxon, was arrested in what remains one of Australia's largest drug busts. 'Saxon was going to be doing Tracy Chapman's tour, but after he was arrested I ended up doing it. That's when things really took off for me.'

It was a roller-coaster ride through the 1990s and onwards for Pope. Being a likeable guy who was very good at his job helped. Many international bands bonded with him and insisted on having him on the road with them, regardless of who the promoter was.

But as the cliché goes, you're only as good as your last tour. Promoters ride waves, and tour managers fall into and out of favour, often because of the most ridiculous reasons. Pope has had many years when his annual income has been measured in six figures, and some when it's been at the low end of four. It's a tougher, more competitive business now, he says. 'It used to be that on every tour you had a day off in each big city. So you'd have a barbecue or a boat cruise or a cricket game. Those days are gone. Everybody wants more bang for their buck – the agents, the promoters, the acts, the managers. It's tougher for everybody.'

Pope misses the reckless old days, with the true characters of the industry. 'Sometimes the crew were all drinking by 10 am. We all used to drive around pissed. Would we do it now? Of course not. I was fined once for doing 187 kph on the Hume Highway. In those days that was just a fine. These days your licence gets taken away. I actually didn't even know cars went that fast until then.

'In those days you certainly had a bond of feeling bullet-proof, especially if the crew was a tight unit – and most of them were. You knew people would have your back if some shit went down. Mind you, some crew guys were pretty unhinged and unpredictable, and you didn't know if they were going to back you up or take you on.'

Then Pope almost drifts into a reverie about days gone by. 'The good old days . . . two – or three – naked girls in a room. I remember how easy it all used to be . . . but everything's changed. Everyone who did the crazy shit is too old to still be doing crazy shit – or dead.'

A couple of nights after we chatted, I run into Pope again. He's outside the Forum in Melbourne, chatting with a few friends. He's tour-managing for American country band Old

Crow Medicine Show. There are no private jets on this tour, but Pope is still out on the road working with great artists. He has survived where so many others haven't – and that's something he appreciates.

25

Tony Wilde and Norbert Probst

Tony Wilde exists in a fantasy world of yesteryear. His work-place – he has a production equipment business – doubles as a private museum for his remarkable collection of memorabilia. Located in suburban Melbourne, it is full of racing cars, vintage taxis, planes, petrol bowsers, phone booths, number plates, model cars and planes, replica milkbars from the 1950s and 1960s ... it's a nostalgic playground. And there's not a skerrick of rock'n'roll memorabilia among it.

The hyper-energetic Wilde started as a roadie in the late 1970s. Like most road crew, including his close friend Norbert Probst, there was no planning: he just drifted into it as a way of making some extra cash. 'I left school when I was 16 and was heading towards being a trainee auctioneer, working with livestock, property and wool broking, but getting up at 5 am to start at the Newmarket saleyards at 5.30 am wasn't good for my body clock. A mate of mine was working for a mobile disco that morphed into working with live bands as well. So, I started working with him at some suburban beer barns and a few residencies around the place.'

This friend turned out to be a dodgy operator: he had to sell everything to get a passport and get out of the country. Wilde bought some of his PA gear and took over his truck, an EK Bedford. It was a gem, but he got a shock when he went to pay out the loan on it and discovered just how much was owing. He told them he hadn't brought enough money with him, and he'd go to the truck to get the rest, so he walked away from the office, jumped in the truck and disappeared. He also found out it was registered as an EH Holden, and the plates had expired five years earlier.

'But I did somehow manage to get it registered, and started to rent it out to bands. Then I bought another truck. I think I thought I was going to be like Lindsay Fox – keep buying trucks and renting them out. The bands were paying $45 for the truck and $40 for me every gig, so I was making $85 a day.'

Wilde worked with countless bands. It was the heyday of Australian pub rock and there was lots of work on offer. He did a long stint with Jo Jo Zep & The Falcons after their stage guy, Geoff Lloyd, was promoted to tour manager. Wilde worked constantly, both in Australia – with everyone from The Church to Jimmy Barnes – and overseas. He was with The Angels in the States when they changed their name to Angel City, and he went to Europe with The Church, and with Dragon when they had to change their name to Hunter.

Like all roadies, Wilde has lots of stories. He once had to drive Stevie Nicks to a gig in Melbourne because she wanted to see Venetta Fields. 'Never meet your idols,' he laughs. 'Nicks was such a gutter-mouthed Valley Girl in the '80s. I was so disappointed, especially after all the hours we'd spent holding up the *Rumours* album cover with one hand . . .'

Wilde recalls the time a legendary Australian roadie, John Swiney, asked if he could hitch a ride to Melbourne in a truck Wilde was travelling in. 'It was an airline strike and Swiney rang me as he needed a lift to Melbourne. Regardless of the strike, he'd spent his air ticket money. I told him there was already three in the front of the truck and he said he'd travel in the back of the truck with all the gear. Of course this was highly dangerous. We stopped at Yass for a wee, and then he gets back in and takes a couple of Serepax.

'We got to Melbourne around 6 am and pulled into the Diplomat in St Kilda, which was where everyone stayed in those days. The bloody Serepax had really kicked in and we couldn't wake him – but believe me we tried. We just couldn't even stir him to get him to get out and come with us. We couldn't leave the truck open in St Kilda, so we had to leave him asleep in the locked truck and go to bed ourselves. The phone starts ringing in my room at 10 am as there's reports of someone bashing and yelling from the inside of the truck. He wasn't happy, but what could we do?'

Then there was the time Wilde and another Jo Jo Zep roadie were running late for a plane. They had to drop the hire car keys back but they became distracted, and each thought the other was going to return the keys. Only once they got on the plane did they realise they still had the keys – and the car was parked in a two-minute zone.

A classic piece of roadie ingenuity came when Wilde was in Western Australia with The Church. 'You'd usually use PA and equipment from a hire company in Perth unless you drove across. We get to the gig in Bunbury and there's no drum carpet in the hire truck. We have to have one or otherwise the kit and Richard Ploog, the drummer, would have fallen off the stage. The dressing room was actually a hotel room at the venue, so I got an idea. I moved the bed over, got out my Stanley knife and cut out a carpet square and then took it and put it on the stage. When we finished the gig I put it back where it should have been in the room and pulled the bed back over it. Everything was fine until someone moved the bed, and I had Michael

Chugg, who was managing the band at the time, screaming at me on the phone.'

After nearly a decade, Wilde started to get jaded with the work, but he was never bored. 'I came back to Australia and the three biggest acts were INXS, Midnight Oil and Jimmy Barnes. INXS were all covered for crew, and I didn't want to know about Midnight Oil because of the guy in charge of their crew, so I got a gig working big venues with Jimmy Barnes. Then Jimmy and his management decided to do a pub run with the same level of production. Bloody semitrailers of gear for shows in Coffs Harbour. I was done. It was a bit like Neil Armstrong after landing on the moon – nothing was going to be like the bigger shows after that. After working the big shows, it's hard to go back to smaller venues. They just don't compare for intensity and excitement. I was tired and I had other options. I had a business with staging, and I didn't want to go back to doing pubs.'

For his part, Probst is a classic old-school roadie. He's probably worked with more artists than he hasn't, such that after a while they tend to blur together – both in his mind and in conversation – as one magnificent, hardworking experience.

As a youngster, Probst used to hitchhike to places like Dandenong Town Hall to see his favourite artists, Bobby & Laurie. He would offer to carry their gear in for them so he could get into the gig for free. Then he became a 'terrible bass player' in a band called Mercy, who did a few gigs opening for Daddy Cool.

'Before the show the guy doing the sound that night had a buzz in the PA. I fixed it and he asked me to stay back after my band's set and help him mic stuff up, and that's how I got into working with bands and PAs. I used to work building little PAs, and then I'd go and set them up for bands and mix the sound for them.'

There are funny stories amidst Probst's recollections from those days – the sort of experiences that only road crew have.

'One day I was working with Mondo Rock, and one of the other roadies turned up for work. Nothing unusual about that, but then I noticed that there were two guys in a car watching us, and then they started following us as we drive from where we'd loaded the gear to the venue for the show that night. So I asked the guy what was going on, and he said they were his bodyguards as he was a witness in the Mr Asia court case. They followed us everywhere on the whole tour – I guess so they knew where he was and that he was alive.'

Then there were the experiences that don't seem so amusing until much later. Like the time Probst was in charge of the dry ice machine, creating smoke for a Tina Turner club gig in Melbourne. 'I'd overheated the water and not clipped the top on properly. I put the plunger down but no smoke was coming from the hose. The bloody thing was going to erupt everywhere, so I sat on the thing, trying to keep the pressure down.'

And then, during a stint with Men at Work – well, you know what roadies are going to do, don't you? Of course they did. 'We actually had witches' hats and Men at Work signs we'd pinched off the roads so we could put them up for the trucks if we were blocking traffic for a load-in or load-out.'

Listening to Wilde and Probst trade stories and experiences – stories they've probably told hundreds of times before – takes you back to the basics of being around road crews. These men have worked with so many big names that they're totally unfazed by that part of the job. They are rock'n'roll soldiers – and like old soldiers, there's nothing they like better than a yarn about the old days. The bad old days and the good old days. And there are lots of laughs. Always lots of laughs.

26

Motley Takes on KISS

There are fairytales in the world of road crew. However, for them to come to fruition, a lot of hard work is usually involved, plus incredible skill and maybe a bit of luck. As a kid, Sean Hackett – let's call him Motley, as everyone else does – was a massive fan of KISS. Maybe they weren't his number one band, but they were right up there. He wanted to work for them – and even if he couldn't, he had his eyes set on being employed by a big international band and travelling the world with them.

For more than a decade now, Motley – whose nickname came from him turning up to work at Jands one day wearing a Mötley Crüe T-shirt – has been a lighting designer for KISS, one of many Australian roadies working in the higher echelons of the international touring business.

'Most people didn't have this grand plan for what they were going to do with their career. We just lived for the moment. But I did have a grand plan. I saw the potential and knew what I wanted to do. I knew someone had to work for all those big bands, so I started working towards that.'

Motley had already seen the downside of road crew work, and was determined not to go down that path. 'There was so much alcohol and drugs around the crew world that so many of these guys came off the road and became alcoholics or drug addicts and then got to their late 40s and looked around and wondered what they were going to do with themselves. They had no money, no partner, no nothing. I didn't want to be on that side of things.'

The start of Motley's ascent to world domination (or at least a gig with KISS) was pretty standard. He began helping out a bunch of guys who lived in his suburb in Canberra and played in a band. Eventually the band scored a support show with The Angels. Motley went down to the gig to help with the load-in. 'I think eight guys loaded in and one loaded out,' he laughs. 'From there I met a few people and heard about loaders who got paid $15 a job. I did that at a big venue in Canberra, and kept seeing all these cases coming in with the word JANDS stencilled on them. So I went, "Okay, all the big bands use Jands."

'I'd always loved the lighting side of things, so I gravitated towards that and watched what those guys did. In those days there wasn't technically a lot to learn. You needed to be at least six feet tall to reach up and hang the lights, but there wasn't much to it. There wasn't anything like the technology we have now.'

Motley met Kevin Richards, who ran the lighting department at Jands, and every week for six months he rang him to ask for work. Finally Richards said the company was busy and could give him a week's work in Sydney. Motley slept on a friend's floor in Redfern. One week turned into three weeks, which turned into three months, which turned into three years. Motley had also begun an apprenticeship as a cook, which taught him discipline and gave him a good work ethic.

'It was 1986 when I started at Jands. Around the time things started to change in the lighting world. It still wasn't that complex to keep up with, but then around 1989 the first digital desks came in, and that change was major. Lights moved to digital way before sound did. So when the sound guys became exasperated, we went, "Now you know what we went through."'

Aged 22, Motley decided to try his luck overseas, realising that English and American crew earnt a lot more than their counterparts in Australia. He had a British passport, $800 and a one-way ticket to London. He went backwards and forwards, alternating stints in the United Kingdom with more work at Jands, before hearing that Noiseworks were looking for a lighting designer. 'I knocked on the door of their manager Michael Browning's office and said, "Hi, I'm Motley – I'm going to be your new lighting designer."'

Motley did that job for a time before moving on to work with Diesel, then Savage Garden and Jimmy Barnes. But always, whenever he was between work, he made his way back to Jands. 'I knew that you needed the right skill set and to meet the right people, and for me meeting the right people was meeting people who worked on the big tours – and they all gravitated around Jands.'

Next came a long stint with INXS, which encompassed the last world tour with Michael Hutchence, then the tours when the band was fronted by Jon Stevens, Terence Trent D'Arby and J.D. Fortune.

By this time Motley had worked with KISS on tours of Australia but he hadn't been directly employed by them – and he'd certainly not worked with them overseas. Then KISS's singer, Paul Stanley, returned to Australia and Motley received an email saying that the band's regular lighting designer wasn't available, and would he like to be in charge of lights for that tour. Naturally, Motley went for it. At the conclusion of the tour, Stanley said he thought the Australian did great lights, and it was a shame he didn't have an American visa as KISS was looking for someone to join their US crew.

Motley actually had a visa to work in the States with INXS, but he wasn't sure if that would allow him to work with other artists. As it turned out, KISS needed someone for four shows straight after the run of INXS dates. Motley was in the right place at the right time. He was now in the KISS camp. The band returned to Australia in 2008, and he did that tour plus a jaunt in Europe. He was still not the band's main lighting guy, but was eyeing the prize.

'Their main guy was leaving to work with Mötley Crüe so I filled in for him for a while, and then a year later their overall lighting designer went off to work with Aerosmith. That's when I went from running someone else's design and show to being in charge of it all myself. Being a fan, I knew pretty much what they wanted. The first major international show I saw was KISS in 1980 in Sydney. I'd come up from Canberra with friends, and visually it just blew me away. So when I started having a say in all this, I made something big and simple and they liked it, so it's evolved from there. Sometimes I'm given a completely free slate to design something; other times I'm told the stage and environment and told to design and direct around that.'

The members of KISS are very hands-on with all aspects of the show, including what Motley does. 'They video everything then watch it back, and after the second show of a tour there's usually a meeting with all band members, the pyro guy, the video director, production manager and band manager, and they go through what they'd like changed. On the first couple of tours I would get three pages of notes, but these days it's hardly anything. They pretty much leave me to it – but you can't get slack. If your quality starts dropping off, they'll get somebody else. I don't take any of it for granted.'

Even so, Motley seems pretty casual about what he does. He doesn't like being called KISS's Lighting Director, and would prefer to just be known as their lighting guy – 'but Americans love titles'.

Despite impressions to the contrary, Motley says it's not exactly a crazed, drugs-and-girls lifestyle with KISS. 'It's business. Those guys are businessmen. They work hard.' And Motley himself, having reached this level in his career, is keen to maintain it until he decides to leave the road. He concedes that his body will make that decision, and at 52 things are starting to hurt. But psychologically he knows how to play the game, how to do his work and not rock a boat that doesn't need rocking.

'The crucial thing is to always remember that they are the employer, you are the employee. That never changes. From my earliest days with Noiseworks on, I've always remembered that. You're there to do a job for them. You're not there to be their best friend. If for some reason you become friends with those guys, that's great, but you're fundamentally there to do a job and provide a service. Thinking you're part of the band is the biggest mistake you can make.

'You're allowed to have an opinion, but sometimes even if you think what the band wants is wrong, it's better to let them do it and then see it's wrong and suggest that you fix it the next day, rather than having an argument where you tell them they don't know what they're talking about. That's complete job suicide.

'And keep your ego out of it. It's very easy for roadies to sit back and criticise a band or management and the way they make decisions. But that's what they're employed to do. Let them make the decision and roll with it. If you jump up and down and make a big deal about it, you're the one who's going to get shot in the foot. I learnt that from the old guys.'

So, what's the key to being a successful road crew person? For Motley it's pretty simple. 'I worked hard, I worked a lot, I made my mistakes, I kept my mouth shut and learnt from the older guys. I was taught to learn from other people's mistakes, not just what they got right. I knew what I wanted, and worked to get there. With KISS, failure wasn't an option I entertained.'

27

The Heart and Soul

Jimmy Barnes doesn't hesitate when the name Eric Robinson is brought up. 'Eric was the heart and soul of Australian music over the past 30 years,' he says.

Robinson began in the music industry in 1970 with a small sound company working with the likes of Billy Thorpe and the Aztecs. Jands had been formed in 1968 by the talented and respected audio engineer Bruce Jackson and his partner, Philip Storey. When the two founders started quarrelling, they disbanded the company and sold it to Robinson and Paul and David Mulholland, who were operating a small lighting company called Jubilee Gaslight on Sydney's North Shore. Over the next 45 years, the Mulhollands and Robinson turned Jands into Australia's largest sound and lighting company.

As an industry figure once commented, you can draw a line through the Australian entertainment industry very easily: there's before Jands and after Jands. Put simply, Jands has for decades been the dominant concert production company in Australia. Robinson was its public face and a driving force behind its success.

More than 25 years ago, Robinson made a lasting gift to the road crew world. A Jands in-house training scheme taught, mentored and pushed out into the world legions of highly skilled, resourceful and talented crew. All had put up with life around Robinson; most would thank him more with hindsight than they did at the time.

As Robinson's best friend, concert promoter Michael Coppel, reflects, Robinson's career has parallels with that of the great but cantankerous jazz pioneer Miles Davis. 'What they said about Miles is that people who went into his band as sidemen left as band leaders – Wayne Shorter, Chick Corea, Joe Zawinul, Herbie Hancock, all those people. It was the same with Eric. So many people who went through Eric's employ, starting when they were 16-, 17-, 18-year-old roadies, went on to found successful businesses themselves, or be production managers and people who went and worked overseas and are in high demand and hugely respected.'

According to Coppel, Robinson concentrated on bringing people into the industry. 'He used to say to me, "All you promoters want to do is pay the least amount of money possible, and with no thought to what happens next year or the next decade or the decade after that." He said that unless we bring people into the industry, and train them and give them an apprenticeship and a career path, then when this generation of road crew disappears, what are we going to do?'

Robinson started an apprenticeship system in which young guys – and some girls – would work and learn. He'd insist on meeting their parents and getting a sense of whether they had the potential to succeed. Then he'd bring them into the company and train them. This wasn't subsidised by the government, as such training often is now, nor was it funded by his clients.

Robinson was closely associated with Cold Chisel for a very long time. In their poignant eulogy, read at his funeral after he succumbed to cancer in 2015, the band pointed out that he personally managed every detail of the production on their Ringside 360-Degree shows in 2003, the band's huge reformation show at Homebush Olympic Stadium in 2009, and the 2011 Light the Nitro tour.

'He was one of the smartest people I've ever known – in every way,' Jimmy Barnes says. 'He was a genius when it came to putting a show together. And he came from a crew background. He was just like a sponge. He took absolutely everything in and he learnt everything. When Chisel put shows together, we couldn't have done it without him. From the truck driver through to Don Walker, everyone asked him how to do the gig, how to put it together and make it work. He was incredible.'

Ask anyone who came into Robinson's orbit over the decades and they'll have a version of the same story. He was arrogant. He was rude. He was confrontational. He was in-your-face. He treated you like shit. But despite all that, it's hard to find someone who didn't ultimately love and respect this man, who became a father figure and guiding light for generations of Australian road crew.

'He *was* hard,' Barnes laughs. 'He could be vicious but he was fair. When I went to his funeral, everyone I spoke to said pretty much the same thing: they all said that despite his gruffness, he gave them their start. When no one else would give them work, he told them to smarten their ideas up and to come and work with him. Eric had a gruff exterior, but he really cared about every aspect of the crew and what was being done. He was as tough as nails but if you got your job done, he was the one who looked after you. I adored him. My whole family did.'

Robinson travelled with Cold Chisel on the Light the Nitro tour, and around the time of the Sydney shows he fell ill and was diagnosed with cancer. He battled the disease successfully for several years, but finally succumbed.

In their eulogy, the band said that Robinson's hands-on involvement with the show extended to their set list. He hated their song 'Letter to Alan', which mourns two roadie mates of the Chisels who died while working in 1980. 'Who's interested?' he'd say. 'It was never a hit, and no wonder!' With a respectful smile, Chisel entitled their eulogy 'Letter to Eric'.

The most successful of the post-Davies generation of Australian artist managers, John Watson, says that in his early days looking after Silverchair, he and other managers and artists of the time actively avoided working with Jands, and therefore with Robinson, in favour of Johnson Audio. 'They were the cool guys, and Jands were considered old-school,' he says. 'We didn't like their attitude. We wised up later. Eric had this whole thing going on where he was both incredibly rude and incredibly funny. A lot of people didn't get it, in which case they just thought he was incredibly rude. But if you got that it was meant to be acidly, darkly comic, it was particularly entertaining – particularly in high-stress situations. He managed to remove all stress with dark sarcasm.'

Despite their closeness, Michael Coppel was not immune to Robinson's in-your-face manner. 'People really would run the other way, they were so frightened of him. He had this trait when he first met you: he would test you to see what you were made of. He would confront you straightaway, and if you shied away or couldn't take the challenge, he would mark your card. That was his way of assessing what you were worth. If you could stand up and hold your own when he came at you full-on, you were okay. He wasn't really heavy or aggressive but he could pick people's weaknesses. He pushed a few buttons with everybody and saw how they responded.'

Coppel notes that Robinson was always on the front line when there was work to be done. 'There was nothing he asked his people to do that he wouldn't do himself. But his greatest strength was delegation, and I've never learnt that – even though he frequently counselled me on it.

'Eric could assess what needed to be done and then tell different people to do elements of it to produce the end result he was looking for, rather than, as a lot of us do, doing too many things yourself because it's quicker than explaining it to someone else. He was never like that. He would always have a sense of breaking tasks down and how to simplify things to get them done the best way.'

Robinson really was the pivotal figure in Australian crewing and production services for decades. It's impossible to talk about the Australian live music industry without mentioning him and Jands.

In many respects we are now in an after-Jands world. Not only is Robinson no longer with us, but after fighting so success-fully against the incursion of overseas production behemoths into this country, and being the first and only Australian company to secure a world tour contract with a major artist (Pink's global dates in 2013), Jands (now incorporating Johnson Audio) has been sold to Clair Brothers, so there is no longer an Australian-owned major audio or lighting company operating in this country.

Robinson's death attracted personal condolence notes from figures such as Sting and Elton John, something that never happens with production crew in a remote music market that most international artists only visit briefly every couple of years. Such was Robinson's reputation and impact.

At his funeral, attendees included Roger Davies, Paul Dainty, Michael Gudinski, Michael Coppel, Jimmy Barnes and many others, marking it as one of the few times outside of awards ceremonies where a myriad of industry figures were in a room together, amicably sharing a drink and reminiscing about their shared deep friendship with and respect for Robinson.

But it was not only the heavyweight industry figures who felt the loss of Robinson so keenly. The vast majority of the Australian road crew community had in some ways all been impacted upon by Robinson. He was one of a kind.

28

Boy from the Bush

Former roadie Bob Grosvenor was brought up being told he wasn't good enough, but his perception changed when he stood onstage in front of thousands of people. 'Well, here I am – good enough,' he told himself. He admits that sometimes he thought he was a bigger star than the people he was working with, but at other times he felt he didn't deserve to be there. 'Certainly there were big periods of self-doubt. I'd think to myself, "What am I doing working for Eric Clapton? I'm a boy from the bush." It was the closest I ever came to being in a band.'

Grosvenor worked on the road in Australia through the mid-1970s and into the '80s, before getting out at age 35, when the wear and tear of the lifestyle was becoming too much. He's been sober for 27 years now, and spends a lot of his time talking to recovering alcoholics and drug addicts.

Like so many Australian road crew, Grosvenor drifted into the work, swapping a more precarious life of misadventure for a louder, more rocking one. 'I came back from Indonesia, where I'd been up to no good. It was around the end of 1973, and I'd gotten mixed up with some desperados over there and

I'd been robbed, so I came back to Sydney, thank God. When I arrived back in Australia, I think the authorities must have known. I got the complete going over – bum search, the lot. All I had was a phone number on a business card.'

That phone number belonged to legendary roadie and tour manager Wayne 'Swampy' Jarvis. In the old days Grosvenor had hung out in Newcastle and helped Jarvis pack trucks, so they were passing acquaintances. 'I was about 17 or 18 when I met Swampy. Newcastle was wild in those days. It was also the pot centre of Australia. Up around there you'd pick it by the tea chest. It was a beautiful time. Swampy was working with the La De Das, so we'd just hang around and help him, be with the band, that sort of stuff.'

This was also when Grosvenor met another famous Australian roadie, Swampy's best pal, Mick Cox. 'Mick's claim to fame in those days was that he'd pierce your ear with a matchbox, a nail and some dry ice. Mick in those days was *the* coolest – and the toughest.'

Grosvenor wandered out of Sydney airport, pulled out that business card and rang Jarvis. After a quick hello, Grosvenor said that he needed some work. Jarvis asked if he still had a truck driver's licence. When Grosvenor said he did, Jarvis told him he had a job available that night, rolling up leads and transporting gear for Roberta Flack. Then came a tour with Fairport Convention, who were on their final visit to Australia with singer Sandy Denny, and a few years of fairly regular work with Jands.

Nothing had changed in roadie world. Have truck licence, will work.

Soon it was one tour after another. As Grosvenor reminisces, he mentions artists such as Dragon, Suzi Quatro, The Bay City Rollers, Gary Glitter, Frank Sinatra, Renée Geyer, David Bowie, Billy Joel, Jeff St John, John Mayall, Helen Reddy . . . the names blur into one long list of artists and tours. Four weeks here,

six weeks there, one concert, a string of shows – wherever the
gig was, Grosvenor was there.

As well as an array of star musicians, there were encounters with the who's who of the Australian roadie world. Early
on, Grosvenor did a six-week tour with $crooge Madigan. The
client? The Seekers. 'No wonder a man took drugs,' Grosvenor
laughs of this tour. '$crooge was into a guru's spiritual phase
and I was in my mandrax phase. Believe me, with The Seekers
you needed them. The same repertoire, night after night. Away
from the spotlight they were a decent lot. But $crooge used to
put these bloody Maharaj-ji tapes under my pillow because he
didn't want me to take drugs. It didn't work.'

Grosvenor smiles at the memory of another job he did:
building the stage and set-up for the American evangelist Billy
Graham when he toured Australia in 1979. 'There were 160
people building stages and scaffolds at Randwick Racecourse.
It was fucking hard work. Graham packed them in, but he still
needed roadies to build the stage and set everything up for
him. It was a mega-show. He came on and did his bit and the
crowd went mad. It was just like a rock show. They loved him.
He was talking good shit, I suppose – one of those American
things where it's all about saying that if you pay me money, I'll
get you closer to God.'

At one stage, Grosvenor and Jarvis went on a run of dates
with the English glam rock band The Sweet, which provided a
scenario for a classic piece of roadies' smoke-and-mirrors genius.

'The lead guitarist would cry and carry on every night
because he couldn't get his guitar in tune. In those days you
had to do it by hand – there were none of those tuning things.
I didn't know what to do because that wasn't my thing. Swampy
heard what was going on and grabbed the guitar and said he'd
sort it out. He walked around the back of the stage, had a
cigarette and came back and handed the guitar to the guy and
said, "Here you go." He hadn't touched it. We'd do the same

thing every night. Didn't touch the fucking thing once but the guy was happy, as he'd got to carry on and have someone else deal with his supposed problem.'

There were some good perks on offer when working with international acts. Grosvenor did one stint with Motown artists The Temptations, who were playing the cabaret circuit by that stage. 'It was all very choreographed: they'd walk down the stairs and onto the stage. My job was to be behind the stage making dry ice for a fog effect. I was clearly doing my job a little too well, because the next thing I remember hearing is this voice shouting, "No more fog, man!" I hadn't been paying attention. I looked up and you couldn't see the audience because of all this fog, and The Temptations couldn't see the steps to walk down to the stage.'

Grosvenor doesn't hesitate when asked what his main job on tours was: 'Supplying the drugs.' But even when he did crash and burn, he managed to find an upside. 'I got sober and was living with my grandmother. Swampy called me up and said I had to go back on the road. He said that I couldn't hide, so I went and did a lot of other shows. I mean, everyone knew me – all the promoters and agents knew me – because I used to sell them drugs.'

Of all the tours Grosvenor worked on, the worst was a 1975 visit by Eric Clapton. 'He wanted drugs and the drugs were procured for him,' Grosvenor recalls. 'But they were cut and he got really sick. Someone in the road crew got greedy and cut the dope. It was shit cocaine, even though heroin was his thing. It was the worst tour. He was spewing backstage and had to cancel a show halfway through. They said it was because of food poisoning. Patti Boyd was with him. Clapton also brought his sound guy with him, a little guy everyone called Womble and he looked like a fucking womble. They bought him a suit of armour and come show time they couldn't get him out of it and they had to call a locksmith.'

And why, one has to ask, did Womble get bought a suit of armour in the first place?

'Because he wanted one. Those were the days.'

The unhappy tour continued around the country. One show was at the Adelaide Oval. Grosvenor was working backstage and kept hearing one of Clapton's crew on the walkie-talkie, calling out, 'Need more! Need more! Need more!' But it wasn't more equipment he wanted, it was more coke. 'I had to go out and pour more on his console for him,' the roadie smiles.

Over the years Grosvenor also worked for Peter Rix Management, crewing for the likes of Marcia Hines and Jon English. But his days with the company came to an end after a particularly memorable drinking session, which began a descent that led to his decision to sober up.

With Jon English he'd worked two shows in Melbourne: one in the Port Phillip area and another at Bombay Rock, in Brunswick. Grosvenor had just been promoted to tour manager, and he and the band's keyboard player, who was musical director and had just received a pay rise, decided to celebrate with a bottle of Hennessy cognac – a bottle each. So come show time, Grosvenor was three sheets to the wind and then some, and he managed to fall through the drummer's kit.

The band continued on to Sydney, where they were to play a massive show on the steps of the Sydney Opera House. It was headlined by Thin Lizzy, along with Wha-Koo, The Sports and Jon English. 'It was a good show. Some mics broke down but I was able to fix them. I thought that everyone would forget about Melbourne but then Peter Rix said he wanted to see me, and he told me that I was a really good bloke but when I drank . . . he told me he had to let me go.

'But that's life on the road. Every day is Christmas and every night is New Year's Eve when you're young and in the business. There's no hangover, and if there is you have another line.'

So there was lots of hard work but also lots of drugs to get through the work and the endless long drives. For crews, it was mainly speed. Cocaine was too expensive and didn't last nearly as long. Eighty bucks for a double O cap of speed and you were going for days. And then there was whiskey to take the edge off the speed.

'You'd buy a bottle of whiskey and one of Coke. You'd pour half the Coke out and fill it with whiskey, and then off you'd go from Sydney to Melbourne in the truck. Throw in three or four lines and you're away. Then there's the longer drives, the ones where you could really go for it. You're travelling across the Nullarbor, and the first guy who spots a kangaroo has to roll a joint. Have you any idea how many kangaroos you see on the Nullarbor?'

According to Grosvenor, there was a lot of in-fighting among crew working at Jands, with everyone wanting to get on the best tours, but in the end the management would always decide who was doing what. The undisputed boss at Jands was co-owner Eric Robinson, whose tough exterior was matched by his demeanour and his tongue.

'Eric was a prick, but he was so good to me, mate. I was mixed up on smack and things when I went there, and Eric and Peter Rooney gave me work, and lots of it. Everyone wanted a piece of Eric because he was successful. And he was well educated. He knew what was what. He could have fired me – and he probably should have – but he used to say, "Bobby, I like what you do." In those days Eric was sitting next to us, driving the truck. I've driven nonstop from Sydney to Adelaide with Eric driving the truck and smoking pot. Eric was a fiend where pot was concerned.'

Looking after the acts was the most important thing at Jands, so they picked the best people to do each tour. Grosvenor laughs that this meant someone else got Rod Stewart and he ended up with Percy Faith. 'But whatever the tour it was, we all had pride in what we did. That's what we had. The stage had to be just right. You were working with the best and you wanted to give them the best.'

Grosvenor calls gaffer tape 'the roadies' saviour'. 'You can make everything *really* neat,' he says. 'I could tell a stage that Swampy had done because it was so neat. And it had other uses. I had to gaffer-tape a drummer to his seat and the stage once so he wouldn't fall off as he drank so much.'

'They say crew are invisible if they're doing a good job, but the band knows. We wanted to go to work, we wanted to do a good job – we wanted to show everyone, including the crew from other bands, that you knew what you were doing. You wanted to be able to show the crew from another band – like Skyhooks, for instance – that you were doing a good job and that you knew what you were doing. You can bet they were checking.'

While he is saddened by the huge number of road crew who have committed suicide, Grosvenor isn't too surprised. 'I think the work attracts that sort of person. When you're really busy and in the middle of it all, you're focused on the work you're doing and you don't have to deal with what's inside. And lots of drinking and drugs after the show masks all that too. A lot of crew guys keep going – and going – to avoid dealing with all the emotional stuff.

'And the job does strange things to some people. There were a lot of shy guys on crews who seemed overnight to turn into fucking monsters. You could work with them setting up stages, but any spare time you had, you wouldn't spend around them. The road fucks people up – but also a lot of fucked-up people come to this job. It's like running away to join the circus.

'We thought we were invincible, too. To walk backstage at those really big gigs and know you belonged there – sure, you felt something special. We were proud of what we did.'

29

The Yogi, Bear, Pineapple and Ray Show

Put four of Australia's best known and most revered road crew members together in one room and what do you get? You get a whole host of stories about some of the most legendary and infamous Australian bands and international visitors. You get tall tales, anecdotes of crazed behaviour, hard work, on-the-road shenanigans. And a lot more.

Grahame 'Yogi' Harrison, Gregory 'Bear' Horrocks, Steve 'Pineapple' Alberts and Ray (just Ray) Maguire are close friends. They all live within driving distance of each other in the Gold Coast and Coffs Harbour area and often socialise together. Their shared experience of the world of the road and rock'n'roll bands has forged a lifelong bond.

Many road crew figures didn't make it through, while some who did haven't fared too well. Roadies not only tend to look after their comrades, but also nurture the bond of the road. They hang out together, recall – and often embellish – the stories, and keep each other close. My day with these larger-than-life characters is spent at Bear's home on the Gold Coast, where Yogi is visiting. They do this a lot. They've been close since the late 1970s.

Bear entered the rock'n'roll world as a 17-year-old, helping out local bands who played at the Hornsby Police Boys' Club in Sydney. There was no money, and he didn't even think of himself as a roadie. The same went for Yogi, who began by helping the band Maple Lace when they played a gig at the Little Bay Psychiatric Centre in Malabar. That's a long story.

How did Yogi get his nickname? One night at the Whiskey a Go Go in Sydney, another roadie looked at the bag he was carrying, knowing it contained 'goodies' (aka marijuana). 'Hey, Yogi, get the goodies out of your bag and roll me a big fuckin' joint,' he called out. From then onwards, Grahame was Yogi.

Horrocks became Bear one day after a game of touch football in Lane Cove National Park. The group included a few tennis players (Horrocks himself was one) and some real footballers. 'One of the footballers got really rough, so I tackled him into the water. It was the then North Sydney and later Parramatta prop forward Bob "The Bear" O'Reilly, so all the guys started calling me Bear and it stuck.'

Bear worked with a variety of bands, earning a reputation for being 'reasonably strong and not an idiot'. He'd do stints with Geeza, Ol' 55, Skyhooks, Sherbet, Moving Pictures and many others. But despite this diverse experience, it's Rose Tattoo that Bear's name is synonymous with.

'I was there from the beginning – before the Tatts were the Tatts. I was at Ian Rilen's house in Paddington when they brought Angry up from Melbourne. Initially Mick Cocks drove him up before joining himself.' In those early days of Rose Tattoo, the crew was usually three: Pig, Panther and Bear. 'There were a number of different animal groups involved. We burnt through crew fairly often.' Bear was the only crew member on a retainer, though.

He and Yogi were never without work. In fact, Bear claims that Yogi kept a calendar of Bear's movements with the various bands he was working with. 'That was to keep track of your women,' Yogi laughs. '"Sorry, Bear's not here at the moment"!'

For his part, Yogi moved from Maple Lace to a band called Head, which mutated into Buffalo, a group he worked with for about four years. Then there was Sherbet, followed by Hush, then it was back to Buffalo. After that he worked for a PA hire company and did some crewing for AC/DC, before finding out – via a production company he worked for – that he was scheduled to head to England with The Saints in April 1977. Circumstances eventually dragged Yogi back to Australia and he moved on to working with The Radiators, then reconnected with Rose Tattoo.

Bear and Yogi shared a place in Bondi in the late 1970s. Yogi was also working for Dragon during what he calls 'the bucket years'. 'We always had a bucket onstage for Marc Hunter to throw up into between songs. And we would set up a mattress behind Paul Hewson's keyboard, so when he nodded off during the show he wouldn't hurt himself when he fell on the floor.'

Yogi too had done a stint with Sherbet, and – like all roadies – knows the real story about just about everything that's happened in the rock'n'roll world. Although he wasn't on the tour when one of Sherbet's roadies was killed, he knows what went down.

'The band went to Tasmania and were told not to take any dope with them, but Tony Mitchell took a Buddha stick,' Yogi relates. 'The cops raided the hotel and the drummer, Allan Sandow, jumped through a window and into the crew's room, and told them to get out of town really quickly because the cops were raiding the motel. One of them – Jeff Evans, a 19-year-old lighting guy – was given some speed, which he'd never had before. They drove away, came over a hill and hit a flock of sheep. He was killed and the other roadie with him broke his back and never worked again.'

Yogi also has the insider knowledge about the deaths of Alan Dillow and Billy Rowe, the long-standing Cold Chisel roadies, while they were working for Swanee. He then switches from the sombre to the scurrilous and tells a story about a bisexual band manager who 'got his band signed to a major label because he fucked the head of the company. We're not supposed to know this – we're roadies'. Roadies who are happy to share this info if they trust you.

With the air of a man experienced in the lessons of karma, he tells of the time a band manager forced him to drive a crew car from Cairns to Shepparton – 3000 kilometres – just to save a $400 drop-off fee. But the universe had other plans. One town before Shepparton, Yogi had an accident and spent a night in hospital. He takes some pleasure in knowing that the excess bill for the car would have been a lot more than four hundred bucks.

There was a road trip from Melbourne to Perth with a brick on the accelerator, a bag of dope, a bottle of scotch and a few grams of speed. As soon as they reached Perth they went straight to work.

Bear chimes in: 'It was the booking agents who put those tours together, and then the managers just agreed to it. When I worked with TMG it was crazy touring. At least 400 kilometres every day, a 92-date tour around the country, with eight days off on the whole thing.

'With Rose Tattoo we were constantly driving between Sydney, Brisbane, Melbourne and Adelaide, then back to Melbourne and up to Sydney – all of that every two weeks. The band were driving as well, but they had those extra couple of hours of sleep that we needed to load in and set up, and then load out. They could go to a hotel and shower and change. It wasn't very often that we got to shower and change – sometimes not for three days.'

It was band after band after band. Following his stint with Rose Tattoo, Bear was poached to work for Moving Pictures. Yogi went to Sunnyboys and The Johnnys. It was around this time, in 1986, that Yogi decided he'd had enough of the road. He was offered a job at Turramurra Music in Sydney, and stayed there till 2001, then moved to Coffs Harbour in 2005.

'I'd well and truly run out of bands I wanted to work with by the mid-1980s. I'm 67 now, but people still ask why I'm not out mixing bands, and I say, "Do you know anyone who wants to be mixed by their grandfather?"'

Does Yogi miss the road?

'Do I miss cunts making you drive from Cairns to Perth? No, I haven't reached that point yet.'

Bear moved to the Gold Coast to work at various venues and small companies, before starting his own production installation company. Then he joined Entertainment Lighting, which later merged with another company to become Entertainment Sound and Lighting. Bear worked there for 26 years before he retired.

In walks Steve 'Pineapple' Alberts, who at 55 comes from the generation of crew after Bear and Yogi. He is clearly still in awe of his friends and what they accomplished. 'You guys wrote the book. You toured the world and worked with some of the best bands. Look at the success of guys from your era. That's because we had and still have a great work ethic in Australia. Crews here aren't any more talented than crews anywhere else – we just have a greater work ethic.'

Pineapple came into crewing towards the end of the reign of the likes of Bear and Yogi. And he learnt a huge amount from them. 'A lot of those guys took me under their wing – partly because I could score good drugs easily,' he laughs.

'And you were likeable,' Yogi chips in. 'We had to have one crew guy who was likeable.'

As a teenager, Pineapple had been a cadet journalist with the *Australian Jewish News* in Melbourne, but also wrote reviews for the magazines *RAM* and *Juke*. After he gave a positive review to a band called AEIOU, they asked him to be their manager. He was 18 and knew nothing about how the music industry actually worked.

'Then one day our lighting guy got thrown through a plate-glass window before a gig where we were supporting Uncanny X-Men, and the band said I had to do lights. That's seriously how I got into it. At the end of the night I had to pay myself $25 for loading in and out and doing lights.'

Lights became Pineapple's calling card, and he honed his skills by working with Goanna and Little River Band. 'LRB were the first band to pay me $300 a week. I thought I'd made it. This was 1985.'

Pineapple then started working for Jands in Melbourne, before relocating to Sydney. There he worked for and alongside some of the greats of the lighting world. 'I loved the brotherhood of roadies. The music wasn't a big thing for me, but the brotherhood and lifestyle was. It didn't matter what you looked like or what you did, so long as you didn't steal and you did your gig. They were the two big things.'

According to Pineapple, lighting wasn't all that hard in those days, and audio guys had it much harder. 'As a lighting guy, it wasn't hard to do your job off your chops. I was very successful at it for a long time. Took it to a new level, actually. I was living in a fantasy world working with all the guys I did. Today I'm called a technician, but I don't have any certificates or formal training like all the guys working in the industry now. The younger ones have read the manuals. What's a manual? It's what you roll a joint on or do a line off the cover.'

To diversify, and give himself a rest from the constant grind of crew work, Pineapple started a crewing service that operated from 1991 to just before 2000. He also worked in corporate events, doing up to 250 of them a year. 'Rock'n'roll got its break from me and I got a break from it.'

Six years ago the lifestyle caught up with him and Pineapple got clean and sober. Having become a Buddhist, he got a gig as a technical director for the Dalai Lama, as well as running a charity called the Big Umbrella with a friend in Melbourne. The Big Umbrella rescues kids off the streets of Nepal who are victims of child slavery and trafficking. They have rescued 34 kids, feeding and clothing them, and putting them through school.

But Pineapple still works on big tours from time to time. At the time of this get-together, he had just finished stints with Paul McCartney and Cat Stevens.

Pineapple is extolling the values of McCartney's show when Ray Maguire strolls in. At 70, he's a touch older than Bear and Yogi, but is still active in the industry, doing a variety of gigs. He has business interests in Austin, Texas, and does corporate events and entertainment at sporting events.

While his three comrades had relatively straightforward introductions to road crew work, Maguire's experience was the opposite. For starters, he was studying to be a priest. Yes, you read that right. Maguire was in his third year of a Bachelor of Theology degree at the Methodist Training College and Bible School in Kangaroo Point, Brisbane, when he took his first steps into the world of entertainment and road crewing.

In between, he worked at Wesley Hospital, getting £3 a week to dispose of hospital waste. 'You pushed a trolley from one end of the hospital to the other, collecting food scraps, kidneys, hearts – whatever was around – and took them to be burnt in the furnace.'

Maguire frequented the Red Orb club in Brisbane. One night, this would-be priest cum hospital waste collector was dancing away when a guy came up to him. He was a friend of Bert Potts, an American gangster who had come to Australia with a boxing match and stayed. Potts's man opened his jacket so that Maguire could see his gun inside, and told him to come outside.

'He told me they were going to make me a go-go dancer and pay me £15 a week. I didn't know what a go-go dancer was, but for £15 a week I was in. Within seven weeks I was the best catcher of beer jugs in Australia. I'd be dancing in a club, someone would call me a poofter, I'd throw him a kiss, he'd throw a jug of beer at me and I'd catch it without spilling a drop.'

Improbable as the last bit of that story is, it's certainly how Maguire entered the rock'n'roll world. As for the roadie bit . . . well, that began soon enough.

Go-go dancers weren't popular with every artist, which was the impetus for Maguire to expand his activities. 'Max Merritt wouldn't have go-go dancers onstage, so a guy called Ivan Dammon asked if I could drive a truck. I could, so I started doing that. Then I went to Melbourne and auditioned for the play *Oh! Calcutta!* and I got one of the lead roles. But on the first night I was arrested because the play had nudity in it.'

Maguire continued driving trucks for bands and putting up posters, did some work for Daddy Cool and then ended up working with Sherbet on a tour where, as he says, he and Howard Freeman 'probably broke every rule in the book – daily'.

'Howard used to go into a bar and hang out with all the locals and the truckies. Then I'd walk in a little later in a white suit we'd bought at an op shop, with a hat on, and I'd order a Pimms. Howard would wind up the truckies, saying, "I think we should teach this poof a lesson – let's kill him," and then I'd pull out a fake gun and say, "If there's any killing to be done, I'm doing it," and then I'd walk out. Later, Howard and I would meet up and have a laugh about it. It all went wrong in Broken Hill one night when the barman pulled a sawn-off shotgun from behind the bar and put it to my head.'

Plenty about being on the road is really about coping with boredom. Bear weighs in with yarns about rewiring the air conditioner in a hotel room so it would explode when the next guest turned it on. Yogi recalls that when the crew weren't treated well at a hotel, they might unscrew a light fitting, place prawns around the rim of the lights, screwing it back up and leave. Apparently this was most effective in summer.

But Maguire seems to have been the king of the on-the-road pranks. 'It was sometime in the '70s when cattle were cheaper to shoot than slaughter, and I went to an auction in a town and bought 150 head of heifers. Cost me about $240 for the lot, including delivery. I told the guy to deliver them to this motel that had pissed us off, and to herd them in front and make sure the gates were closed as I'd pick them up later. Somewhere else I bought 500 chickens. We used to fill hotel rooms full of chickens. Why? Because we could.'

Pineapple is laughing hard now. 'Goats were good, too. They'd just eat anything.'

And of course there are gun stories – lots of gun stories. Maguire recalls seeing a sign in Queensland that informed the public that due to a recent change in the law, you could only buy 3000 rounds of ammunition at any one time. 'On a Sherbet tour, Garth Porter and one of the other guys used to build remote-controlled airplanes, and the rest of the band and crew had M16s, and we would shoot the shit out of them as they flew around.'

Then Maguire has the room in stitches as he recalls – for probably the hundredth time – the story of the night in Mount Isa when Tony Mitchell from Sherbet decided he wanted a toasted cheese sandwich at 2 am in a motel that most definitely did not have room service at that time of the night.

'Tony rang the manager's phone and woke him up. The guy told Tony in no uncertain terms that there was no room service and to go back to sleep. Although I'm pretty sure he hadn't been to sleep. Tony could see the manager's residence from his room, so he started shooting arrows through his window at the manager's quarters while Howard and I tried to calm him down. That was the night Tony turned the bow and arrows on Howard.'

Pineapple weighs in with a yarn about the time he was working with former Easybeats singer Stevie Wright. 'We were staying at the Cosmopolitan in Bondi, and Ray Arnold was in charge of stopping Stevie getting out of his room and going to score smack. I'm in my room and I see these sheets hanging down past my window. Then I see Stevie climbing down the sheets. He sees me looking, stops and tries to wave. Twelve feet from the ground he runs out of sheeting. Ray Arnold's down below, going, "Jump, you little cunt, I dare you!"'

This is roadies at their best, trying to outdo each other with yarns of life on the road.

Maguire ups the ante with a tale from a Sherbet tour. 'I only ever got to drive the Sherbet truck when it was broken down. One day I'd been working on the thing, and I walked into a restaurant where Sherbet and Howard Freeman and Roger Davies were eating. My clothes were covered in grease and the maître d' told me I wasn't suitably dressed, and would I mind leaving. So I go outside this glass window and see a frog. I put it arse-first in my mouth. I just thought it was a big frog with warts, but it was a cane toad. I've walked back into the restaurant and put my head over Harvey James's shoulder – he was eating a bowl of French onion soup. Anyway, the toad jumped out of my mouth, into the soup, and then bounced around the restaurant. Real Keystone Cops stuff. Eventually I get the frog by its back legs, and I went, "Fuck it," and bit its head. God knows what I was thinking. Howard had to hold me down while they got an ambulance. I thought I could fly. I ended up spending two nights in hospital.'

By now Maguire is in full flight. He's straight into a story about touring with Debbie Harry of Blondie, whom he still considers a friend. 'Billy Miller from The Ferrets was the support. On the bus to a gig he drank a whole bottle of riesling and then pissed in the bottle. He looked at me and said, "I hear you're a smart cunt – make this disappear," so I drank it. From that moment on, he did whatever I said.'

After the first Blondie tour, Debbie Harry and the band asked Maguire to continue on with them to Japan and then to America. To this day, he continues to work with Harry from time to time. Part of the reason they bonded might be because Maguire saved the singer after an incident at the Park Royal Hotel in Brisbane.

'There was a riot in the venue when it was announced that she wouldn't be appearing,' he remembers. 'I convinced the Queensland coppers not to go and check on the room. I said she'd OD'd on cherries, as they didn't have as much fresh fruit in NYC. I told them she'd played in Lismore the night before and eaten too much fruit.'

Next, Maguire is telling the room that the legendary drummer and wild man Keith Moon made him an honorary member of the Keith Moon Appreciation Society after people introduced them and told Moon about some of Maguire's antics. 'I did a lot of stuff with bands who just liked having me around. I learnt early in life to entertain the entertainer.'

After eight hours of yarns and reminiscences from the Four Musketeers, I have to leave and catch a plane back to Sydney. Of course they drive me to the airport. If you get on with roadies, they'll never let you take a taxi. That's not what they do.

They still make road crew, but they don't make them like Yogi, Bear, Pineapple and Ray Maguire anymore.

30

The Real *RocKwiz* Roadie

Dugald McAndrew is a roadie by day and by night – and a roadie on your television screens if you're a regular watcher of SBS's long-running rock'n'roll quiz show *RocKwiz*.

Ask McAndrew how he ended up as one of Australia's best known and most respected road crew, production and stage management figures, and he really can't tell you much beyond the fact that he was drawn to it. And for reasons he can't really explain, after more than three and a half decades he's still doing it.

'I just really wanted to do it. In my first year out of school on the Sunshine Coast I worked on a family friend's farm, and one day we went up to Noosa to see one of a series of outdoor concerts at the footy oval. I saw all these guys working, and fuck knows why but I thought, "This is what I want to do." For some reason the whole idea of what they were doing resonated with me and I was attracted to it. That was more than borderline weird, I guess.

'I have no idea what the attraction was, because I really had no idea of what they actually did. It was not a job that had visibility to anyone outside of those that already worked in the industry. But I looked at it and thought, "I think that's for me" – and here we are.'

McAndrew's initial gigs as a roadie were in the early 1980s. The very first was Sacred Cowboys at the Grainstore Tavern in King Street, Melbourne. 'I used to volunteer at radio station 3CR, where their manager, Michael Lynch, had a show, and Terry Doolan, the guitarist, was music programmer. On the Friday I must have said, "Do you guys need a hand?" and at 2 pm the next day I found myself humping gear up four flights of rickety fire escape stairs at the rear of the building for the princely sum of $20.'

After his stint with the edgy and intense Sacred Cowboys, McAndrew became absorbed into the mainstream rock'n'roll community, working with Stephen Cummings and then the Sweet Conspiracy managerial company roster that included Redgum, the Eurogliders and Wa Wa Nee. From there the gigs just rolled on, seemingly endlessly. Later there were periods with Paul Kelly and The Messengers and Hunters & Collectors.

Even in the 1980s there was still no formal training for road crew; you learnt on the job. But McAndrew did study, buying books on electronics and guitar repair and how to set up and maintain instruments. And there were life lessons along the way, some of them brutal but important.

'I was on a Eurogliders tour, and it was long and gruelling. I was having a bitch and one of the senior members of the crew turned around and said, "If you don't like it, then fuck off." It was Colin Skulls, and that was probably the best bit of advice I've ever been given.

'Then there was Charlie Zarb – Mondo Rock's guitar tech – who scared the bejesus out of me. I did some gigs with Stephen Cummings when he was opening for Mondos, and Charlie had me doing everything except restringing guitars. I lived in fear.

He turned out to be one of the gentlest of gentle guys, but back
in the day . . .'

McAndrew moved to work in film for a few years – including
on Richard Lowenstein's *Dogs in Space* – before coming back
to rock'n'roll road crew work through a lengthy period with
Hunters & Collectors. The PA set-up the band used kept
McAndrew very busy. 'The advantage was that the truck was
owned by the band and the PA by John Archer, the bass player,
so a lot of mid-size club promoters would book the Hunters
production because it was a one-stop shop: you got the truck,
the PA and the crew with one phone call. When the Hunters
weren't playing, the PA and crew hire was their other income
stream. We did dozens and dozens of indie club acts.'

Around 1993 McAndrew started working with Crowded
House, a job that would last for the next six or seven years,
but he opted not to tour with them in the early 2000s as he
was studying industrial design at university and only wanted
to do weekend crew work. But the relationship with Crowded
House continued, and McAndrew worked on the four shows
they did at the Sydney Opera House in 2017.

'I remember having my final interview to see if I'd be accepted
into postgrad studies at a different university to where I'd done
my undergraduate degree while I was on tour,' McAndrew
laughs. 'I was on a conference call to the faculty in Melbourne
from the stage at the Metro in Sydney during soundcheck. I'd
told everyone that the call was coming through, so I think I
interrupted soundcheck in order to have the conversation. And
the Metro had pretty bad phone reception. But I got in.'

Not long afterwards McAndrew got into the world of television. At the time he had no idea that he'd end up spending over
fifteen years 'playing' a roadie on the TV show *RocKwiz*. 'For
many years I played a social game of footy on a Sunday and
Wednesday down at St Kilda with a team called the Bangers,
made up of a bunch of ratbags, and Brian Nankervis was one

of those people. He was shooting a pilot for a TV series and he needed a roadie – or roadies, at that stage – so me and David Mayer rocked up for the first pilot, which was filmed at Chapel on Chapel. Then there were auditions a couple of weeks later, and 15 years later here I am. It's been a pretty sizeable part of my life.

'Brian had a loose idea that he wanted some roadies running around, and that became absorbed into the show. In the actual show I play a roadie but I also do the technical stuff. I'm the band technical guy so I set up the band's gear and the guests' gear and look after all the technical requirements for both. So I'm playing at being a roadie and also being an actual roadie. On *RocKwiz* tours I'm production manager and work as a technical roadie, and then go and play a roadie during the show, so it's double-dipping.'

These days, when not doing *RocKwiz*, most of McAndrew's work has been as a stage manager, usually at festivals and other large events. But there are very few Australian bands who can afford or need a standalone stage manager for their shows. 'I spent fifteen years on the Big Day Out, and I've done Soundwave and Falls Festivals and lots of others.'

McAndrew stage-managed the last couple of Cold Chisel tours, and also the Australian leg of the 2017 Midnight Oil tour.

'The role of a stage manager is difficult to define,' McAndrew admits. 'The production manager does the big blocks and builds them, and then my job is to run the day of the show and devote what resources I have to the various departments at the right times. With Midnight Oil, for instance, their production manager, Alex, looked after the big-picture stuff and then I go and run the day for him. I understand what he wants and how he wants the day to run, and my job effectively is to represent him and to be the go-to person on the day.'

When I remark to McAndrew that at the big concerts I've observed there's an almost Zen-like calmness around the stage and site in the hour or two before the concert starts, the veteran of hundreds of such events is not surprised. 'There should be calm. There are pretty tried and true methods as to how a show comes together. But every show is different. On Midnight Oil there's four or five trucks of gear; on the Big Day Out it was thirty or more.

'There's a big difference between working for one act and working for an event. On the big festivals the goal is to try and give every band the opportunity to present themselves in the best possible way – to give them the resources to be able to put on the best possible show. In those instances there is zero Zen. No Zen. There is no Zen to be found. It's craziness from the creak of the first truck door opening to the last one shutting. These are big, busy days.'

As an outsider, I'd observed McAndrew and the rest of the crew unpacking massive semitrailers before the Midnight Oil shows at the Domain in Sydney. Perhaps I'm naive, but I was staggered at the fact that at least one person knew exactly where – and in what order – everything fitted together in these trucks. For McAndrew, it's nothing special at all. It's what he and others do.

'The method to the madness is in the packing and unpacking of them. If you break a show down into small compartments, all those compartments have to work cooperatively to put a show on. Trucks are the same. It only works if you break it down bit by bit. Midnight Oil's shows are fairly simple – there's no stage set, no pyrotechnics, no dancing girls, no costume changes. So it's pretty straightforward.'

McAndrew has managed to navigate his way through the world of sex, drugs and PAs for all these years and emerge as a seemingly well-adjusted, healthy individual. 'I have a really grounded, happy family life. I'm married with two fantastic daughters – one's not at home anymore, and there's a 14-year-old.

We have all the same aspirations as any other middle-class family. I just happen to be involved in a fairly odd job.

'It is an industry that casts aside some of its less fortunate folk pretty easily, and it can be brutal in that respect. Maybe my circumstances are atypical but they're becoming more the norm. I think most road crews these days are not drawn from the pool they were in the past. It's a changed scene with contemporary crew. If you are even thought to be drinking at work or stoned, for instance, you'll probably be replaced. You just can't get away with that anymore. People expect 100 per cent professionalism. That stuff might have been seen as a lifestyle choice once upon a time, but not now.

'It's partially because of issues of heath and safety, but the expectations have changed. The shows have a far greater technical element, and you need to be a little more on your game. Technology is changing rapidly and you need to keep abreast of all of that. People of my generation are digital immigrants. We've had to absorb technology, as opposed to our children, who are digital natives, and it will always be part of their experience. They're totally intuitive with technology, whereas we're not.'

McAndrew started out as a music fan and still is. However, he's not a crew guy who can't stand working with artists whose music he doesn't like. 'These days it's not so much about the band. If you've got a good bunch of crew around you, the product is almost secondary. Crew get to close ranks pretty quickly, so if a tour is well organised and going well it doesn't really matter who the band is – just so long as you have good people around you. And people who have each other's backs. When you work in that environment, you can make the best of even a poor situation.'

For McAndrew, one of the keys to longevity is not to dwell on things that haven't gone well. 'Sentimentality is not the crew's best friend. You need to be able to brush off whatever happened last week and move on to the next job.'

And not become too close to and familiar with the artists you're working with?

'I don't think that ever ends well. Bands are going to move on, and whether they take you with them or not is another matter. You're there to provide a service. That's not to suggest that you can't be friendly or have moments when you're social- ising, but I don't get too involved. A friend of mine worked with Silverchair from the first day to the last. That's pretty unusual, to have such a long association with a band, but he said that he never socialised with them – even in Newcastle when he was sorting out gear and Daniel invited him around for dinner, he just said no. Kept it completely business-like the whole way through.'

McAndrew is keenly aware of the toll taken on road crew over the years, and has lost many people he knew well and worked with. 'Their world can get pretty small. No one in this caper ever had an exit strategy. No one thought ahead to what they'd be doing in 20 years' time, unless they moved into sales or corporate, a more passive role in the industry. If you've got issues to bury, this is the industry to keep them buried in. This lifestyle will only exacerbate them. It's not therapy.'

31

Let's Delay Soundcheck

It wasn't his intention at the time, but Mike Emerson's decision to give his crew an extra hour's sleep before a load-in at Newcastle Workers Club before a gig in late December 1989 saved many, many lives. He couldn't have known it, but the city was about to be struck by a massive earthquake. His call to put back the load-in that day came from years and years of experience on the road – in New Zealand, Australia and further afield. He'd done the hard yards, and had a mindset of looking after his fellow road crew.

Emerson grew up in New Zealand as a music fan – a serious music fan. At 17 he took a week off school and travelled via train and ferry from his home in Dunedin up to Auckland to see a concert by Jethro Tull on their Thick as a Brick tour. The round trip took him almost the entire week. He still describes it as the second-best concert he's ever seen. Before you ask, his number one gig was by Yes at the LA Forum in 1978.

Soon after seeing Tull, Emerson started hanging around a band from Dunedin called Mother Goose. They're the bunch who had a really big hit with that annoying 'Baked Beans' song. After taking the typical road crew beginner's path of wrapping up cords, loading gear and so forth, Emerson became Mother Goose's sound guy. He saw it as a potential ticket out of his home town. 'I would have done anything to get out of Dunedin,' he laughs. So in October 1976 Emerson accompanied the band to Australia, where they spent a lot of time touring, initially in the Gold Coast and Brisbane area.

After achieving significant success in Australia, Mother Goose moved to Los Angeles in June 1978 to pursue opportunities with US managers and record labels. Emerson was with them. 'We went to LA and lived there for ten months on the smell of an oily rag, waiting for a record deal that never really happened. When we first arrived in LA, two of us bought a hamburger and shared it. Things were that tight. There were fifteen of us – the band, me, wives, girlfriends – all living in a big house in the Hollywood Hills. After five months there, the band had played one showcase gig, so I started to look for other work.'

The Mother Goose entourage eventually drove across America to New York, and things looked more promising for a while. They were playing a lot more but still all lived together, this time in a house in New Jersey. The exception was Emerson, who, by this time in his early 20s, met a girl who took him into her apartment in New York's East Village. 'After every gig the band would be heading back to New Jersey, but I just had to go to the Village with this girl. I remember – this is true – she had a parrot that used to say, "Let's hear it for Jackson Browne."'

Mother Goose was constantly courted in New York, creating situations that frequently blew the mind of a young sound guy from Dunedin. 'KISS's management came to a show. They took the band and I out in this Cadillac stretch limo. There was a black dude driving, flutes of champagne – glass ones – on a table, lines of coke and we were driving through Central Park at 4 am. Nothing ever happened but that was pretty cool.'

Eventually Mother Goose came back to Australia, and Emerson parted company with the band. He began working with Russell Morris, while also honing his audio engineering skills. He worked crazily long hours with Morris and others for little remuneration. And there was lots and lots of driving the highways of Australia. 'I reckon I drove more in five years as a crew guy than most Australians drive in a lifetime.'

Along the way, Emerson got up to the sort of escapades that are typical of Australian road crew. On one trip to Perth, Emerson and another crew guy pulled the truck he was driving into the Nullarbor Station Roadhouse to get fuel. At the same time, a Chrysler Valiant going in the opposite direction arrived to do the same, and six guys piled out. It was a band heading to Melbourne. 'They asked if we had any pot. Having just come from Adelaide, we did, and they offered to trade us the LSD that they had. I drove the next 30 hours tripping.'

Emerson also did some stints as a monitor guy, controlling the sound the musicians hear. 'What's the difference between a monitor guy and a toilet seat?' he jokes. 'A toilet seat only has to deal with one arsehole at a time.'

After that, Emerson headed to the United Kingdom on a backpacking holiday, but quickly found work. He honed his already impressive sound-mixing skills on tours and gigs with artists such as Graham Parker & The Rumour, The Ramones, Mike Oldfield, Magazine and Ultravox.

Back in Australia in the early to mid-1980s, Emerson worked as a sound engineer with Mondo Rock and Goanna, also adding road manager and production manager to his skill set. Who did he work with? Try U2, ZZ Top, Sting, Bob Dylan, Elton John, Stevie Nicks, Neil Young, INXS, Eurythmics. The list goes on and on – and on. Emerson was one highly skilled guy, much in demand.

Which brings us to the very end of the 1980s, when Crowded House was preparing to perform its End of the Decade concert in Darling Harbour, Sydney. Also appearing, and in fact head-lining, was that other legendary New Zealand band, Split Enz, which re-formed specially for the occasion, five years after breaking up. The two bands shared numerous personnel and crew, notably Neil Finn and Paul Hester. They decided to do a mini-tour of four shows, which would get the bands warmed up for the New Year's Eve gig. They were supported on this tour by Boom Crash Opera.

On 27 December, the three bands – with a full-sized coach for the crew, a semitrailer and an eight-tonne truck – set off for Mudgee. Emerson had previously been production manager on a couple of Crowded House Australian tours, and was appointed in that role again for these dates. The Mudgee gig, he recalls, was a total blur, but he recalls the next period of time in minute detail.

'Trying to fit three acts of that size into a pub was always going to be excruciating, to say the least. We also discovered that this was a later gig than previously advised. Stage manager Peter McFee told us it would be at least 3 am before we would finish the load-out.'

Alarm bells went off in Emerson's head. The next day they'd be doing the Newcastle Workers Club, with 36 stairs to climb for the load-in, which was booked for a 10 am start. He called together the bus and truck drivers and they examined the map. It was at least a five-hour drive from Mudgee to Newcastle. They wouldn't get to their hotel in Newcastle until 8 am. By the time they got to bed, they'd be lucky to get an hour of sleep. With the crew facing a huge day of work, Emerson made an executive decision. 'I rang Newcastle and changed the load-in time from 10 am to 11 am. Two hours' sleep is better than one.' When they made it to Newcastle and finally hit the sack, it was twenty past eight in the morning.

'For some reason that I'll never know,' Emerson continues, 'I set my alarm for exactly 10:27 am. Just time for a quick shower and to walk a few hundred metres to the Workers Club, ready for the 11 am load-in. Or so I thought. At 10:27 am my alarm went off. I rolled out of bed and tried to stand up, only to find my legs buckling underneath me. I knew I was groggy from lack of sleep, but this was ridiculous. The whole room was swaying. I pulled back the curtain and saw a plume of smoke in the distance. Was it an explosion? No, an earthquake!

'Moments later, Jock Bain was running down the corridor, banging on the doors and yelling, "It's an earthquake – you have to evacuate, *now*!" I quickly pulled on a dirty T-shirt and jeans and ran down the fire stairs to the entrance. No shower today. The hotel staff ushered us outside onto the footpath. We would not be allowed back inside to get our bags in case the building collapsed.'

There was nothing they could do but walk down the street to the gig. There were cracks in the footpath, and everywhere the sound of sirens wailing. A shop verandah was leaning down precariously. Reaching the Newcastle Workers Club, Emerson saw the tour's two trucks parked on the road outside. He had played the venue many times before, and from the outside it appeared unchanged.

'What I didn't realise was that I was only looking at a façade. The front brick wall of the building had stayed intact, but behind that, the top-floor auditorium had collapsed down into the second-floor gaming lounge, which had collapsed down into the first-floor bars and restaurants, which in turn had collapsed down to the underground car park.'

Emerson's mind turned immediately to his crew colleagues. 'Where was our semi driver, John "Face" O'Shannessy? The driver of the eight-tonner was present and accounted for; hopefully Face was somewhere downtown, having breakfast.'

Some of the crew investigated nearby cafes, but to no avail. Outside the Workers Club, emergency vehicles were gathering, and injured people started to emerge from the building. It was clear this was a major catastrophe, but still the front wall of the buildings looked intact; the devastation behind it was hidden. Emerson found a manager from the Workers Club and introduced himself as the production manager for Crowded House/ Split Enz. 'In the spirit of "the show must go on", I asked him, "Do you think we can still do the gig tonight?" He looked at me incredulously and explained that there was no building left behind the front wall – and that there were possible fatalities inside.'

The crew spread out and continued the search for Face, but as time wore on it became apparent that he was probably inside the building when the earthquake struck. It was later confirmed that John O'Shannessy was one of 13 people who died in the Newcastle earthquake, which struck at exactly 10:27 am on 28 December 1989. Nine of those 13 dead had been inside the Workers Club.

If the crew had not changed the load-in time from 10 am to 11 am that day, up to 30 loaders, plus a virtual who's who of Australian crew, including Steven Swift (lights), Julian Spink (front-of-house sound), Bob Daniels (monitors), Michael Waters, Jock Bain (sound), Garry 'Brick' Chamberlain (lights), Peter 'Sneaky' McFee, Paul 'Arlo' Guthrie (stage/backline) and Emerson himself would have been on the casualty list.

Yet it could have been much worse, Emerson says. 'Imagine the extent of the tragedy if the earthquake had struck 12 hours later. Over 2400 punters, all of the musicians, crew, plus wives and girlfriends. The international music community would have been indelibly changed if we had lost Crowded House at the height of their career, not to mention Tim Finn and Split Enz and others.'

Emerson and the other crew members spent the rest of that day sitting on the median strip of King Street, Newcastle. They weren't allowed back into the hotel in case it collapsed, but the staff retrieved their bags and delivered them to them on the street outside. The crew coach had already returned to

Sydney, and didn't make it back to Newcastle until nearly five in the afternoon. The drive to Coffs Harbour that evening was conducted under a pall of gloom. The tour continued, but the End of the Decade concert was not the joyous occasion everyone had hoped it would be.

Emerson recovered emotionally from this horrible event and continued on, working regularly with international artists such as Tom Jones, Diana Ross and Paul McCartney, and then had a highly successful career as a freelance production manager and technical director before retiring from full-time work at Acer Arena in 2011. He still does occasional sound mixing for the likes of Irish singer Mary Black and some former members of Goanna. His has been a remarkable career.

Emerson hands me a copy of his stupidly impressive CV, and smiles as he says, 'I still couldn't get a job if I wanted one – all I've done is this.'

32

One Man, One Van,
One Band – for 50 Years

Ronald Clayton knows a lot about the Ted Mulry Gang – possibly more than anyone on the planet, except the surviving members of the band. In fact, there's every chance he recalls more than even them. Clayton has worked for TMG for close to 50 years. There has been no other band for him. He is literally the only Australian roadie who has given his whole working life to just one band. Crazy? Maybe. Dedicated? Certainly.

And to add to his uniqueness, Clayton is the only Australian roadie to have written a book detailing his career. *It's a Roadie's Life* is a warts-and-all recollection of his time on the road.

Clayton's dedication to TMG is the stuff of legend – so much so that when roadies get together, he feels a little like an outsider. He's the guy who started with one band and stayed there. He didn't move on and evolve in the roadie world.

'I kind of sacrificed my career, and my knowledge as a roadie probably suffered because of that. All the other guys went on and learnt a whole lot of stuff from each other. I was self-taught in the early days, and it was only when TMG got the John Swineys and Nicky Campbells and Billy McCartneys in that I picked up a bit of knowledge about stuff, and that was only short-lived. I went up with the band and down with the band, whereas everybody else kept on moving on.'

Clayton started with the musicians even before they were known as the Ted Mulry Gang. In the early days, the band was the Velvet Underground – the Newcastle one, not the New York one featuring Lou Reed. 'I started with them not on a professional basis, just as an amateur, like everyone else did. I turned up and loaded gear in and out just to get into the gig for free, to save 30 cents.'

As well as Herman Kovac, who became a mainstay of TMG, the Velvet Underground featured a guitarist by the name of Malcolm Young – the very same one who went on to find fame and fortune as a central part of the AC/DC machine. Clayton remembers Young's first ever performance onstage, with the Velvet Underground. 'January 29, 1971,' he says without hesitation.

When Clayton started in the roadie world he was 17, but like so many young men of his era, he also had a trade as a fitter and turner – just in case. 'Malcolm Young was a sewing machine mechanic. I used to pick him up, as he worked near the railway at Hestia. Daryl Braithwaite was a fitter and turner too. That was what you did. In those days you left school and got a trade. A lot of people got into a band but it was assumed that wasn't going to last. But the thing that we didn't know then was that rock'n'roll wasn't just going to last for a couple of years – it's gone on for 60 years and it's still going.'

Clayton was there when Ted Mulry began using the Velvet Underground as his backing band, and eventually they became the Ted Mulry Gang. Until 1976 Clayton was TMG's only crew guy, although towards the end of 1975 the band had done a tour with Sherbet, Hush and John Paul Young, so all the crew members gave each other a hand. As TMG's popularity grew,

Clayton found that he needed an extra pair of hands permanently, so he took on an assistant, John Cobcroft.

The most significant difference between TMG and most
other bands of the time was that they owned their own PA and
truck, which meant they never needed to use the established
PA and transport companies, except for running repairs on
the road. Clayton had purchased a 22-seat bus and converted
it for the band and their gear. Then, as all of TMG lived in
a house together, they pooled their funds and bought a basic
but functional PA.

The workload was rigorous and endless. 'There were a lot
of lunchtime gigs at schools. Shows in indoor sports arenas at
schools or basketball arenas. These were at around 12.30 to
1.30 pm, and then often there were after-school gigs where the
bands played between 3.30 and 4.30 pm. I remember one in
Pendle Hill, in Sydney, which was TMG, AC/DC and Buffalo,
passing each other as we loaded in and out – and that was just
a school gig!'

As things began to escalate, Clayton and TMG found that
some decisions – particularly financial ones – moved out of
their immediate control. Now managed by Roger Davies, TMG
went on a national tour with the Newcastle band Rabbit. The
Disturbing the Peace tour required a bigger crew, which was
provided by Artist Concert Tours, so the likes of Bill McCartney
and Nicky Campbell became involved. As the A-list crew guys
moved in, for the first time Clayton felt marginalised.

The Disturbing the Peace tour was typically wild, like others
in that era. To the participants at the time, though, it seemed
just like any other tour, complete with plenty of girls and guns.
'We all had guns because we were able to. On the days off,
when you were out in the middle of nowhere, what else were
you going to do? We'd go shooting. You can't go to the beach,
so you'd just go out in a paddock and shoot bottles or cans,
and occasionally you'd get invited out on a pig hunt.

'Ted got done a number of times for having unlicensed guns. He bought an air pistol in New Zealand, and it came back with him through customs without any questions being asked. And then he got done for it later when he started using it and showing it around. It was a pretty harmless thing but he got into a lot of trouble.

'In Perth we had a few irate parents coming to look for their daughters, and Ted appeared with a gun, which caused us a bit of trouble. Parents looking for their daughters were always a problem. That was without the appearance of any guns. Particularly in small country towns, the local girls didn't want to have sex with the local boys because they'd get talked about and get a reputation – but when a rock'n'roll band came to town, it was open slather. Girls used to get totally googly-eyed. A local guy would go out to a gig with a girl and she'd set eyes on the guitar player and it was all over – he'd have lost her for the night. And a lot of girls went for the crew guys. We were often more accessible than the band.'

There was always the potential for trouble, Clayton says. 'In one country town there was a girl who did just about everyone in the band and crew, and she was the police sergeant's daughter. She had a companion who was the local minister's daughter.'

There was also plenty of harmless fun and shenanigans as the bands and crew attempted to stave off the boredom of another night in a small country town. 'One time we were in Mount Isa – we were the first big band to go there and we sold out a bunch of shows, and so there was a reception organised for us by the mayor and mayoress. Howard Freeman and Ray McGuire from the crew decided to stand by the edge of the pool during this reception, kissing with a raw egg dripping down between them. This was in front of all the local dignitaries.'

And in between the country towns were the endless miles on the road. 'When you went down or up the Hume Highway, you never knew if you were going to get to the other end. It was just horrific to drive it, and we were expected to do it all the time. In the early days it wasn't even two-lane roads in places, just a single strip of bitumen. The amount of deaths on the road should have been far greater. Now it's suicides that are emptying the ranks.'

Clayton has thought a lot about the high suicide rate among roadies. 'A lot of people who became roadies had nothing to fall back on. They were fully involved for a time and then things dropped off and a lot of them became redundant. The way of life that a lot of them had had for a long time ceased to exist. When the work stopped, most of them didn't own a house, they didn't have a business. The abilities you have as a roadie don't really carry you into any other work. You are a jack of all trades and a master of none.

'We had to be carpenters and electricians and a lot of things. We went into places where there were no stages and had to find stuff and literally build them. In the 1970s you were going into schools and showgrounds in small towns and building every-thing from scratch. But when the work stopped, even though you could do all these things, you didn't have any recognised qualifications to get another job.

'When I think about roadies, I liken it to the Wild West. The majority of people who settled there wanted to be farmers and things like that – and a few of the others wanted to be gunfighters and rabble-rousers. In the modern world the rabble-rousers became roadies and everyone else settled into normal society.'

Clayton is the rabble-rouser who has stayed loyal to TMG and its members for five decades. He quit briefly in 1978 when his marriage went kaput, but that didn't last. He's borrowed money to keep the band on the road, and he's lost houses and property when the band found themselves in financial trouble and their accounts were linked to Clayton's. But he kept coming back. And he's still there.

Even Clayton can't put a figure on how many TMG shows he's seen. Really, it's easier to recall the ones he's missed. 'I had to go to hospital and missed a week in 1973. Then they did two boat cruises, eight or nine weeks when they went to America and Canada. I was working a job as a fitter and turner then.'

When the going got tough for TMG, Clayton was the one who could – and did – get a job to ease the financial stresses for everyone. His was a complete sacrifice for what he believed in: the Ted Mulry Gang.

Even these days, with TMG being fronted by the late Ted Mulry's brother Steve, Clayton works for the band – for free. He gets an age pension now and owns the TMG merchandise, so sales of T-shirts and other products bring in a bit of extra income.

The workload can still be intense. 'The band just did four minutes on television and I worked 17 hours for that to happen. It was a public holiday on the Friday, so I picked up the truck on Thursday, drove it to get the gear, then to home in Windsor, then to the television studio the next day, then five hours at the studio for those few minutes, and then the gear and the truck had to be returned.'

Clayton is one of a kind. A likeable, hardworking guy who loves his band.

One man. One van. One band. One life.

33

Australia Looks Small on a Map

'I wasn't really into bands – I was more into the commerce of running a production business. That's the difference,' says Julius Grafton, who has spent his working life managing a production hire business, working with and as a road crew member, publishing a magazine, and running conventions for people in the production business. Grafton has put in the hard yards on all fronts, but he's come out of it well and remains comparatively undamaged by the rigours of the road and the lifestyle.

It's the experience of being on the road, providing equipment, dealing with hundreds of road crew, and writing about and working in the field that gives Grafton a perception of the music world that is broader than most. 'I came from a different mindset. Most roadies are frustrated musos – but that makes for a better roadie, because they can talk to musicians on their own level. That's why roadies and musicians have always been so entrenched.

'In the early days, the barriers to entry in the roadie world were not set much higher than you had to have teeth and be breathing. On parole? No problem. On the run? No problem.

That's one of the reasons all of the crew guys had nicknames, as so many of them didn't want to be found for one reason or another. It really was the wild frontier.'

Grafton's introduction into the roadie world began in the early 1970s, when he started out doing lights for bands. 'It was originally a psychedelic light show, mood lighting. Then stage lighting came in when bands became visual, and they needed to be seen and look like they did on *Countdown*. That was the era of Sherbet and Skyhooks. Before then, you'd had the likes of Tamam Shud and Tully, and all the head bands who didn't want to be seen or didn't think it was important. But Daddy Cool wanted to be seen. Skyhooks wanted to be seen. Television went from black-and-white to colour with *Countdown* and things changed – both for bands and for crew.'

Grafton started using cinema audio technology, and in about 1974 learnt how to move things so the sound hit you in the chest. 'Suddenly you started going to a gig and it was like a cinema. The band would punch you in the guts with their sounds, *and* they were colourful and in sequins. I was lucky to be there. That door was opening and I walked through it.'

Based in Sydney, Grafton started his own lighting company in 1974, and in 1980 opened a production company. The first band he worked seriously with was the ska revival band The Allniters.

Grafton and his company were around in the much mythologised era of the early 1980s. 'That was the time of the mega bands – Midnight Oil, Cold Chisel, INXS, Little River Band, Air Supply. All the guys who made all the money peaked around that time.'

And the 1980s were a different time for road crew. Nothing was properly regulated, including pyrotechnics – the explosions during a rock'n'roll show. Pyro can be problematic even in the most controlled environment, and it could be seriously hazardous in years gone by, especially when set off in a crowded venue.

'Of course, there was an inherent need not to hurt yourself, so there were acceptable practices that everyone knew and understood. But we were still putting ladders on road cases to get to heights and taking what now seem like unnecessary risks, and blowing shit up in the name of pyro and fun. We were using gunpowder and magnesium powder for pyro stuff because it was way cheaper than buying the real stuff. And you could go to a gun shop and just buy it.'

At one time it was a genuine risk: pyrotechnics killed a few audience members in accidents in the 1970s. 'There was one incident in Ipswich at a dance. There was this guy who had his pyros in an ex-army ammunition box that you used to be able to buy at those army disposal stores in the 1970s. He thought he'd put a micro switch so that you couldn't fire the circuit, but someone slammed the lid hard and it broke the switch and when he set the pyro off the box exploded and killed a girl. It was madness. There were no real standards then. Everyone was mindful of efficiency, because you always wanted to be able to set up and take things down quickly. It was all about time.'

Reflecting on the relationship between roadies and artists' managers, Grafton agrees that road crew were frequently considered to be dispensable and even bulletproof. They were often expected to do things that managers and musicians wouldn't consider doing themselves, such as an extremely long drive after virtually no sleep.

'But we *wanted* to do it. Don't forget that. We'd get the worksheets from Harbour or Premier or whichever booking agency you were working with and roll your eyes. Worksheets were known as "the book of lies". You'd get them and go, "Fuck, we've got to go from *there* to *there*. Can't these fuckwits read a map?"'

These were known as dartboard tours, because that's what it seemed the agents had used to plan the shows. 'Australia does look really small on a map,' Grafton laughs.

In his opinion, most bands – despite paying lip-service to the contrary – traditionally didn't have a lot of respect for their roadies and crew. Sure, they often hung out and drank and did drugs with them, but at the end of the day they were the band and the crew were the ones who did all the hard driving, lifting and setting up. Road crew come and go; they're disposable. But another guitarist like *me*? Who are you trying to kid? I'm in the band.

'I tried to avoid getting close to bands. I loved music but I didn't like a lot of the humans. By its very nature, performing brings out the worst in a lot of people. And a lot of musicians were obnoxious and somewhat toxic. I had disrespect for a lot of musicians, and I think it probably sprang from them disrespecting their crew.

'The disposability of crew was infamous. I'd do it myself – go on tour and fire guys because they were doing drugs and staying up all night and losing their minds because they were doing too much speed. You'd just get rid of them and look for someone else. And if you couldn't find someone quickly, you'd just call the dole office or whatever Centrelink was called. Often you'd physically go to their offices and say you needed a guy for a road crew and they'd give you three numbers, or there'd be a guy sitting there and he'd say that he'd do it. That's often what we used for loaders in those days. Call the dole office and they'd send them over.'

During the 1980s, Grafton watched as more and more money started to appear in the Australian music industry. As it did, bands and managers moved to cocaine as their drug of choice. But not road crew. 'They couldn't afford coke – unless they were selling it, and a lot of them were. Speed was the scourge. With heroin, they'd just nod off or drop off and you'd get rid of them. Some crew had heroin users but not that many.'

And then there were girls – there were always lots of girls, for both band *and* road crew. 'Relationships were disposable, and if you wanted to have random sex every night of the week with groupies, you just could. It was just there – even for crews. There were some guys I worked with who were smelly and sweaty in a way that you would definitely notice. They oozed unhealthiness, but they had this magnet-like thing about them that attracted girls – like bees to honey. My mates and I could never work it out. They'd literally be rooting under the back of the truck.'

Ask Grafton who is and who isn't a roadie, and he's adamant. 'A roadie is anyone who interfaces with the band equipment. Anyone who handles or operates any form of band equipment is a roadie. And every band needs equipment. Unless you're going to stand on a street corner and sing a cappella without any amplification, you need a roadie because you need gear – or you move it yourself.'

Grafton also sees comparisons – and some differences – between roadies and circus workers. It's often said that the two are alike, as both run away to a lifestyle of entertainment on the road. 'In many ways they are like a carnie, a circus worker. They call them "warbs" – that's what the circus calls the stage-hand – and carnies are like the lighting operators. On one of his final tours, John Farnham did a regional tour and he did it in tents, so he took a circus crew with him. But the rock'n'roll crew and the circus crew couldn't get along, because they were actually very different people. The circus is more about canvas and rope, and roadies are into plugging shit in, so it's more technology-based. There's a cultural difference. But there's also a lifestyle that's pretty much the same. Warbs live in caravans and drink themselves to death. And like your average roadie, they'll root anything – each other, sometimes.'

When asked why there have always been so few women working as roadies, Grafton doesn't hesitate. 'Being a roadie didn't make sense to your average girl. They could be a groupie. Or in a band. So why should they put themselves through what road crew went through? Don't forget that most road crew are failed musicians. They couldn't get in a band or get a gig as a musician, so they became roadies to get close to bands. Women had other ways of getting close to musicians.'

Grafton has studied all the reports about road crews and suicide and mental health issues. While he is saddened by the statistics, he's not surprised. 'Some did well out of the industry and their time on the road, but 99 per cent didn't. Most are failed musicians. And the vast majority are in it for the lifestyle only. They were working *for* the band but considered themselves *part* of the band. That's a big part of why they suffered the fall from grace as soon as it stops.'

Life on the road can be incredibly claustrophobic, Grafton says, but that only makes the absence of it more pronounced when it's over. 'Everybody who works in entertainment suffers the same sense of loss when they're off a show. They go from being part of a team that's very tightly knit to competing against the others in the team for the next gig. And they often have no one to talk to except the people they're competing against. It's the isolation factor, you go from living together on the road and partying together, to suddenly being home and alone in your room.

'In that community the death rate is incredibly high and the general health level is appallingly bad. Most guys carry back injuries, as well as other things. That's from incorrect lifting techniques. And also they were anaesthetised through alcohol and drugs, so they ended up injuring themselves even further without actually realising it.

'And there were a lot of car and truck accidents, especially in the mid-1970s. There were no DUI checks, so we were all routinely drinking and driving. I took a bottle of Southern Comfort to Melbourne with me once. It got me there – and I was driving a truck. That's just what we did.'

34

Blowing Smoke Up Madonna's Arse

Stan Armstrong has had back surgery and a new hip. He likes to joke that he's the $40,000 man. He can smile about it now, but there are very few Australian road crew members who haven't had surgery or wanted to. And those body repairs aren't cheap. Some roadies suffer painful injuries that they just have to live with.

Armstrong is chatting one Thursday afternoon as he sets up guitars and other gear ahead of a Mark Seymour show at Sydney's Basement club. He worked with Seymour's band Hunters & Collectors between the mid-1980s and the late 1990s, also juggling work with Weddings Parties Anything. Now in his fourth decade as a road crew member, Armstrong looks in good shape.

'It's like misfits who are attracted to running away to join the circus,' he says when I ask why he and so many others find themselves spending decades on the road with rock'n'roll bands. 'You've got to be a little unhinged, a little whacky in the first place. That's why people do it. Why does a musician become a musician? Because they love playing music and they don't want to sit in an office and then go home and play guitar in their room. They're people who won't be satisfied with that.'

Armstrong's road to the roadie circus began when he moved out of home aged 16 and spent the next half-decade driving up and down the east coast, surfing and living in share houses. Really, he was working full-time at avoiding a so-called normal working life.

Eventually, Armstrong found himself involved in the much-mythologised Sydney punk venue The Funhouse, in Oxford Street, Darlinghurst. He was hanging with a guy who mixed a band called The Psycho Surgeons, and because Armstrong had access to a truck, he started hauling their gear around. Then Mark Taylor from that band gave him an occasional job in his hip import record shop called White Light. About six months later, The Psycho Surgeons sacked their singer and Armstrong stepped up. He sang on the infamous 'Wallaby Beat' single, the cover of which the band splattered with cow's blood.

The band ultimately went pear-shaped, and Armstrong drifted into working for a little company called Sound On Stage in Darlinghurst, which rented PA gear to bands. 'My first gig was loading gear for Barry Crocker. It was whatever came along. We were all living in squats around the areas, so $20 a day was good money. I was in the infamous Villa de la Filth in Francis Street in East Sydney with Peter Tillman, who's now a corporate lawyer, and a couple of other guys like Bob Short.'

Armstrong was content. He was loading gear in and out of gigs, setting it up, driving equipment in trucks. He did that for a few years, eventually hooking up with The Nauts – former members of Supernaut – and did their lights, stage monitors and driving. Along the way he was doing what every roadie did: learning the job from actually doing it. There was a stint with one of Chris Bailey's incarnations of The Saints, before Armstrong became a kind of in-house roadie for the independent label Citadel Records, whose roster included Died Pretty and Porcelain Bus.

Armstrong was like many others during that time who fell into a serious drug addiction for a few years. He was trying to work at the same time, but the two pursuits weren't exactly complementary. His salvation came in the form of Hoodoo Gurus.

'I hooked up with them around the *Mars Needs Guitars!* time. Clyde Bramley was in the band then, and he was an old mate from The Funhouse days. They tried to get me cleaned up. It was a saviour, really. I did clean up and did a three- or four-month tour with them, doing lighting, and then I became a guitar tech. Brad Shepherd was breaking his guitar strings all the time, so I just fell into the guitar thing then. I'd done a lot of lights, so I'd set up their stage gear and then go out front and do lights.'

This was the mid-1980s, and Hoodoo Gurus were putting together their first big crew and stage set-up after a string of successful radio songs. Along with Armstrong, there were two other lighting guys, a front-of-house mixer and a couple of others. There was a tour manager, a truck and PA – all the bells and whistles for a band breaking through in that era. Armstrong remembers being paid about $300 a week, which was a pretty good wage in those days.

He worked a lot with Hoodoo Gurus at that time, and did stints with Don Walker and The New Christs. Then Sydney venues began to be taken over by the dreaded poker machines, which turned a good profit and didn't make lots of noise or require sweaty road crews to load them in and out. Work for rock'n'roll bands – and therefore roadies – started to dry up, so Armstrong moved to Melbourne, hooking up with Hunters & Collectors and Weddings Parties Anything for extended periods. It was the heyday for both these iconic Australian bands.

For all sort of reasons – not all of them related to their love of touring – Weddings Parties Anything were on the road fairly constantly, which was good for Armstrong. His wage by now was about $600 a week – not top-rate, but not too shabby, and the band treated him well.

Life is full of chance opportunities. About the time Weddings were slowing down, Armstrong met a woman. She was moving to England and with little immediate work beckoning him, Armstrong packed up and relocated too. He and the woman got married and are still together. And there was plenty of work around for an Australian roadie who knew what he was doing, although he had to start again from the bottom of the industry. 'I was getting five quid an hour to set up at Hyde Park for Sting and people like that. But it was work.

'I set up as part of the Madonna crew. There were more than 80 of us, with a dozen different spot operators, stage guys, props guys. One of my jobs was to be underneath the stage, basically blowing smoke up Madonna's arse.'

After this, Armstrong was in the right place at the right time and pulled a gig with Elvis Costello; he was with him for five years. 'Costello's a workaholic, which was great for me, so if he wasn't doing band stuff he was doing the duets thing with Steve Nieve, the piano player. Then he wrote an opera and toured that. I was Elvis's "little man" for the years 2000 to 2007, with little breaks in between.'

This was a big cocaine period, Armstrong says. All the crew except for him were old-school English guys who'd been with Costello since The Attractions were his backing band. Most of the touring they did was in the United States, and there was cocaine everywhere among the road crew. 'Many spent their per diems on an eight-ball of coke each week,' Armstrong says. 'There were seven core crew guys, so that was 25 grams a week. The band were teetotallers and a couple of them had had heart attacks. They'd gone through the vodka and cocaine period, which used to be their thing. Everyone knew that the crew were out of it, but as long as we got our gig done it was okay.'

And the money was good: with Costello, he was on £1600 a week. That went straight into his Australian bank account, and the exchange rate at the time was favourable. 'Plus he flew me business-class, and there were per diems of a couple of hundred American dollars a week. So basically I banked my wages and lived on backstage catering and per diems for five years.'

Back in Australia, Armstrong picked up with artists he knew, such as Mark Seymour, by then in a solo career after Hunters & Collectors, with whom he had worked consistently, went into an indefinite hiatus; and Rob Younger from Radio Birdman, whose last tour he worked on, having known the band since 1977.

But the work has changed. There's not the touring circuit that there used to be for Australian artists, and most of the gigs are built around weekends. It's fly in, fly out stuff. Fly to Brisbane on a Thursday or Friday, do a couple of shows and fly home on Sunday. For the rest of the week Armstrong picks up a variety of casual work to make ends meet. But a good crew member like Armstrong can do all right from weekend work alone – so long as he's working more weekends than not.

'I get paid per show. I have a rate and that's it. If I'm away from home I get a good wage for a night, and if I'm away for three nights I end up with a good weekly wage just from those three nights. But then you have to take into account your downtime. Two grand, like some crew get, is great if you're working every week, but you're not – not even close to it.'

And Armstrong says he's fortunate that he has a domestic life that actually supports his crew work, which is a rarity. 'Having a good partner is the catalyst. She knows I don't want a nine-to-five gig. She's an actor and knows the vibe. She can tell when I'm getting restless, and she'll say, "Get out of the house and get a gig."'

And make no mistake, Armstrong loves the work. Loading in and out and setting up with the rest of the crew is hard, but then comes that magical moment called show time. 'Oh yeah, it's the same buzz that a musician gets when they go onstage and go from being an introvert to an extrovert – or sometimes it's the other way around. Bang – show time! We're on. If you haven't got your shit together, there's 200, 2000 or 20,000 people out there who have paid good money to come and see an act, and if you fuck up, the act fucks up. But on the upside, you get as much buzz from a great show as the band or artist does.

'No one who doesn't do this job realises the skill involved. With Mark Seymour, I think I have 14 guitar changes in a 30-song set. Unless you've done it, you don't realise the skill involved in keeping 14 guitars in tune. They slip in and out of tune as the room temperature changes. You have them ready for the show, and then as people come in the room heats up, and they go out of tune so you have to re-tune them all. Your worst nightmare is when they're all set and the venue turns on the air conditioning and they all go pear-shaped.'

Although there's less violence at gigs these days compared to the 1970s and '80s, Armstrong has seen his fair share of biff and bash over the years. And he concurs that it was often the crew who were the target of the aggression.

'It was a case of, "Let's get really pissed and pick on the crew while they're trying to pack up." Gigs like the Pier at Frankston were notorious for that. You'd have a couple of mic stands set up at the back of the venue or the back of the truck ready to fight off trouble. You could just feel when there was going to be trouble. It's like being a really good security guy – they can pick what's going to happen before it does actually happen. Those guys can look into a crowd and go, "Those guys over there are going to have a fight in five minutes – I'm going to go over there now and separate them." You mixed up speed and booze, and when you had lots of both you could bet that things were going to get ugly.'

Sometimes people were just stupid. 'I remember one night packing up and there was a crew guy up a 20-foot ladder trying to take some lights down, and there were these guys shaking the ladder thinking it was pretty funny. So I told them to fuck off and that turned into a fight. The guy on the ladder was holding a 25-kilo lamp and perched up there. People are just dumb. They don't realise that you've already spent six hours setting all this up and you're tired.'

On the day we talk, all the crew Armstrong's working with – setting up for a Mark Seymour gig – look to be of about his vintage. They have a pragmatic approach: get it done smoothly, quickly and professionally. There's little chatter. Everyone knows their job, and they get about doing it.

'Getting fucked up just doesn't happen these days with crews. Maybe there's a bit of it with younger crew, who are trying to live the dream, but everyone's getting older and the job is more professional.

'There's a new generation of crew guys coming through for sure, but it's hard to get a young guy with experience because they all do the courses. It's classic. You get a guy who's done the mixing course and then he gets to a live gig and asks us who's going to plug his stuff in, and you say, "You are," and he tells you he doesn't know how to because at the college where he's studied, it was already plugged in. But there's also guys who do it the old-fashioned way, and go and work for a PA company and learn from the ground up.

'There's definitely been a change. There's a lot of guys who hit their 50s and couldn't deal with all the changes, all the digital stuff, and they fell by the wayside and couldn't get a gig. They wanted to live in the past, going out, getting fucked up and rooting girls, but it wasn't happening like that anymore.'

Armstrong laments that it's hard to find good crew. A lot of crew guys think they're more important than the band, he says, but they don't last long. 'As you know, it's a family on the road.' And he is adamant that any road crew member with a good relationship is lucky. 'If it's a good situation, your partner will look after you, but if it's not your partner will be sick of you being away and is jealous. And when you come home, all you want to do is sleep, so it's easy for things to go pear-shaped.'

Whenever he stopped after a long period of touring, Armstrong didn't feel tired until a week or two later – and then he'd sleep for a week. The body clock takes time to readjust, he says. 'After this run of dates I'll be awake till 2 am for quite a few nights when I'm home, as I'll be back in that zone.'

In earlier days, the burnout rate among roadies was extremely high. The crews were pushed to the limit. Not only did band managers think they were infallible, but crews themselves thought they were bulletproof. It was nothing to do a gig in Melbourne on a Friday night, drive to Sydney on the Saturday for a show that night, and then continue on to Brisbane for a Sunday-night show.

'No one questioned it. Everyone was taking speed, and then drinking to take the edge off the speed. I went down that road and was really depressed for a time. The psychologist pointed out that I'd been living my life doing so much stuff and drinking and masking it all with drugs. Then when you settle down and stop drinking as much and taking drugs, all those things – including depression – come bubbling up.

'The age of crew guys committing suicide is around 50. They get out of the business and the industry, and they haven't got anything to replace it with. I've been lucky enough to have a good partner and family, and maintain a solid amount of work, plus maintaining my health.'

What does the future hold for Armstrong? He's not about to stop working as a roadie anytime soon. 'I'll probably do it until I can't do it anymore. I do stage-managing for the Golden Plains and Meredith festivals, and have done that for almost 20 years now. I can see it getting to where those are the two gigs I do a year. At those gigs I just point the finger and tell people where to put things. That's okay.'

35

Building a Pyramid
for Elton John

'They started the build on Tuesday – you'd better get down there soon,' says the email from Michael Chugg, co-promoter of Elton John's regional Australian tour in October 2017.

The build is for a concert in Wollongong, where Elton John will go onstage at around 6.30 pm the following Sunday. I look at this email and think I must be misreading something: they're building the stage *six days* before the show? Setting up a concert can't take *that* long, can it? Yes, it can and it does.

Although I've been around the rock'n'roll scene for more than four decades as a writer, manager, promoter and so forth, I've never actually seen the build for a major international show. I realise that a concert staging set-up isn't just plonked into a venue by some almighty helicopter system – I'm not that naive. But until this show in Wollongong, which some 22,000 people will attend, I had no idea how much work was involved in putting together one of these set-ups.

Christian Pepper from Force Events emails me to lay out exactly what is going to happen. In essence, by the end of

Tuesday – if all goes well – the stage deck will be built. On Wednesday the roof will be constructed, and if there are no screw-ups or hold-ups, they will start to lift the roof by the end of that day. On Thursday they will be 'lifting the roof with stage at full trim'. I'm not entirely sure what this means, but I get the general idea. Come Friday, they'll be building the front-of-house mix structure and finishing off the stage. Production loads in on the Saturday, and the show takes place the following day. On the Monday the roof and front-of-house will come down, the stage deck will go out on Tuesday. So a full week after they started, Wollongong will have its football field back again. It will be like Elton John and the hundreds of crew workers were never there.

When I arrive at the backstage area, the stage is built, the lights are on the stage, and the PA stacks are partially assembled but not yet fully raised. There are two video screens in a semi somewhere. Dozens and dozens of loaders and crew are busily doing stuff. There's actually a sense of calm at the site: no one is panicking, and everyone is just doing what they do. They are all being directed by Tom Michael, Christian's partner at Force Events.

I watch as the PA speaker stacks are lifted off the ground and positioned high above the stage, so the sound will fill the venue. Anyone who's been at a rock'n'roll concert, and particularly close to the stage, has looked up at the speakers and lighting rigs suspended from the ceilings and scaffolding. If it's an outdoor show, you can often see it moving in the breeze. You look at the chains and hooks keeping all this very heavy gear suspended in the air, and you wonder if it ever falls. It hardly ever does.

The crew members who have 'flown' these PAs all have proper work safety tickets. It's very technical, regimented and supervised. They're on a chain motor. The guy who attaches the motor to the truss must have a certificate to do that work; if he doesn't, the production company has to get a sub-contractor to do it. Even so, one veteran crew guy comments: 'Having seen it done hundreds and hundreds of times, I wouldn't stand under them.'

Before I arrived, the whole football field was covered in white turf protection mats and around 12,000 plastic seats. By 3 pm the first semitrailers with production gear come through the gates. Some have travelled from the last gig in Mackay, others from Sydney. They're greeted by around 80 loaders supplied by Showcall. They're a diverse collection of individuals, including a lot more women than I expected, but they're united by two things: high-vis vests and an ability to quickly and efficiently follow a series of surprisingly basic and direct instructions: 'Those trucks are full – let's empty them.'

For the next few hours I wander around marvelling at it all. I'm impressed that someone actually knows how to pack and unpack those semis, and where everything goes and in what order. And I'm amazed the way the production crew onstage know precisely how to fit this myriad of cables and boxes together. I'm reminded of how a pilot once described the wiring and workings of a jet plane: 'Imagine an explosion in a spaghetti factory,' he wrote, 'but somehow it all fits together and planes fly.'

And I'm staggered by the attention to detail, particularly in this day and age of terrorism at major events. On show day I chat with Momtchil 'Momo' Vassilev from Avert Risk while every seat in the venue is inspected, just in case someone has planted something. He shows me the grassed area behind the stage where Elton's helicopter will land at 3 pm. When I ask what would happen if there was an incident once the gates had opened, Momo tells me that there are various evacuation points, and the people on the floor will be ushered to the grass area where Elton's helicopter is to land. But what will happen if Elton's helicopter is en route and close to landing? Momo tells me there is a contingency plan for the chopper to put down. When I ask where, he looks at me, smiles just a little and says, 'I can't tell you.'

Elton does land in the designated area, but a half-hour early, as there are concerns about the increasing winds. Meanwhile, his crew do their soundchecks, the final touches are put on the staging, and the gates open at 4 pm – right on time. Everything backstage is still strangely calm. Even so, I have the sense that a calamity is just seconds away. It turns out everyone is thinking the same, but no one says anything.

A Queensland duo called Busby Marou opens the show, and then Elton appears right on the stroke of 6.30 pm. He plays great, and nothing goes wrong. The crowd is delirious. No one dies. No babies are born. There appears to be no bad acid. Elton utters his best line of the night: 'Two words I never imagined myself saying – "Hello Wollongong!"'

Twenty minutes before the show ends, I wander backstage. The loaders are in their high-vis again and ready to go. Elton comes off and is driven to the helicopter before the house lights go up. The band follows five minutes later and hop into a waiting van. Less than ten minutes after the show ends, the stage gear is being loaded down ramps and into trucks. It's almost 9 pm. Four semitrailers will be on the road tonight to Melbourne so they can get on the *Spirit of Tasmania* and sail south for Elton's concerts in Hobart. If they miss the boat, it will not be a good look.

The crew work feverishly till midnight. I wander back at 6 am the next day as the stage is being dismantled. The matting and chairs have already been rolled up and packed. 'This is what we do, Stuart,' one of the production crew tells me. 'We build pyramids, then we take them down and move them on.'

36

Smoking with Marley

'Grandpa, can you tell me that story again? The one about how you ran out of pot on a Bob Marley tour? Please – that's a really good one.'

Like all road crew, Ian 'Piggy' Peel has a thousand stories of being on the road with some of the most legendary figures in music. But it's hard to top his Bob Marley yarn. Peel worked on Marley's only tour of Australia, which was in 1979. The affable and amusing roadie winks when he says that his memories of that tour 'are all a bit cloudy – none of us can remember much'.

But he does recall a few moments, and they're priceless. First up was taking Marley to a press conference in Perth, where there were about 50 assembled media. As Peel remembers it, a journalist asked Marley what he thought of Perth's reggae bands. On many levels, this was a fairly dumb question. Aside from the fact that Perth (like most other Australian cities) wasn't known for its reggae bands, Marley and his band had just lobbed into the country and so hadn't had a lot of time to assess the nascent reggae culture.

But according to Peel, Marley confronted the question head-on. 'You are not Rastafarian here,' he said. 'You do not play reggae.'

Peel also remembers that none of the touring party would refer to him by his roadie nickname. 'They don't eat pork – there was no way they were going to call me Piggy.'

Anyway, the Marley entourage eventually ended up in Melbourne. The assembled masses in the band and their immediate Jamaican crew had been travelling with 100 buddha sticks and a pound of heads. The Australian crew weren't so well-supplied, though, and ran out of dope.

On the day of the show at Festival Hall, things were moving slowly. Load-in was not going well. The crew were listless and taking much longer than usual to get things set up. Marley's sound engineer, Dennis Thompson, approached the crew and asked why everything was running behind schedule. Eventually, one of the crew blurted out that they'd run out of dope to smoke. None of them was stoned, and it was affecting their work rate.

'Dennis told us to wait where we were, and the next minute Bob and all the band are filing into the backstage area and looking at us. They're all grinning. Then the tour manager handed us a package and said, "Go away now – go to the band bus, and do not come back until you have smoked all of this." The package was a half-ounce bag of this filthy-looking shit. So we've come back in fucking shitfaced, and the tour manager has said, "No worries, Bob, they are now *normal*."'

That was the tone of the whole tour. At every show, grateful audience members were throwing packages of grass onto the stage. Marley and his band members wouldn't touch it as they had their own first-rate supply. The Australian road crew weren't as choosy.

'One of my friends was working onstage,' Peel says. 'I was doing follow spotlights, and I'd spot stuff and tell him that there was something onstage that he needed to look at, so he'd scamper across the stage and grab another bag of pot.'

Peel's journey leading up to working with Marley – and many other international artists in the era – began casually enough.

In fact it was a total fluke that this became his work. After finishing at Prahran Tech in Melbourne in 1972, he was working at Art Design and Folio in St Kilda. Already a music fan, the first concert he ever saw was Led Zeppelin at Kooyong in 1972. He remembers that they started with 'Immigrant Song', and it was 'loud as hell. Loud. Loud. Loud'. Next up was a concert by Frank Zappa. Peel was doing okay in the concert stakes.

One night Peel was driving home from work in his Kombi van, heading down the Nepean Highway, and he picked up a hitchhiker by the name of Grant Jennings. It turned out Jennings was a lighting guy. When Peel dropped him off, it was at the home of John McKissock and his wife who had a business called Clear Light Lightshows. Jennings invited him in, and after a bit of a chat McKissock offered Peel some weekend work with his business. Who knows what Peel would be doing now if he hadn't picked up a hitchhiker that night? As it worked out, Peel spent a year putting up lights at the Hard Rock Cafe, at school gigs, at town halls – wherever Clear Light was supplying lights.

One day Peel's parents asked him if he smoked drugs. After fessing up, he was kicked out of home and moved to a house in Chapel Street, Prahran, sharing with a bunch of arty types and road crew guys. Soon Peel was asked to do lights for The Redhouse Roll Band, so he was responsible for the onstage atmospherics while the band did their covers of songs by The Doobie Brothers, Deep Purple and others.

Then came another lucky break: Peel met Peter McCrindle, who was doing lights for Ariel, and he asked if Peel wanted to join their crew. '*Everybody* wanted to work for Ariel,' says Peel. 'They were unbelievable musicians.'

By now Peel was firmly ensconced in the Melbourne crew scene. He still has no idea – or won't say – how he gained the nickname 'Piggy'. (In fact, there was another legendary 'Pig' before him: Glen Loyd, who worked with Rose Tattoo.)

Peel already knew 'Wrongway', a roadie who, on the way back to Melbourne from Adelaide one night, pulled over for a quick sleep, woke up in a daze and headed off in the wrong direction, which he didn't realise until he saw the lights of Adelaide. Then there was 'Atlas', who – of course – could lift anything. These and a myriad of other characters were part of Peel's world. They'd pass each other on the road, see each other at truck stops, or head to well-known venues together after gigs. Peel recalls that Martini's and the Tiger Room in Richmond were popular Melbourne hangs, while in Sydney it was always the Manzil Room. 'You could get a bottle of champagne and a dozen oysters for ten bucks at Pinocchio's in the Cross, and then head down to the Manzil, which was just down the road.'

After Ariel wound down, Peel found himself working with Renée Geyer, before eventually joining Concert Lighting Systems. There he began working with international artists and their tours, many of which were brought to Australia by Michael Coppel and Zev Eizik at Australian Concert Entertainment (ACE).

One of those tours was by the American singer/songwriter Tom Waits. Peel was dispatched to collect Waits from the airport in Perth, as no one else was available. It was only when he got to the airport that he realised he had absolutely no idea what Waits looked like. This was decades before Google and mobile phones. He drove to a phone box and called the promoter's office in Melbourne, where his question met with a gruff response. Usefully, he was told that Waits was 'short and wears a hat'. Well, that cut down the possibilities. Walking around the airport, Peel saw no short men wearing hats. Eventually he went to the counter and asked them to page a Mr Tom Waits. The next thing he saw was a head pop up from a couch where Waits had been sleeping.

Peel also worked as a lighting designer for tours by Melanie, Mike Nesmith, Chick Corea, Smokie, Bob Dylan, Boz Scaggs and John Denver.

Peel's road yarns seem intrinsically intertwined with Perth. He recalls a great day there during Bob Dylan's 1978 tour. 'We had a day off and there was a knock on the door. It was $crooge, saying that we should do something different. So all the crew took a half a tab of acid each and decided to go to the beach. It was like the Keystone Cops – eight or so guys just walking around together. Then we got bored, didn't we, so we headed back to the Sheraton. Dylan's technical people had heard about what we were up to. Some of them didn't like drugs, believe it or not. One of them came up to me and said, "So, Piggy, what's it like on Mars today?" Then they headed off in a bus.

'I'm back in my room and there's a call saying that there's a party in the executive suite, so I head up there. Dylan has put it on for everyone – food, drinks, the lot. Everyone from Dylan's crew had gone to Alan Bond's place, but when Dylan realised that the Australian crew hadn't been invited, he said, "I'm out of here," and hopped on the bus and came back to the hotel and said, "Party for the crew."'

Soon after, during a José Feliciano tour, Peel was introduced to the production people for Olivia Newton-John, who liked what he did. This resulted in him doing a world tour with her, before lobbing in England, where he worked with Madness for a year. He also did stints with The Tourists (who evolved into Eurythmics), Mike Oldfield, Chris de Burgh, Yes, Lene Lovich and Status Quo.

'The conditions were fantastic in the UK. I was getting 350 quid a week, plus per diems, so more than double what I'd been getting in Australia. And you were driving around Europe, so I didn't mind getting in a crew car. The next gig might only be 100 miles away, and there was this amazing variety of things you saw travelling through Europe.'

As time went by, Peel started to experience visa issues in the United Kingdom, plus he fell in love with an Australian woman, so in July 1981 he returned to live in Sydney. He received offers to work with bands such as The Angels and Midnight Oil, but Peel found it tough to commit. 'Everything was twice the price it was when I left, and wages for crew were terrible compared to what I was used to.' To keep the money coming in, Peel did some work with Mondo Rock, Tangerine Dream, Leo Kottke and Leon Redbone.

Then Peel went fishing – literally. For twenty years. After teaming up with a friend, he moved into tuna fishing, exporting the catches overseas. He didn't miss being a roadie, feeling that the industry had changed in ways he didn't like.

The years went by, and one day Peel met up with some old roadies from his era. The talk turned to what had happened to all their fellow crew guys, and Peel and his mates started making lists. Soon the dead list was a lot longer than the living. The group realised that a surprising number of crew had taken their own lives. Peel decided to start a Facebook page for old Australian road crew, and old friends started emerging.

'A few people had tried to do this before, but I hadn't. It should have been done 30 years ago. I just thought I'd have a crack at finding everyone and started ringing around. I was sick of only catching up with people at funerals.'

Things grew, and more and more crew got in contact with one another again. Then Gerry Georgettis died.

'That was really the cruncher,' says Peel. 'When he committed suicide, everyone just freaked. Here was a case of someone that everyone had on a pedestal, and going, "Why?" Then came the idea of getting together for a reunion. Leaving all the tour grudges behind and buying another old crew guy a beer because they're still there.'

The first reunion took place at the St Kilda Bowls Club on Sunday, 25 November 2012. Initially it was open to road crew who had worked prior to 1982. On the day, 176 old crew, musicians and friends turned up.

Someone had suggested to Peel that the reunion be on a Saturday night, but then another said if they did, they might get other people crashing it. Peel laughs. 'I said to them, "Who's going to crash a party with a couple of hundred roadies and expect to get out alive?"'

The impact of what became known as the Australian Road Crew Collective was immediate. (The collective evolved into an association, and is now known as ARCA.) 'After the first reunion I received at least four emails from people saying things like, "Thanks for inviting me – I was going to top myself," so if we've saved even one person it's a good thing. There's been five suicides since ARCA started, and none for the past two and a half years. Two guys that didn't come to the first reunion are among the ones that have suicided.'

Since that initial reunion, there have been further gatherings in Sydney and Melbourne, as well as projects such as Desk Tapes, where mixing-desk recordings of live shows from well-known Australian bands are sold to raise money to assist – via the Support Act organisation, which helps musicians in need – road crew going through tough times.

For Peel and the other figures behind ARCA, it's about committing to looking after hardworking and talented road crew who perhaps didn't look after themselves as well as they could have. Many found themselves without a support network to help them deal with psychological, physical or financial issues. These are often very damaged people, who have emerged – sometimes only just – from the dark tunnel at the end of what seems a very seductive lifestyle.

'Sex, drugs and rock'n'roll – that's a powerful attraction. It's like, "Wow, this is *really* good!" But what people don't realise is that everyone else is having a party while you're working. And by the time you finish working and want to go partying, there's usually no one left. It's a high-intensity industry. We were working five or six nights a week on the pub scene, and there was no real opportunity for a break.

'Creatively, we were all enjoying the bands we were seeing and the work we were doing. Everywhere we went, we set up to the best of our ability, made it look and sound the best it could. The stage guys made the band feel comfortable and they had good gigs. All the time you could go anywhere and see great gigs. A lot of bands became famous because of what crews did at gigs. People saw the live shows and went and bought the records.

'A lot of good crew got dumped when the bands they worked with went overseas, and the record label or management said they should leave the crew at home and pick up other people overseas. So there were a lot of crew around looking for gigs. After five or ten years of working as a roadie, what do you do? You may not have qualifications in anything else. And no super, no protection. It was high-intensity for years and then it stops.'

At the reunions, old crew members often talk to each other about things they wouldn't talk to their families about. And they talk about physical pain.

'A lot of the guys ended up ten years down the track with degenerative diseases. They *couldn't* work in the industry so they had to retrain or find something else, and it *never* has the same feeling as what they've done. Thirty or so years later, people sit back and go, "Wow, we actually did a really good thing back in those days." You're never going to see it again. There will never be that amount of amazing bands and gigs ever again.

'There was a camaraderie that happened between crew and bands. It was family. You were always looking out for each other. One way to describe it is that we all built the industry with our bare hands.'

37

Gerry Georgettis

Gerry Georgettis was one of the most loved and respected Australian road crew members – which is why the extreme nature of his death caused such waves through road crew ranks.

Roadies had died before, some in accidents, others by taking their lives. No one really thought too much about it. It was the way of the road – just what happened. Then Gerry Georgettis died in the most unspeakable circumstances. It was a turning point. People started to focus on the mental heath of Australian road crew. Who are these people? What's happened to them? How do we look after them? How do we protect them?

Georgettis was born in Goondiwindi Hospital in 1949. His family ran the local cafe. After finishing school, Georgettis took a job at the Bank of New South Wales, but he and the bank weren't a good combination. When the Georgettis family moved to Boggabilla in the late 1960s, Gerry went with them. The family opened another cafe, and Gerry gravitated towards rock'n'roll bands. He became the roadie for Compulsion. Then there was a stint with the La De Das.

By the early 1970s, Georgettis was a roadie for a band called London Express. He was big. He was strong. He had a van.

And he wanted to be a professional wrestler. When that band broke up, Georgettis moved into touring, and eventually relocated to Sydney. There, after stints with various other bands, he started working with Cold Chisel.

Jimmy Barnes recalls Georgettis with incredible fondness, and had known the roadie well before Chisel days.

'I spent many years travelling with and hanging out with the crew. They were just more like me. Before Gerry joined Cold Chisel he was the only roadie for Kevin Borich, and he'd worked with the La De Das. He carried so much gear by himself. When I was younger I used to hang around and help him load the truck. He was like my hero. He'd carry the whole PA, set it up and then mix. So we wanted him for Cold Chisel.

'He was the best sound guy, the hardest-working guy, and he was the King of Cool. Gerry Georgettis turned me on to more good music than any other musician I've ever met. He played me The Meters, John Lee Hooker, Captain Beefheart, so much music. He played me the *Rejuvenation* album by The Meters back in like 1976.

'In those early days I'd finish the gig, the band would head off and I'd hang around and drink and travel with the crew. They were *the* guys – they were the salt of the earth. It wasn't that I didn't like the guys in the band, but the roadies were much more fun and entertaining. Where the band would do a show and then rest and do another one, the crew would just roll on. And that was the way I was.

'I really loved the crew and I loved hanging out with Gerry. Along with Harry Parsons, Nicky Campbell and Mark Keegan he was our main guy for a long time after Alan (Dallow) and Billy (Rowe) died. Prior to them it was Peter Moss, Mossy's brother – he was the one-man crew.'

Jen Jewel Brown, the then partner of Don Walker, recalls Georgettis's time with Chisel. 'I spent a helluva lot of time around the king of sound Gerry Georgettis in the 1980s . . . from my favourite perch beside the mixing desk, I got to appreciate how this steady, caring, dry-witted and 120 per cent trustworthy man was the heart of Chisel live, delivering precision set-ups and happy, on-time crews that Chisel and their manager Rod Willis never had to spend a moment freaking out about. They loved him with a passion.'

After finishing up with Chisel, Georgettis relocated to America. He worked on the Lollapalooza festival and with numerous major international artists, including the Red Hot Chili Peppers and Bon Jovi.

Ted Gardner, co-owner of Lollapalooza, said of Georgettis: 'He was the sane one, on the road with 140 people. He was a champion guy.'

Georgettis moved to Miami, Florida, and began working in a theatre. He had a partner and a family around him. On a superficial level, everything looked to be okay. Then, on 4 February 2006, Georgettis bought a new car: a new Ford Escape from the Metro Ford dealership at 900 NW Seventh Avenue. When he got the SUV home and started having a look through the sale contract, though, something didn't seem right. He believed he'd been stiffed on the deal.

Georgettis stayed up all night, unable to sleep. The next morning he went back to the Ford dealership and drove the new car through the business's front window. He got out, opened the trunk and pulled out a can of petrol, which he poured on the car. Then he lit a cigarette and threw it at the car. The resulting fire caused more than US$1.35 million worth of damage.

Georgettis, who had calmly walked away from the carnage, was soon tracked down by police. Reportedly he had been shouting, 'Kill me, kill me!' Taken into custody, Georgettis was charged with first-degree arson, which carried a maximum 30-year prison term. He was later released on a bond of US$15,000, before appearing on US television saying he was ashamed of his actions. 'Yeah, man, I was just stupid,' he said. 'I'd like to get out of it . . . I think I made a mistake.'

Georgettis quit his job as manager at the performance art theatre, telling his boss he needed the severance pay to hire a lawyer. It was becoming clear to Georgettis that he was in deep shit. No one knows what was going through his mind at this stage, but he boarded a flight to Los Angeles. Then he hanged himself in a toilet cubicle mid-flight.

His death prompted an outpouring from friends, fellow road crew and music industry figures. In many ways it was a pivotal moment for the road-crew community – the realisation that they needed to look after their own.

38

She Am I

Leesa Ellem came to the world of road crew later than most. She had a secure job as a hairdresser for the majority of her working life. But she was also always around music.

Slowly, and totally by chance, Ellem started driving artists around on an occasional basis for her friend, the tour manager and band manager Haydn Johnston. She'd met him via the partner of Jed Kurzel from The Mess Hall, which Johnston managed. Through the same connections she met Dan and Matt Rule, the two brothers who ran the rock'n'roll melting pot that was the Annandale Hotel in the 1990s and 2000s, before it was sold and modernised.

Ellem had pretty much decided she didn't want to be a hairdresser any longer, so she kept driving for Johnston, and supplemented that by helping the Rule brothers with marketing and publicity for their venue, along with booking a new music night for them. Gradually she became more of an assistant to Johnston.

'Maybe because I was a bit older and because of my hairdressing background, but I knew how to deal with people and how to take care of them. So I just got involved, and then one day I remember saying to Haydn, "I think I want to do this job – I like it." And he said, "No, no, no, you don't want to do this – it's horrible."'

Ellem's break in the road crew business proper came via You Am I. The band had a very good monitor guy called Davros, who was also their tour manager. The only problem was that he was *very* good, and therefore in demand. He also worked with Nick Cave, and in 2006, when Cave's and You Am I's schedules clashed, he decided to stay with Cave.

It was coming up to the Big Day Out, and You Am I needed someone to organise them. Johnston told the band's bass-playing manager, Andy Kent, that he should give Ellem a go. She was still comparatively new to the caper, having been a promoter rep for Johnston but not a lot more. 'I sorta knew what to do but . . .' she smiles. 'So I went and did You Am I, and I thought it would be just a one-off thing, but I've been with them as their tour manager ever since.'

Now that Ellem is closely associated with You Am I – and their rather notorious hard-drinking, hard-partying, law-unto-himself frontman Tim Rogers – there is a sense in music and band circles that if she can corral that band, she's capable of anything.

'Exactly. But there you go. There's your female element that works perfectly. Women do things differently on the road. It's a funny one. I knew straightaway that he [Rogers] respected me, and I think he liked the female energy. And it wasn't from a sleazy thing. It was a gentlemanly sort of thing, because at the heart of him Tim's a real and total gentleman. They're all darlings. I love them to death. They're my good friends and good people.'

Even so, Ellem thought the BDO was a one-off. But about a month later Andy Kent called and said the band was doing an album tour, and they wanted her to do it with them. 'People have got to know me as You Am I's tour manager. It was a baptism of fire, being thrust into that world with that band at that level, and with such a big, larger-than-life frontman.'

What makes Ellem different? She thinks a lot of it is ego management. Male managers and tour managers often find themselves in a strutting, testosterone-driven, bloke-against-bloke confrontation over issues and ways of doing things.

'I think a female brings an element where they're not going to challenge you so much just because they can. I think they actually behave themselves more. I've been called "Mumma" by You Am I for over eight years now. I'm Mumma. "Mumma, what are we going to do? Mumma, when do we leave?" That's actually pretty much it in a nutshell, the way I see myself as a tour manager. It's taking care of the family on the road. That family on the road is *my* responsibility – on all levels.'

As well as being responsible for the band, a tour manager like Ellem is equally responsible for the road crew. And You Am I have had a fairly consistent road crew. After many years the band lost their sound guy, Tim Carton, who had done their front-of-house 'forever', but eventually the changing nature of touring and the desire for more financial consistency won out. You Am I also lost Chris Howell – 'Troph' – who became a father and didn't want to be away from home for extended periods.

Gone are the days when Australian bands tour for the majority of the year. It's just not possible anymore. The lucky bands are out for four or five months a year, and their tours usually involve gigs from Thursday till Sunday. So if a road crew member isn't jumping from one tour and band to another, it's often impossible for them to make a decent living.

Working as a crew member for a band like You Am I is a highly skilled, demanding job. 'They are not an easy band to do stage for. Tim Rogers has really intricate guitar changes – and a lot of them. So to work with that, you have to be really good, and therefore it's not easy to find someone to just sub in and work a few weeks with You Am I. With guitar tuning, even a breath of breeze can change a tuning.

'My partner Alex Grant did a stint guitar-teching with them, and one night he did 56 guitar changes for Tim Rogers and Davey Lane. Very few people can do that. I've had people subbed in to do guitars for You Am I, and I've just watched them crumple side of stage. There's just so much to do. Tim Rogers is a lead guitarist and lead singer, and his guitar playing is out of this world. His tunings are really weird. There are a lot of drop tunings that aren't easy to do at all, let alone quickly in the middle of a gig. It takes skill. A hell of a lot of skill.'

After her introduction to the world of tour managing, Ellem learnt quickly – and bluffed a lot. She also employed the famous 'phone a friend' approach to getting through. She was on a massive learning curve.

'I seriously knew nothing much about anything at that stage. People would ask me about amps and things, and I'd just pretend I knew. So many times I'd call my old friend Haydn and go, "What are they talking about when they go 'bass cap heads combo' – what is this?" And he'd tell me what to say and I'd go back and start the conversation with, "What I think we should do is . . ." and they would go, "Cool." I had to do that because a lot of the touring work I'd done was low-level stuff, where I'm production manager and tour manager, and I'm driving and wearing many hats in the day. A production manager is an amazing thing to have, but most bands can't afford to have that sort of crew, let alone someone to organise that crew. So I was just thrust into it, but I had enough humility to always ask people.

'At the start of a You Am I tour Andy introduces me to everybody else involved and says that I'll take over from there. I *love* building tours – that's my most favourite thing to do. I build it from the grassroots and take it out on the road. And I use my crew to build my tours as well.

'Most bands can't afford to get extra stuff, so the crew are usually working with less than good conditions, but they still have to produce the sound that the band want to hear. It's a tricky situation – constantly.'

Economics means that even a band with You Am I's popularity don't take their crew overseas. Another factor is that they're somewhat seasoned at this caper, and can pretty much look after themselves on the short tours they tend to do overseas. As Ellem explains, they head off with ten guitars and a cymbal pack and just deal with it, with the help of a guy in the States who travels with them and assists.

Once Ellem was established with You Am I, she was offered a gig tour-managing Eskimo Joe, who were then at the peak of their popularity. For her, that was the next level of touring as they already had a long-standing and established crew. It's always a difficult situation when a new tour manager walks in and has to interact with a bonded team.

'I don't like to pull the female thing, but I still remember walking onto this stage in North Queensland. The crew was already there as they'd arrived the day before and were setting up. I flew up with the band and went to the site to meet the crew. It was the first time I was meeting them, and I thought I'd do that before show day. They knew me on email and through phone calls. That was all. So the lighting guy – in front of everybody – just yelled out, "You know what you're doing, don't you? You've done this before?" and I was cheeky and went, "Nah, this is the first time – let's just see what happens, hey?" And everyone laughed. They were established crew and guys that had been around for a long time.'

Her Eskimo Joe experience was invaluable for Ellem. Among other things, it taught her that with crew it's often the little things that matter. Even things that might seem trivial can be a very big deal to the crew member concerned. 'This was my first time where I was principally the tour manager and just that.

They had a good production manager, Casey Hilliard who's an old-school tour guy and amazing. He taught me a lot about it all. He said Ross, one of the crew guys, likes to know when the sandwiches are going to be ready. One of the other guys liked to know what seat in the plane he was going to be in, and how close to the front he was going to be. And the flight must be able to earn points. It's such a big thing with crew that every flight they're on earns points.

'Some of this stuff seems ridiculous and it drives me crazy but he pointed out that I wasn't dealing with their little idiosyncrasies, but the little things they needed to get them through the long days. I realised I had been going, "do you really care when the sandwiches arrive" and snapping, "YES, YOU'RE ON QANTAS" but then I realised that all I had to do was make that stuff happen, and tell people what they needed to know and the whole day was that much easier. You're pre-empting and thinking about what makes everyone happy so that everything runs according to plan – your plans and theirs.'

There were times when there was resistance to Ellem, a woman in a world dominated by men, but that doesn't happen anymore. In her early days as a tour manager she recalls being at a festival site and heading to the backstage area where the band she was working with had their trailer. She'd get stopped by a security guy and told that she wasn't allowed to go back there. Then she'd pull out her pass and say that she was the tour manager. The usual response: 'Well, do you have anyone who can prove that?' It's not a conversation that is likely to happen these days.

There was also a patronising attitude from guys. Even if it was meant affectionately, it was still condescending. 'One of the You Am I crew guys – whenever I did something, he'd say, "Good girl." They'd do that to wind me up. But he would never have done that to a male tour manager. I was going to smash him at one stage.'

Everyone has a breaking point. For Ellem it was one night when she and the band and crew were checking in at the Holiday Inn at Melbourne airport, after driving three hours from Ballarat. 'It was about 2 am and I was getting the room keys, and there he was over my shoulder trying to tell me how to do a hotel check-in. Andy Kent took three steps backwards, as he'd seen the look on my face and knew what was coming next. I just turned to the crew guy and very calmly looked at him and said – very evenly – "You need to shut the fuck up right now. I do not tell you how to do your fucking job, and do not tell me how to do mine."

'That's one thing with crews. Someone always knows how to do it better than the tour manager. They often think we have this easy job, but what they don't realise is that everything that is happening for them today or tomorrow is because of something that we've done already. They see us walking into the office and working on stuff that's not related to what's going on then. That's because it's all done, and it's their job to do what they need to do and yours to work on what's coming up.'

Ellem first toured overseas with Eskimo Joe in 2009. She ended up doing five European tours with the band, which she found a great learning experience. But her very first international tour was with Gotye.

'That first time with Gotye. It was just me, his drum tech and his sound guy. We were in a van, and whoever had put the tour together had done *the* worst routing possible. The only way we could make it from one place to the next was to leave after the show and drive three hours to get a head start on the next day's travel. I was tour-managing, doing merchandise selling – and driving. It was horrible.'

Over the years, Ellem's reputation spread. She also became Clare Bowditch's tour manager, and a promoter representative for Chugg Entertainment, something she's done for the past ten years.

A promoter rep essentially means that she goes on the road with international tours as a representative of the Australian promoter. She works with the crew that the international head-lining artist brings to this country with them. On significant tours the artist will bring their own tour manager, production manager and crew, and Ellem works with them to help get everything done.

One of those promoter rep gigs led Ellem to what is currently her major role. She was working with Feist in 2008, and quickly established a good working relationship. 'At the end of that first tour, Feist invited me to have breakfast with her and her manager. I wasn't sure what was going on, but during breakfast she got on her knees and said, "I propose that you come on tour with me." So initially I was her manager's assistant. That was amazing, as I learnt how to be a tour manager on another level completely as she was doing massive shows all around Europe.'

For Feist's *Metals* album tour, Ellem did all of Europe as well as Asia and Australia. After a five-year break, Feist returned and Ellem did her tour globally, which took up pretty much all of her 2017. During that period, You Am I did a short tour with Hoodoo Gurus, which meant that for the first time in a decade she couldn't work with them. 'I went to see them at one of the shows, at the Enmore Theatre in Sydney. It felt weird being there and not working.'

As far as Ellem is concerned, being a production manager or tour manager is still being a member of the road crew – it's just that people in those roles have a different level of respon-sibility. 'We're crew, all crew,' she says adamantly. 'Crews are the forgotten people on tours most of the time. They work *really* hard.'

Ellem understands better than most just how hard a road crew works. She brings up the famous observation by Tom Petty: 'I think the general public has no idea what roadies do. Bless 'em all. I just play the songs. They make the show happen.' Ellem gets it. She has seen it – and been it. She has great affection for road crew, and she doesn't have a lot of time for people in the music industry who don't respect them and appreciate what they do.

'My favourite people to work for are people who appreciate what crew do. People think road crew get paid a lot of money – and they kind of do – but my working day when I'm on tour in my position starts . . . well, I have to be there when those doors open at a venue. Not to let the audience in, but to start the set-up. As the truck doors get opened, I have to be there to make sure everything's going right. And then I'm there to the end.

'That day can start anywhere from 6–10 am in the morning and it can end anywhere between midnight and 3 or 4 in the morning. And you're working that whole day. Sure, there's moments when there's a lull after you've set up and you might have a little break, but then the band arrive and there's soundcheck and all the last minute stuff before the doors are opening and the show is happening. Crew work hard. Really hard. There is so much detail that goes into every show!'

For Ellem, one of the biggest challenges on the road for the crew (and artists) is to maintain a healthy lifestyle. 'There are a *lot* of unhealthy people on the road and working in this industry. It's the hours we keep and a lot of other things. You have to be mindful of what you're doing – or not doing – to your body. It's so easy to sit down at 1 am every night and start drinking. It's compacted drinking, too. Two hours later and you're drunk, and it can go on night after night. Breaking that is hard, and it takes discipline. I get worried about people on the road, but having said that, there's a lot more healthier crew now than there used to be, the younger crew people especially. The old-school guys, some of them still like to get stoned in the afternoon – and again before the show.'

Ellem is not a fan of crew being even remotely out of it when they're working, and agrees that it's an unacceptable practice these days with health and safety regulations. Her kinda, sorta exception is lighting directors. If they want to move into another stratosphere before a show, she understands where they're coming from.

'LDs are different,' she laughs. 'They're almost like another band member, and they often need to be slightly out of it because their show is done to the music. I've seen many of them go off with their bottle of booze, and they work the lights and drink while they do it.'

There's certainly a new breed of crew around these days, Ellem says, as many of the old-timers didn't want to progress as technology changed. 'They were used to a big analogue desk. Some of them still use them, but not many. Times have changed.'

These days crews come from a variety of places. Some study in audio colleges and then look for work on the road, while others are still getting their start in the time-honoured way, like Ellem did – through a friend. 'They might be the guy driving the backline or they come and help load in at a venue. When they show that they really want to do it, someone gives them a break and they start tuning guitars and things like that.'

Opportunities are still limited in Australia, though. There's not a big touring circuit anymore, and not many bands earning the sort of money that allows them to retain a significant crew. The front-of-house operator frequently doubles up as the tour manager.

Ellem knows that she was lucky to break into the international touring world when she did – and also to have her promoter rep gig. 'I don't do sound. I can sort of tune a guitar, and I love doing lights when I get the chance. I did them a few times for You Am I. But I'm not a lights person.'

For someone working primarily as a tour manager, opportunities are limited.

The nature of the crew that is required has also changed, as the days of artists building their careers slowly are largely over. Increasingly the artists that hit big do it quickly and in a spectacularly immediate fashion. And when they do they require the best available crew to deliver the top standard and level of production, sound and lighting for them – so they go for the experienced crew, leaving fewer opportunities for young crew people to hone their skills alongside an artist as they all grow.

'A lot of the big names today have this instant success,' Ellem says, 'and it happens very suddenly. They're not having to do the hard yards like bands like Hoodoo Gurus or You Am I, for example, those bands that have learnt it all on the road and have gradually become bigger and bigger. These days an artist puts out a song and it becomes huge, and suddenly they need to have all this crew, and they've never known how to do it any other way. And they become very dependent on that set-up. They'll bring in the big guns of the crew world – they'll cherrypick from the established crew people around the world.'

Another recent development has been the emergence of what's known as a tour coordinator. 'They pick all the crew and appoint the tour manager and production managers. The managers do the deals and stuff they do, and these companies set up these mammoth big tours.'

With one Australian electronic artist, for instance, 'He had a couple of crew he'd had from the beginning and still had them – but it was a mishmash of crew with others who had been brought in. Then it had to be sorted out because it had become a shit fight with a lot of bickering. Basically it was a mess. So the tour coordinator came in to clean it up, which meant firing a lot of people and turning it into a working unit.'

Road crews – good ones, at least – are for the most part a pretty cohesive unit. They're a little like a travelling team of boy and occasionally girl scouts, living and working together and looking out for each other. When cracks appear in crews, they're usually in one of two areas. Towards the end of a tour, there's often anxiety about where the next gig is going to come from. Tension can develop as crew members might now be competing against each other for a new gig. And if the artist they've been working with for months is taking a brief break from the road, the crew might be uncertain as to whether they'll be asked back for the next leg of the tour – or replaced.

The other danger to crew is the artists themselves. As Ellem has seen and heard time and time again, friends of the band who fundamentally don't know anything about crew work can affect how artists view their crew. 'Bands are so influenced by dickheads around them,' she says bluntly. 'They'll pay so much attention to a friend saying the sound or lights were crap. And before you know it, someone is being sacked and someone who actually isn't that good is brought in. Maybe they'll save a bit of money by doing that, getting someone less experienced who doesn't charge as much, but they'll ultimately lose out in terms of quality.'

Conversely, one of the biggest traps a crew member can fall into is forgetting or confusing the fact that they are employed by the band or artist – they're not *in* the band. 'You have to always remind crew that are getting too friendly with the band that they have to keep a level of professionalism. Crew can get too pally and go out partying and hanging out with the band. Then if something goes wrong – maybe a guitar isn't tuned correctly, or the monitors aren't as good as they should be – that band member doesn't know how to deal with it, so the easiest option for them is just to get rid of that crew member rather than confront it. It doesn't make sense but that's what happens.'

With You Am I it's different, Ellem says, as the band and crew do operate like a big family. But in general it's important to maintain a level of professionalism.

'Often I have to pull rank with crew members. With Feist I had a crew member who was unreal, but I was really concerned about his health. He was drinking heavily and not turning up for lobby calls. I had to pull him aside and say that it was a final warning, and that next time he wasn't ready in the lobby we were leaving without him. I need to be respected in my job. Someone has to play bad cop. You can't be pals all the time.'

Another no-no as far as Ellem is concerned is crew complaining to the artist – even when the crew have gone to extreme lengths to get things sorted for a show. 'Bands often have no idea what crews do. And nor do they need to. We did this gig in Portland with Feist, a shitty venue. We have these massive parts for the light show, and we had to get the loaders to take them upstairs because they wouldn't fit in the lift. It was them plus my crew plus me doing this. There were twelve of us on each piece, just to get it up the stairs. It was the only way we could get into the venue. The band had no idea this had happened – and guess what, they don't need to. I hate it when crew tell or complain to bands about how hard a load-in has been. I tell them they're not allowed to do that. They're getting *paid* to do this. If it's too hard, then get another job. Bands don't need to know. They need to be kept away from stuff like that.'

Ellem knows all too well that one of the most confronting times for crew members is when a tour ends. When they come home and there are no more worksheets, no more backstage catering, no more camaraderie. There's no real structure to life, as there is on the road. That's hard to deal with for a lot of crew, particularly those who aren't in a good place emotionally.

'When I come home it can be a really weird thing. How do you do fairly basic things? How do I live normally? Just basic taking-care-of-yourself matters that you get out of practice with.' She's in a decade-long relationship with someone who does the same work as she does, and that helps. They can go for months not seeing each other if both are on the road and in different countries – but they both understand the world they work in.

It can be a really hard world to comprehend from the outside, even for a partner.

'You live in a bubble. It's very artificial. Breakfast, lunch and dinner is all sorted, then there's the after-show drinks and pizza, and then you go back to the hotel and your room. It can get very weird. And bus touring is even weirder. You're then living in this weird universe that just rolls through the night. You leave from backstage at one gig in one city and wake up in or close to another venue and gig. Buses are amazing, but so bad for your health. It's like you leave the gig and walk into your own moving nightclub. It's a different world.'

Bus touring is almost the ultimate cocooned lifestyle. It's too easy to keep drinking and indulging all through the night, rather than trying to sleep in the cramped bunks. Then it's another day, another city, another load-in, another gig. Bus touring is particularly hard on tour managers who are the first ones up and the last ones down.

What Ellem does is – as she's the first to admit – an often thankless job. She feels that bands appreciate what she and other tour managers do, even if crew members themselves often don't. 'The fights I have are hardly ever with the band. If I have to push back on something, it's usually with the crew. But it's important for me to be good to the crew, because often I have to ask them to do shit and they need to respect me when I ask them to do stuff. I *really* look after crew. I know how hard they work and they need to be looked after. Have they eaten? Are they okay? Because if they're not okay, then things don't happen. They need to eat. If they're doing big tours and there's crew catering, that's okay. But if there's not I'll buy crew lunch out of float money if they're unable to leave the venue to get something to eat. I'll go buy it and bring it back for them. Crew like me because I look after them and I have their backs. It's the little gestures that go a long way.

'If a crew guy wants a cold-pressed drink in the morning –
and one of the Feist crew does, believe me – then I sort it,
because if it's not there, he's not happy. And I need him to be
happy, and it's a comparatively small thing. Artists are easy –
it's crews that can be hard. Sometimes the biggest superstar
behaviour comes from crew, not the band.

'But I love crew. I really do.'

39

Born to Crew

Maybe it's the power of hindsight, but it always seemed inevitable that Benny Harwood would end up as both a musician and a roadie.

The ingredients were there from a very early age. His uncle was a member of Goanna, and his father played in bands around Geelong, as well as being a sound engineer. So from around the age of ten, Harwood was sitting next to his dad while he worked with the likes of Melbourne music legends Broderick Smith and Mike Rudd.

'I was kind of old before my time, as all my friends are around 50 and 60 years old,' Harwood laughs. 'I'd been at the Wangaratta Jazz Festival and Port Fairy Folk Festival when I was a kid. Then Dad started sneaking me into pubs when I was 13 or 14. I just learnt stuff from hanging around and being with lots of interesting musicians and roadies. I'd heard all the stories about legends like Howard Freeman and $crooge when I was a young guy – and I'd heard many different versions of the same stories about their exploits. I saw $crooge at a funeral not so long ago, but I was still too scared to say hello.'

Born in 1983, Harwood felt that his road to playing music and working as a roadie was interrupted only by the need to go to school. Yeah, shit happens, even for a roadie in waiting. Not surprisingly, his father had a sizeable record collection, and Harwood immersed himself in it, usually when he should have been doing his homework. His chief texts in those years were a live Jimi Hendrix album and a Goanna cassette.

'I decided early on what I wanted to do. I needed a black Les Paul and I was going to play guitar. In the shed, as a kid I'd ripped out parts from all the old speakers and hi-fi cabinets and built a little PA with monitors for my sisters and me. We were in primary school. I sort of knew what I wanted to do, so it felt like school didn't really matter. And add to that the fact that I was possibly passively stoned a lot of the time from sitting in band rooms and doing three gigs a weekend with Dad and his other friends, who rolled joint after joint and worked and told stories. I really just wanted to hang out with them – and keep up with them. I had my own little road case, which I'd take to gigs and festivals. Musicians loved me as a young kid.'

It wasn't long before Harwood had his own bands and began playing residencies in local pubs. Of course, he was always the one who jumped offstage and went to fix the sound for which-ever band he was in at the time. At that stage, he got the idea that if he learnt more about the mechanics of sound mixing, it was something he could get paid to do. And when he was in his late teens, Harwood started working at Johnston Audio, a big Melbourne-based PA and sound company.

'I'd made it halfway through a music course, but I thought, "What's the point?" because I'd already mixed all my teachers when they were playing in their bands in pubs. A week after I stopped that and started working, I was doing gigs at Rod Laver Arena.'

At Johnston Audio, Harwood met a host of famous road crew guys. He thought of them as legends. He was paired up with one of them, a Glaswegian guy covered from head to toe in tatts, who'd come to Australia with Gary Glitter in the 1970s and stayed. 'They put me with him so I'd learn things – like how to smoke.'

Initially, Harwood thought he'd become a front-of-house sound guy. Then another Johnston Audio guy – Gouldie – told him there were only three or four great monitor guys in Australia, and he thought Harwood would be suited to it. His first monitor gig was a 'trial by fire' with the notoriously sonically challenging Jon Spencer and his Blues Explosion. Without going into too much detail, if you can do monitors for Jon Spencer, you can probably do monitors for God.

Self-effacingly, Harwood doesn't consider doing monitors to be as challenging as a tour manager's job, but he does concede that 'monitors takes a special kind of musical autism. It's a zone. It's one of those 99 per cent psychology, 1 per cent talent gigs. You're working for up to, say, 12 people onstage, and you're creating their environment the way they want it. You learn to pick up on all the visual cues, and understand what they mean and what that person wants. Someone will give you a signal that looks like something from a Three Stooges skit, and you somehow understand what they mean and know what needs doing. I often wonder what exactly it is I'm doing, but for a musician onstage, peace of mind is a beautiful thing.'

One night Harwood was doing monitors at a hip-hop gig at the Palace in Melbourne headlined by Hilltop Hoods. At the end of the gig, John Hall, who was Cut Copy's sound engineer, approached him and said the monitors were amazing. Did he want to go to Singapore and Japan the next week and do monitors for Cut Copy? From left field, Harwood's destiny was sealed. He would work with Cut Copy until . . . well, until he couldn't take it anymore.

This was Harwood's introduction to the dance music world. At first he wasn't so into it, but it didn't take long before he was seduced by the music and vision of what Cut Copy were doing. It was 2006. In the beginning it was just Harwood and Hall doing everything, but by the time Harwood finished up many years later, the group's crew was getting massive, expanding to 11 people at one stage.

Cut Copy's ascendency was swift, and Harwood found himself crisscrossing the globe as the band played one huge gig after another. With it came a rugged, 24-hours-a-day life-style, which was seductive but ultimately unforgiving. Harwood discovered that he could work really well while also partying really hard. 'We didn't sleep a lot,' he reflects. 'You'd often get back to a hotel room that you hadn't slept in and you'd go straight to the foyer, as lobby call was in 20 minutes.'

For better or worse, Harwood was living the dream he'd had since he was a kid. He'd drunk the Kool-Aid of life on the road.

'I was trying to be like an '80s dude – as the gigs got bigger, the intake of drugs and alcohol got bigger. And soon you're on a Hunter S. Thompson-like diet of self-medication. As a ten-year-old or around then, I was kind of inspired by Keith Richards and all the musos around me – that sense that you had to destroy yourself to remake yourself as a dark soul. That was the plan. To get a studio, tour and go as hard as possible. That's probably why those older rogues liked me.'

But eventually things started to unravel. There were black-outs. Harwood had a particularly bad night after Cut Copy played a Lollapalooza festival in Chicago. 'I was getting through a litre bottle of vodka a day at this point, and rock'n'roll was established.' Yet he pushed on. One day he felt like he was going mad. And still he pushed on. More drinking. More fun. More blackouts. More gigs. More vodka. Get stoned. Another airport. On and on Harwood went. The touring was relentless, and Harwood was in the zone. When Cut Copy took a touring break, he didn't take the opportunity to rest: he picked up other gigs until Cut Copy was ready to tour again.

Eventually Harwood went and saw a doctor. He muttered something about how he thought he was having mini heart attacks while on planes. The doctor asked him if he'd heard of anxiety. 'I told him I smoked so much weed that I couldn't get anxiety. Then the doctor told me that the weed was probably a contributing factor – along with everything else.'

Still, Harwood kept pushing, using all sorts of methods to combat his anxiety – which manifested itself particularly on planes. At one stage he combated his demons by taking up watercolour painting – mid-flight. It helped Harwood find what he calls 'the Zen', and get him through a flight. 'Hosties would hate it,' he laughs. 'Being a typical roadie, I didn't go about it half-arsed – I had a full painting set-up on the tray table.'

Harwood went around the world five times with full-blown anxiety. In his words, he was 'borderline psychotic'. Of the constant touring with Cut Copy, Harwood says he remembers half of it but the other half is a blur. There were shows in Iceland, Russia, everywhere. 'It's so strange – I can get lost in the CBD in Melbourne, but I know my way around Portugal pretty well.'

Harwood was close to falling off a very high precipice. He'd been surrounded by casualties, but still wasn't reading the memo that was right in front of him. 'On tour it was a case of sleeping two hours a night, maximum. And always in different time zones. Then I'd bring the tour home with me – I'd want the adrenaline rush to continue. You get addicted to the stress. It's a weird life. You do a show in front of hundreds of thousands of people, and then you're back in a hotel room by yourself if you let yourself go there. And then you start talking to yourself a lot of the time, because it's such a lonely existence on so many levels.'

Harwood also found that his relationships often fell apart just before a tour started. 'The other person thinks you're going to play up, or they want company that you can't give because

you're not there. And it's at that time that you need it most.'
After a tour was a strange time, too. 'You can fix something
in front of a crowd of 50,000 people but you can't do simple
things like post a letter or do your tax.'

The tours continued. 'I kept saying I wanted to stop, but no
one listened. And then they kept offering me things, and often
they were things that were on my list to do. I thought, "Okay,
I haven't done Reykjavik, the festival in Iceland, so I better do
that." It was ridiculous. It was like collecting matchbox cars.'

The tours were not only with Cut Copy, but with other artists
who needed a first-class monitor guy. There was an Australian
tour with Flume, for instance. 'That was, I now realise, towards
the end. I knew that I could bail on a flight 15 minutes before
the airport, and even at check-in I could still bail. I was in such
a state that I really thought that 15 minutes into the flight I
could still ask the captain to turn around and go back.'

With Flume there was a top-notch crew: a lighting guy from
Cut Copy, and another guy they'd pinched from Daft Punk.
'These were the new breed of tech guys. They made me feel
really old-school, because they are not the types to just wing
it. These guys are *really* together. There were, like, 16 people
on the crew, but I was really starting to burn out.'

There was also a difficult gig with the legendarily grumpy
English punk/post-punk artist Mark E. Smith and his band,
The Fall. 'That was a tough one. He spat on me and kicked
me in the arse during a gig. I'd picked up a gig on my birthday.
You always book a gig on your birthday so you don't have to
do anything and be like a normal person. My mate was tour-
managing this one, and he asked if I would do monitors. The
guitar tech from Cut Copy was working on it as well. It was a
show at Billboard. We knew it was going to be a bad day. My
tour manager friend had already been slapped in the face in
the hotel lobby by Mark E. Smith. He'd told him he couldn't
smoke in the van driving to the gig. Smith had also hit his much

younger French wife. You could see the speed all over his face, and he was just mumbling away incoherently.

'At the gig he blew up amps and tangled guitar cords around everything onstage. Then he was turning amps off. This was his idea of being punk. During the show, he screamed at me to turn the monitors off. I went, "Cool, man," and muted them. Then he starts carrying on about how the monitor guy – me – is a cunt. He's asked *me* to turn them off, so I gave him the finger. From that point on it was all about me and him warring for the rest of the gig.

'I went onstage to untangle the spaghetti of cords everywhere around the six mics. He'd gone offstage in a huff, and I'm there bending down trying to untangle everything. He's been sidestage dusting his nose, and then he must have come back on and I felt this swift kick right between the legs – this was in front of the crowd – and then he spat on me.

'So you have your ups and downs . . . You have a night like that, and then you go to the next artist and they're beautiful.'

Eventually, it all got too much for Harwood. The final straw was a tour with Sydney dance group RÜFÜS. It was a seven-week run of shows right when the band was starting to take off. There was a major gig in Perth, but Harwood wasn't coping. He realised the only way he could get out of it was just to not turn up. He called the band and told them he wouldn't be there. Where did he go? Straight to a St Kilda house where three roadies were living together. Harwood figured they were the only ones who'd get what he was going through. He was right.

Six years ago, in 2012, Harwood stopped taking all drugs, and now he doesn't drink either. He started rebuilding. 'I'd hung out with a lot of older roadies who'd fallen into heroin and were on methadone. That motivated me. I was 27 years old, and realised that I was broken before I was 30. When I got sober I realised I was still a 17-year-old kid – possibly younger. I had to rebuild all the skills to do the normal human things.

They say that being a roadie is like running away to join the circus, and you can keep running and we often do. I got out with my limbs and at least half of my mind intact.'

Harwood saw a lot of changes in the time he was touring the world with Cut Copy and others. On the technical side, lights became more and more important. 'In the dance world the lights take over. I almost ended up being a lighting rigger by proxy. And the equipment changed so much. I came in at the time of pub rock and went from all this big, heavy PA and sound equipment to something where you walk in and plug a USB stick in.'

Because a lot of old-school sound engineers left the industry when it went digital, Harwood says bands rarely sound like they used to. But there are positives too. 'Digital is great because wherever you walk into, anywhere in the world, you put your USB stick in and hopefully the firmware lines up and you go from there. Having a computer tech at shows was a big new experience for me in dance music. I swear I had grey hair by 25, and clumps of it coming out because of computer and MIDI failures. All the stuff the guys tried to avoid in the '80s. I always thought a real band played instruments and Malcolm Young'ed it – plug it in and play. Now I have a studio set up, full of drum machines and synths.

'There's the audio schools now where people go to learn all this stuff, but they don't really teach that special part of what we do. That bit of paper doesn't impress, because you can't teach intuition. It's like being in the mafia – once people have got your number and know you're good, they'll keep calling.'

Harwood lived and worked through an era when more and more women came into the world of crewing. He saw the evolution of women being merch sellers, then lighting designers and technicians, and then taking on other more immediate crew roles. 'It's so great to have sisters. You get sick of hanging with stinky dudes on the bus. It was never like women weren't invited, but it's not the best culture and there's still guys who say stuff, and I just have to say, "That's just not cool – you can't say that anymore." It's still a role that's earnt. If you do the hard yards, you're there. I never saw it as a gender thing.'

Harwood still works hard, but he doesn't get on planes and go on tour. He loves being able to drive home after gigs. In fact, he had intended to quit doing live gigs and just take on studio jobs, but life has a way of not working out the way you plan it. He does monitors or front-of-house these days, and still puts in the same effort and smarts he always has. But now he does it sober, and close to home.

'I always thought I was going to die in a hotel room. But I didn't. Getting out of it takes practice, like anything else, and I got pretty good at it. For a very long time I was never straight at shows, but muscle memory comes in. I tried to get fired but I couldn't.'

What's his motivation when he's behind the sound desk these days?

'You're always working towards those "pin-drop moments" – or making the hardest guy in the bar cry,' he says.

Benny Harwood probably doesn't realise it yet, but his best days – professionally and personally – are probably in front of him. And after what he's already gone through, that's saying something.

40

Making Them Match-fit

Roadie school? Yes, one exists. It's based in Perth, and run by an experienced roadie named Jared Nelson via his company Behind the Wall. Nelson is adamant that if you want to be a good road crew person, you need to learn some essential skills. He offers training in all aspects of live production, pre-production design, stage management, stage presence and live performance workshops, artist management, industry business skills, along with stress and fatigue management.

Nelson worked his way through the road crew world along the tried-and-true path. Yep, he started in bands in his early 20s, and things there didn't pan out so well. He enrolled in a music industry skills course at TAFE, but found it slow and drawn-out. He wasn't learning much and wanted to be out there working on gigs. How do you do that? Bang on a few doors and get some work.

Initially, Nelson did basic crew work for shows, building fences and setting up outdoor sites. But he wanted more, so he went to a company called Concert and Corporate Lighting. 'They were great. They gave me knowledge. The older rock'n'roll guys taught me to an international standard. I loved the lifestyle, and particularly not spending money at weekends, but making it instead and having a good time as well.'

Nelson worked on all sorts of shows in and around Perth, and as far away as Darwin. 'I ended up concentrating on lights, as loading and lugging speakers was too heavy for me. But lights were heavier too, back when I started. In those days I often worked six weeks straight, 12-hour days. I was doing lighting director work.'

After a number of years, Nelson discovered that road crew work can be a lonely lifestyle. He thought of stepping up from regional work and moving into a full-time life on the road – the work and the shows were exciting, but the constant parade of hotel rooms wasn't. Plus his lower back was starting to give him significant pain. That was when he came up with the concept of training both roadies and local crew, those teams of people hired to lug gear in and out of big shows and venues.

'Early on in my career, I got to a point where I was managing a whole show and in charge of loaders who really had no idea what they were doing. I started imagining what it would be like if there was something like a green card for our industry, and that's where it all stemmed from. The other thing I'd heard was that students doing other courses were not industry-ready when they finished their study. This is across many industries, not just the crewing one; people think they're ready to do a job when they're really not ready and have no experience at all.'

Nelson's aim is to get people who want to work in the crew and technical side of the live music industry *really* ready. 'I'm saying to kids, "Okay, you've done your course studies, now let me show you what sort of person the industry wants." I show them what is expected on a professional level. I say, "Whatever you think you know, forget it – and learn from people who've done it, because live sound is very, very different from what you learn in courses and studios." With students, the chances are that whoever's been teaching them isn't currently active in the music industry, and has told a bunch of tales about how it was when they were directly involved – and often that is quite a long time ago, and that knowledge is out of date.

'The reality is that most people employing crew don't look at the piece of paper someone has from doing a course. They just tell them to go and work on a crew for five years and then come back and talk to them. It's really a case of going to work in a sound or lighting hire factory, or bumping in and out as local crew for two years, and then going and shadowing some experienced crew for two or three years. At the end of that, you're probably ready to be an assistant tech or an operator. You need to learn from the ground up and get the full picture of what goes on.'

And Nelson is well aware that there are two types of road crew. It comes down to a basic attitude towards the work. 'There's the person who goes, "That's too hard," and then there's the one who says, "We can make this happen" – *they're* the ones who last.

'There's also a difference between the sound or lighting guy who comes in and says, "Where's the desk?" and the ones who will chip in and help unload the truck and do other things. They're the ones who also last. It's all about the camaraderie. One in, all in – that's what roadies are all about. It's about all working together. If the shift goes late, we *all* go late. It's not like you clock off and leave others working.'

The roadies' world is one Nelson knows about, and he has a love/hate relationship with it. He realises there are many reasons people are drawn to this world. 'For some it's a lifestyle choice. They want a different type of work and they want to still be a child, even though they're 40. And they want to work a few days a week. It's perfect for them. For others it's obviously a full-time gig. One where you can do 90 hours a week when you're busy and 40 hours a week when you're not. People who love that love the job. It's their career.'

Nelson believes he could probably earn a lot more money if he went to work in other industries, but he knows he wouldn't love the work as much. 'It's the mateship for me. There's that sense of pride in what we do every day. We're the pistons and the cogs in an engine that no one really knows about. Everyone touches the outside of a Ferrari and goes, "That's so amazing!" but what makes the Ferrari so great is what's under the bonnet. Road crew are that to the live music industry.

'We help the entertainers get onstage and do a show. For everyone who comes to that show, it makes them forget about their lives for a few hours, and then they leave and go home and it starts again for them. There's a real sense of pride in being part of that.'

41

The New Power Generation

Sophie Kirov hasn't been home – to Brunswick Heads, just north of Byron Bay – for four and a half months. That's nothing particularly unusual. During the most recent period she's been tour managing American artist K. Flay.

Kirov is one of the rising stars among Australian road crew, a smart, astute, hard-working figure who already has a global reputation in the live music industry.

On the day we spoke Kirov was in a hotel in the middle of the United States, but she was pretty happy. After weeks and weeks on tour buses, the previous day had involved the comparatively luxurious world of planes.

'Yesterday we flew from Moscow to Zurich, and from there to Chicago and on to Kansas City, which is where I am at the moment,' she laughs.

'After being on buses for such a long time the opportunity to fly is a nice relief.'

Kirov, still in her mid-20s, is already a very experienced member of the road crew community. Originally from Perth, the young music fan quickly realised she didn't have the genes to be a performer, but wanted to be around the world of those who did.

What Kirov did have was a logistical mind and an ability to organise things, so she started volunteering at a touring company, eventually moving to Melbourne, and then Sydney – and is now in a world where home is usually whichever town or city she's in that night, broken up with occasional visits to Brunswick Heads.

Kirov learnt on her feet, and bluffed a lot. By her own admission she was telling people she was a tour manager before she really knew what a tour manager was.

'In the early days I was pretty much bluffing it. It was "let's sink or swim here", and as I go along figure out exactly what is involved with this job. I learnt a lot – and very quickly – from being around some really good people.'

So what is involved with Kirov's job? Pretty much everything associated with organising life on the road for artists and their other crew. There's coordinating flights, bus schedules, load-ins. It's spending hours and hours in liaison with caterers, hotels, transport and rental companies, venues, other crews, production houses, merchandisers. There's lots of driving through the day and through the night if a stand-alone bus driver isn't involved. And there's pushing road cases into and out of venues alongside the rest of the crew if there are deadlines to meet and an extra body is going to make the difference.

Many of Kirov's skills were honed during an extended period working in Australia and around the globe with Flume, but she's also worked with the likes of Flight Facilities, The Cat Empire, Art vs Science, Nina Las Vegas and Kimbra, and on large events such as Stereosonic.

Ask Kirov if she considers herself a roadie and she hesitates. Not because she's ashamed or embarrassed by the suggestion, more that she operates in a world that on many levels is – in

2018 – far removed from many of the traditional stereotypes of roadies and road crew.

Part of this is that as a tour manager she feels – and is – removed from the more immediate 'roadie' work, even though she pitches in when it's required.

'I get involved when I need to push cases or whatever is needed to be done but . . . maybe the word roadie is a bit, not so much unfriendly to women, but I think it comes with that very male "we're road dogs" thing.

'I think that maybe back in days gone by an image emerged of the roadie as this scruffy guy who wore the same shirt every day and was out the back of the venue smoking cigarettes and doing drugs and chasing girls. It was all this very dirty under-world of rock'n'roll and it was probably terribly clichéd but now it's not that way. There are a lot of people coming through who take a lot of pride in their work. I'm sure they did back then too – it's just a different world these days.

'Mind you, some days I don't know when I've last show-ered or washed my clothes, so there's still a very filthy, dirty element to it, but I think the word roadie comes with some of those traditional stereotypical connotations as opposed to what happens in the contemporary world.'

Part of the difference between the old and new worlds of road crew is, in Kirov's mind, to do with the changing nature of the work.

'Today's live show is constructed in a far more technical way. There's a lot more computers and consoles that everyone's using. With some of the stuff that's rolled out now you have to be on top of that equipment to do what they're doing. On top of that, these guys – and now girls – also need to have a multitude of other skills too.

'Touring is very expensive now. In days gone by it was maybe affordable to bring multiple guitar techs and a drum tech on the road and everyone just stayed in their lane, but now with all the costs involved you need to have a multiple of skill sets. For me it's like, well I'm the tour manager but I also need to have a production background and need to know how to do X, Y and Z. You still definitely need to have all the traditional skills to even start being able to do that.

'People are needing to know all sorts of systems and play-back rigs but also be able to set up guitars and be a drum tech. You really need to have quite a lot of different skills otherwise there's going to be someone who'll come in who is super skilled in multiple areas and they will take the gig.'

Kirov isn't putting down the old days – just acknowledging the reality of the changing nature of live music technology and the changing nature of the skills required to present it.

But even in the contemporary world Kirov is adamant that regardless of how many music industry courses someone has been through, nothing beats hands-on experience.

'Despite the courses – which are good for learning how to do this stuff – the industry still exists on a basis of learning from experience. I think that's what sets the guy who has just come out of whatever college they've been to apart from the guy who's been doing it for five or six years on the road. They've got more tours under their belt and they've learnt more things from actually having to do them at shows and in venues on the fly.

'In the evenings after shows a lot of the guys will go back to their rooms and teach themselves things, or they'll sit there and pull out their laptops and maybe they're doing an online course at the same time as working, or they'll sit down with a band member who knows things they want to know about.

'These days you need to be across and know how a lot of software works and retain that. So it's a mixture of old and new that's required. You can't do it without a lot of the old values and approaches.

'When I worked with Flume a lot of the time there was only myself and the lighting director/production manager. Basically

I sat down with the team who had designed his show and I had a manual and they had written everything up for me with pictures and instructions. They were like, "Okay, this is what the show is and this is your step-by-step guide of how to set up this show," and we had to take it from there.

'Obviously his crew is way bigger now. Things these days can grow so fast with streaming and all sorts of things and bands can get very busy, very quickly and they need to have the equipment and crew to deliver shows to a high level of expectation.'

With this amount of pressure and intricate computer systems to deal with it's no surprise to hear Kirov say that a high level of professionalism is mandatory for the road crew of today. By that she means it's a different sort of professionalism from the old days – and one that can't really be accomplished if it is infused with what we'll call a 'heightened reality' fuelled by drugs and alcohol. There are now also occupational health and safety regulations that make these activities unacceptable in the live music workplace.

'I think when the truck doors are closed it's a different story. I'm not saying it's a ruckus, or a ruckus like it probably was, but crews still party.

'There's definitely a real sense of professionalism on actual show days. The general crew-person these days is probably eating a lot healthier and looking after themselves more. They care about getting to a gym when they can and there's a greater sense of looking after one's mental health on the road. That's because of what's gone before and the realisation that crew need to be looked after – and to look after themselves.

'It's a really skilled industry – it always has been in its own varying ways – and people take a lot of pride in their work. Partying still goes on and everyone still gets up to all sorts of behaviour, but within the show itself and when people are working there's a different mentality. During that part of the day and night everyone is focused on delivering the best possible show.'

Kirov is excited by the number of women she encounters in many aspects of the live music world but still sees them as being in specific areas of the business – the office side of the touring industry, the back-end of festival sponsorship, management, booking agents.

'There's so many women involved these days in those areas and that's fantastic to see. But as far as the actual on-road aspect, without doubt there's just not a lot. I encounter very few women if we're talking real touring crew. And that's a worldwide thing. If I needed a female tour manager for an Australian band I could pretty much name them all on one hand. I would say that's the same for audio crew. There is a real opening for females who want to work in these areas.

'I'm not sure why it hasn't changed more. I think one of the things is that for younger women coming through that I've spoken to, their perception is that it's still very male dominated and so they're quite scared to get involved because they feel that they've got a very hard path ahead of them.

'That's something I find really unfortunate because I'm so proud of being a female in the touring industry – and I'm so proud of the men that I work with. I'm absolutely respected – well, I hope I am – in the role I work in. And I respect the people I work with in return.

'I rarely come up against anything sexual in nature and there's no inappropriate behaviour that I have to deal with. The men that I work with are the utmost gentlemen. They very much respect my safety and they respect me in my role.

'I think it's actually a very welcoming environment for women. Maybe in the past it was different, but at no time now, in my day-to-day work – and that's wherever I am in the world – am I ever really finding myself in a position where I have to say to myself, "Wow, this really sucks to be a woman doing what I have to do."

'I think it's really unfortunate that young women who are wanting to come into the industry have this idea that it's a really blokey world and that it's going to be tough out there and that you're going to have to act like a guy because that is really just not the case.

'As long as you're able to do the job and do the job well you'll be okay. Yes, you have to be assertive and you have to stand your ground and maybe we do have to work a little harder than the guys do, but if you do that, then you will cement your place within the industry very quickly.'

IN MEMORIAM

The Collective Backbone
of Australian Music

Last Name	First Name	Last Name	First Name
AMSTER	Dave	BURNELL	Glenn
ANTOUFIDES	Tony	BUTLER	Al
ARNOLD	Ray	CARE	Tony
BAIN	Jock	CARTER	Eric
BARBERRA	Mal	CHAPMAN	Andrew
BARRON	Chris	CHUGG	Aaron
BELL	Laurie	CLARKE	Greg
BENTLEY	Andy	COEHICO	Kevin
BISHOP	John	COLLIS	Rory
BLACKMORE	Ron	CONNELLY	Leo
BOWIE	Ian	COONEY	Declan
BRAHAM	Dennis	COOPER	Shane
BRATTAN	Rick	CROSBY	Andy
BRODY	Dave	DALLOW	Alan
BROWN	Peter	DART	Bill
BURKINSHAW	Phil	DAVIDSON	Jason

Last Name	First Name	Last Name	First Name
DeABREAU	Joe	JAMES	Arthur
DEUTSCHER	Chris	JARVIS	Robbie
DEW	Ray	JARVIS	Wayne
DICK	Peter	JENNINGS	Grant
DICKIE	Dennis	KAY	Andrew
DRUMMOND	Ron	KIDNER	Rick
DUHIG	Scotty	KIRTLAND	Steve
DUNN	Graeme	LAFFY	John
EASTICK	Phil	LAFFY	Peter
EDWARDS	Tony	LAYTON	Meg
EDWARDS	Warren	LEGGE	Michael
EMERY	Ray	LEHDAY	James
EVANS	Geoff	LETCH	Shane
EVERET	Brewster	LIDDY	Scott
FARMER	Genevieve	LIPPOLD	Tony
FARRELLY	John	LLOYD	Greg
FRENCH	John	LONGWOOD	Bob
GABBUSCH	Tim	LYSAGHT	Sean
GEORGETTIS	Gerry	MARINI	Sam
GIBB	Billy	MARSH	Lee
GILLIES	Andrew	MARTIN	David
GODFREY	Ray	McDONALD	Andrew
GRANT	Chris	McKENZIE	James
GRAY	Ian	McKERCHAR	Trevor
GREEN	Jeff	McLEAN	Hugh
HARRIS	Rodney	MERRYWEATHER	Jeff
HARTLEY	William	MONDO	Ray
HAYLOCK	Rodney	NESSEL	Gary
HICKMAN	Greg	NORTON	Tony
HITCHENS	Ken	O'DONNELL	Mark
HUGDENS	Watson	O'NEILL	Paul
HUXLEY	Mark	O'SHANNESSY	John
INGHAM	Dave	OSWALD	Rob
JACKSON	Bruce	PALMER	Tim

Last Name	First Name	Last Name	First Name
PEACH	Greg	STELL	Allan
PEACH	Robert	SUMMERHAYES	Jon
PERYMAN	Warren	SUMMERS	Peter
PETKOVICH	John	SWINEY	John
PICKETT	Pat	SWINEY	Norm
POPOFF	Steph	THOMPSON	Greg
POWELL	John W	TIMMERMANS	Graham
PRIOR	Brian	TITTMARSH	Don
PUCKERIDGE	Bruce	TURNER	Jeff
PURVIS	Bob	TYCROSS	Timmy
RAMP	Ricky	VANDEN BROUCKE	Fred
REHE	Tex	VERENKAMP	Jim
RICHMOND	Luke	VILLANI	John
RISBEY	Colin	VINCENT	Deborah
ROBINSON	Eric	WAPLES	Steve
RONDO	Steve	WATKINS	Derek
ROWE	Billy	WATSON	Steve
RUSHMELLON	Harold	WEEKS	Dion
RUSSELL	Nui	WHEADON	Geoff
SANDBACH	Neal	WHYTE	Cliff
SHUGG	Chris	WILLIAMS	Anthony
SMITH	Ian	WILLIAMS	Barbara
SORTINO	Vito	WOOD	Lew
SOUTHY	Beau	WOOLLARD	Jim
SPROCKET	Brian	WRAIGHT	Andy
SPURA	Peter	WRIGHT	Jonathan
STEGERT	Ivan	XYPOLITIS	Chuck

Acknowledgements

I didn't and still don't want this book to finish. Over the course of more than a year I've encountered some of the most amazing people, as I've been fortunate enough to gain entry into the world of Australian road crew.

First up I'd like to thank the roadies themselves who shared their stories with me: John Highlands, Daryl Kavanagh, Tana Douglas, '$crooge' Madigan, Mick Cox, Howard Freeman, John D'Arcy, Nicky Campbell, Clive Lawler, Roger Davies, Peter Wilson, Bill McCartney, Noel Jefferson, Adrian Anderson, Geoff Lloyd, Shane Scully, Greg Little, Louise Le Raux, Noel Bennett, Michael Lippold, Ted Gardner, Kerry Cunningham, Ross Ferguson, John Pope, Tony Wilde, Norbert Probst, Sean Hackett, Bob Grosvenor, Grahame Harrison, Gregory Horrocks, Steve Alberts, Ray McGuire, Dugald McAndrew, Mike Emerson, Ronald Clayton, Julius Grafton, Stan Armstrong, Ian Peel, Leesa Ellem, Benny Harwood, Jared Nelson and Sophie Kirov.

You speak for five decades of Australian road crew and you speak with insight, humour, honestly and poignancy. Thank you.

Many other music industry figures, friends and associates spent time with me giving me insights and recollections.

Invaluable help and support came from Michael Chugg, Michael Gudinski, John Watson, Bill Cullen, Michael Coppel, Jimmy Barnes, Ian Moss, Phil English, Col Joye, Simon Fenner, Ian James, Iain Shedden, John O'Donnell, Roger Grierson, Therese Rutledge, John Foy, Zac Dadic, Andrew Watt, Jeff Apter, Amanda Dweck, Jen Jewel Brown, Eddie White, Ray Argall, Greg Fitzgerald, Momtchil 'Momo' Vassilev, John Gaucci, Nick Chugg, Lucas Chugg, Gaynor Crawford, Craig Barman, Bailey Holloway, Gary Jackson, Phillip Morris, Simon Napier-Bell, Glenn A. Baker, Justin Ractliffe, Max Merritt, John Fitzgerald, John Hansen, Irene Taylor, Mick Mazzone, Gerard Schlaghecke, Darren Cowan, Scott Dimmick and everyone associated with the 2017 Elton John tour who made me so welcome in Wollongong, Alex Grant and all the Midnight Oil crew, Colleen Ironside, Kathy Howard, Cat Swinton, Nardia Drayton, Brent Williams, Brian Taranto, Tim Rogers, Tex Perkins, Jimi Bostock, Neal McCabe, Steven Rackley, Denise Officer, Bob Gosford, Chips Mackinolty, Ian McFarlane, Bridie Tanner, Simon Marnie, and Angry Anderson who spent a very generous two hours with me which was enlightening and entertaining but ultimately didn't find its way into the book as it took its present shape.

I'd also like to thank Jacquie Brown, whose attention to editorial detail frequently left me gasping with admiration.

Last but certainly – as they say in the trade – not least, I want to single out four people in particular.

Howard Freeman has been my go-to guy in the road crew world. It was a big boost of confidence to me when he agreed to be interviewed and being able to mention his name opened many other doors. He and his wife Lil made me so welcome in their home, prodded me to include particular people, answered all my questions, and generally became my sounding board for this whole project.

I met Adrian Anderson when I was researching my biography of Michael Gudinski and through Adrian I heard about the

Australian Road Crew Association. During the whole process Adrian peppered me with an astonishing array of contacts and ideas. If I'd followed them all up I'd still be interviewing people in 2025, let alone writing anything!

This is the third project Matthew Kelly and I have worked on together and it was he who jumped quickly when I first made an offhand comment that I was thinking about a book on roadies. By now Matthew and I know each other well and are good friends. We're also pretty good at navigating the ups, down and twists and turns of a book project with good humour and only marginal damage to our psyches. Matthew's a great publisher and a steady, reassuring voice of reason when it's required. I hope we get to do it all again soon.

As I write this Susan Lynch is sitting at the other end of the table, head down, poring over pages, checking for errors and suggesting ways to better convey what I'm trying to say. She's damn good at it and her input into this book is far greater than even she realises. Beyond that, Susan is the reason I'm the happiest I've ever been in my life and have a sparkle in my psyche that enables me to do this. To have her in my life is a joy beyond words.

SUPPORT ACT is a charity that helps Australian artists and music workers who are facing hardship due to illness, mental health problems, injury or some other crisis.

https://supportact.org.au
General Enquiries: 1300 731 303
24/7 Wellbeing Helpline: 1800 959 500